*Law*Basics

100 CASES

That Every Scots Law Student Needs to Know

AUSTRALIA
Law Book Co.
Sydney

CANADA and USA
Carswell
Toronto

HONG KONG
Sweet & Maxwell Asia

NEW ZEALAND
Brookers
Wellington

SINGAPORE and MALAYSIA
Sweet & Maxwell Asia
Singapore and Kuala Lumpur

*Law*Basics

100 CASES

That Every Scots Law Student Needs to Know

By

Past and Present Staff at the University of Strathclyde
Law School

EDINBURGH
W. GREEN/Sweet & Maxwell
2001

Published in 2001 by W. Green & Son Ltd
21 Alva Street
Edinburgh EH2 4PS

Printed in Great Britain by Ashford Colour Press,
Gosport, Hampshire

No natural forests were destroyed to make this product
Only farmed timber was used and replanted

A CIP catalogue record for this book is available from the British
Library

ISBN 0 414 014 626

DEDICATION

To Daniel McNaghten, alumnus of the Glasgow Mechanics' Institute and, thereby, of the University of Strathclyde.

PREFACE

This is not a case book, at least not in the traditional sense. Far less is it a book of cases and materials. Rather it is an exposition of 100 of the major cases which have either created, or illustrate well, the legal system as we know it today. The book is designed as a learning aid, and as such the cases have been chosen primarily for their use in educating students on important points of law. Some of the cases are self-evidently important in their own right (*Hedley Byrne, Handyside, West*); others are included because though they are unimportant in themselves, setting out no new principle nor setting the law off on a different road, they do nicely illustrate an important point in a way that students, in our experience, find it easy to grasp. Sometimes the cases are from foreign jurisdictions—this is so when the case being presented is one which can lay claim to having a universal importance. The choice, to a large extent, is eclectic, and reflects our own teaching experiences and interests. It was difficult to limit our choices to 100 and it is inevitable that those familiar with Scots law will find some of the omissions surprising. But the book makes no attempt to be comprehensive, nor to provide coverage of all areas of law. It does aim to provide a grounding in a large variety of legal disciplines.

In order to make the text as accessible as possible (every case is written for an audience of first year undergraduates) the tone we have adopted is quite different from that in a normal legal textbook. We eschew an academic disinterest in the cases we present, and have attempted instead to emphasise the human interest element. This was a deliberate policy, for two reasons: first, it is important for students of law to remember that every case that is decided by the courts deal with real issues affecting real people; secondly, cases in which the reader can identify with one (or more) of the parties are cases which he or she is more likely to remember. We have rather indulged ourselves with this freedom from normal academic constraints and have consciously permitted our own opinions of the parties to colour our presentation of the facts. We do not like, for example, Mrs Reavis nor Mrs Lawrie nor Mrs Oliver; but we are rather fond of (on no real evidence to be found in the law reports) Miss Sweet. We are not keen on landlords, as a rule. No knowledge is neutral, far less is its presentation, and the personal views expressed here will hopefully illustrate this universally acknowledged truth. Notwithstanding that there is a lot of law in this book, we would hope that a more general readership will find it both accessible and interesting.

The cases are presented in a strictly chronological order, and reading them in that order gives an interesting historical perspective of the development of Scots law from the Union of the Parliaments to

Devolution—but the book does not need to be read that way and, hopefully, it can be enjoyed by readers dipping into it for particular cases as and when the topic it is concerned with is being explored. The further readings provided with many of the cases concern, by and large, the case itself rather than the point of law at issue.

Individual members of our team were primarily responsible for individual cases and while we all take some responsibility for the book as a whole, expressions of opinion in one case should not be taken to be the considered views of us all. The general editor, however, bears some responsibility in permitting and indeed encouraging such expressions of opinion.

KENNETH MCK. NORRIE
JOHN W.G. BLACKIE
GERRY MAHER
ANNICK MASSELOT
JEAN MCFADDEN
KENNETH MILLER
THÉRÈSE O'DONNELL
PETER ROBSON
BARRY J. RODGER
JENIFER ROSS
JANE SCOULAR
JOHN SINCLAIR
SCOTT WORTLEY

CONTENTS

Contents

Contents

Contents

TABLE OF CASES

TABLE OF STATUTES

Case 1: Greenshields v. Magistrates of Edinburgh
(1711) Robertson 12
(House of Lords, Scotland)

Constitutional law—Legal process—Appeal from Scotland to the House of Lords—Treaty of Union

(See MacLean, "The House of Lords and Appeals from the High Court of Justiciary 1707–1887", 1985 J.R. 192.)

The Parliament of Great Britain came into existence in 1707 as a result of the Treaty of Union between Scotland and England, which was ratified and brought into effect by Acts of the Parliaments of each of these countries. These Acts abolished the Parliaments that passed them, and transferred their powers to a new body, the Parliament of Great Britain. One of the matters left, perhaps deliberately, unresolved was whether an appeal from the Court of Session could be taken to the Upper House of the new Parliament, which had long acted as ultimate court of appeal from the English courts. Prior to the Union, there had been a right of appeal from the Court of Session to the Scots Parliament for remeid (remedy) of law. However, the Treaty of Union made no mention of any right of appeal to the Parliament of Great Britain. Article XIX of the Treaty did, however, declare that "no causes in Scotland be cognoscible by the Courts of Chancery, Queen's Bench, Common Pleas or any other Court in Westminster Hall". The problem was, the House of Lords was not one of the specified courts, and it did not sit in Westminster Hall.

Shortly after the Union, the House of Lords heard, without challenge, a couple of appeals from Scotland. Greenshields' case was the first in which their jurisdiction was questioned. It arose in a dispute of great public import.

The Revd James Greenshields was a Scotsman, and an Episcopalian clergyman. He therefore belonged to a minority form of Christianity in Scotland, and one indeed by which the Established (Presbyterian) Church felt distinctly threatened, for much of the *British* establishment, including the Crown itself, was Episcopalian. In 1709 the Revd Greenshields opened a private chapel in Edinburgh, at which the English Book of Common Prayer was used. The Presbytery of Edinburgh summoned him and prohibited him from preaching, on the ground that he was ministering without their authority (which they had no intention of giving). The Presbytery asked the Magistrates of Edinburgh to enforce their decision and the Magistrates forbade Greenshields to preach on pain of imprisonment. The Revd Greenshields ignored this order, he continued to preach, and the Magistrates committed him to prison. He presented a Bill of Suspension to the Court of Session, but that Court refused the Bill. He remained in prison for seven months and was only released when he appealed to the House of Lords. The Magistrates argued that the House of Lords had no jurisdiction to hear appeals from the Court of Session.

The House of Lords, on the question of the extent of their own jurisdiction, held (as judges in their own cause often do) in favour of extending their power. They resolved that Greenshields' petition and appeal were "regularly and properly before the House", and since then the right to appeal to the House of Lords has been unquestioned.

On the merits of the case, the House of Lords held that although the Presbytery was the legally established church government in Scotland, there was no law of conformity in Scotland which obliged the laity to be in communion with the Church of Scotland, nor was there any law which prohibited ministers of the Church of England from exercising their function or the laity from joining in worship with them in a private manner. The Magistrates had no jurisdiction to inflict penalties on such ministers or laity. Greenshields' imprisonment was, therefore, not warranted by any of his acts and his appeal on the merits succeeded.

This decision caused great dismay in Scotland, not so much because of the House of Lords affirming their new jurisdiction, but because of the nature of the case in which they did so. Since the Union of the Crowns the Scottish church had felt vulnerable to domination by the larger English church, leading to many extreme views and actions in the late seventeenth and early eighteenth centuries. The decision in *Greenshields* was perceived as an English court interfering with the affairs of the Scottish Kirk. The subsequent actions of the Union Parliament did nothing to assuage the fears of the Scots. The Toleration Act of 1712 lived up to its name by making plain that the Episcopal clergy in Scotland were entitled to use "the liturgy of England"; less tolerantly, and leading to the first serious challenge to the Union itself, the Patronage Act in the same year restored to Scottish land owners the right to choose and appoint parish ministers (a tradition which the Scottish church with its egalitarian—presbyterian—principles had long fought against and finally abolished in 1690). The patronage dispute rumbled on for centuries, leading eventually to the Great Disruption in the Church of Scotland in 1843 when around 40 per cent of the ministers walked out and formed the Free Church of Scotland, because the Kirk had grown accustomed to and would not fight against patronage. So it is that Great Causes in the courts can have social effects far beyond the parties involved.

THE SCOTTISH SEDITION TRIALS

Case 2: Thomas Muir (1793) 23 St. Tr. 117
(High Court of Justiciary, Scotland)

(See also *James Tytler* (1793) 23 St. Tr. 1; *John Morton, James Anderson and Malcolm Craig* (1793) 23 St. Tr. 7; *John Elder and William Stewart* (1793) 23 St. Tr. 25; *James Smith and John Mennons* (1793) 23 St. Tr. 33; *Walter Berry and James Robertson* (1793) 23 St. Tr. 79; *Thomas Fyshe Palmer* (1793) 23 St. Tr. 237; *Alexander Scott* (1793) 23 St. Tr. 383; *William Skirving* (1794) 23 St. Tr. 391; *Maurice Margarot* (1794) 23 St. Tr. 603; *Charles Sinclair* (1794) 23 St. Tr. 777; *Joseph Gerrald* (1794) 23 St. Tr. 803)

Criminal law—Sedition—Bias of judges

(See Cockburn, *An Examination of the Trials for Sedition in Scotland* (1888))

Europe in the 1790s was profoundly influenced by the French Revolution. In Scotland, and Britain as a whole, the ruling establishment was deeply afraid that the events in France might be repeated at home. On the other hand, inspired by the French Republic, many lower and middle class Scots took up the call for adult suffrage and annually elected Parliaments and set up organisations to further that end politically. Thomas Paine's *The Rights of Man* (published in Scotland in parts in 1791 and 1792) was circulated widely though considered seditious, while local groups such as the *Friends of the People* agitated locally and also joined together as a national Convention of Delegates in Glasgow and Edinburgh and corresponded with equivalent groups in London. Many activists were arrested. They were tried for sedition, mainly for issuing seditious literature (including *The Rights of Man*), reading seditious writings in public (particularly at meetings of the Convention) and making seditious speeches, all calling for suffrage and annual elections. None of these trials alleged that there had been any call to violence to overthrow the current Government. The trials were widely condemned throughout Scotland, and elsewhere, by radicals and establishment alike because of the oppressive sentencing. Subsequently more general legal and historical opinion also condemned the conduct of the court itself as unfair and partisan. Probably the most prominent of all the trials was that of Thomas Muir, an advocate who conducted his own defence (a defence much criticised by Lord Cockburn in his book cited above). He was one of five accused who were sentenced to fourteen years transportation. Muir escaped from Australia in 1796, and spent some time in France as a guest of the Republic, before his death in 1799.

The crime of sedition is uttering words, written or spoken, which tend to foment popular unrest against the state and government. No unrest needs actually to have been fomented. Nor is it necessary to prove that the accused intended to foment unrest: it is sufficient that the objective tendency of the words was to have that effect (*John Grant* (1848) J Shaw 51). What may also make the words seditious may be the political climate in which they are uttered. Sedition is thus a political crime. In modern times prosecutions where there is a political element tend to rely on the general criminal law of conspiracy, with a requirement to prove an intention to use criminal (violent) means, rather than sedition.

Sentences imposed for sedition were not usually so severe as those imposed on Thomas Muir, William Skirving, Maurice Margarot, Charles Sinclair and Joseph Gerrald. John Morton, James Anderson and Malcolm Craig, three young printers, were convicted of sedition. They had gone to Edinburgh Castle and, in the presence of soldiers, they toasted "George the Third and last and damnation to all crowned heads", invited the soldiers to join in and tried to persuade them to leave the army and join the *Friends of the People* or the *Club for Equality and Freedom*. At their trial Lord Henderland commented on these organisations: "I like not their names..... Freedom is a name we all revere, and we enjoy it; but if, by equality be meant an equal division of property, it would be downright robbery to introduce it." They were sentenced to nine months imprisonment and a fine. One other consequence of this and other episodes was that the general practice of billeting soldiers in the houses of ordinary people in towns where they were stationed was stopped, and barracks were built.

There are many reasons why the trials of *Thomas Muir* and the others have been so severely criticised by history. There was the method of choosing the jury: the trial judge selected jurors from lists drawn up by the sheriffs in the relevant counties. At Thomas Muir's trial all of the jurors were personally known to the judge, all held offices of some kind under the Government and all had previously subscribed an Address denouncing the *Friends of the People*. One of the jurors, a naval officer, had attempted to disqualify himself as he felt the force of these objections, but he was not allowed to do so by the judge, the Lord Justice-Clerk, Lord Braxfield. He presided over the majority of these trials and it was particularly his behaviour which brought the trials into disrepute. During his address to the jury in Muir's trial, he advised them that two things needed no proof: "First, That the British constitution is the best that ever was since the creation of the world, and it is not possible to make it better." Secondly "that there was a spirit of sedition in the country last winter which made every good man very uneasy". Thomas Muir's being an advocate was almost certainly an aggravation, and also his "haranguing such multitudes of ignorant weavers about their grievances". To the jurors who heard the trial of Maurice Margarot, who was the President of the Convention of the *Friends of the People* and who also defended himself, Lord Braxfield said that "the crime charged is sedition; and I think he took up to four hours in a defence, which was sedition from beginning to end; finding fault with the constitution, and I think a speech of a very seditious tendency." At the trial of Joseph Gerrald he told the jury that the Convention had already been characterised as seditious by two previous juries. Although the most outspoken, and also popularly viewed as coarse and brutal, he was not out of step with his fellow judges who similarly displayed their fear of ordinary people ("the rabble") being called on to assert rights. In the trial of William Skirving Lord Swinton said "Calling upon the rabble! How are the rabble to do it? Can they do it in any manner but by outrage and violence? Is there any instrument in their hands but that of outrage and violence?" In the trial of Thomas Fyshe Palmer Lord Abercrombie told the jury: "... the right of universal suffrage is a right which the subjects of this country never enjoyed; and were they to enjoy it they would not long enjoy either liberty or a free constitution. You will therefore consider whether telling the people that they have a just right to what would unquestionably be tantamount to total subversion of this constitution, is such a writing as any person is entitled to compose, to print and to publish." The convictions were as unsurprising as they were scandalous.

THE MELVILLE MONUMENT CASE

Case 3: Walker v. Milne (1823) 2 S. 379
(Inner House, Court of Session, Scotland)

Economic loss—Nature of wrong—Contract, delict, unjustified enrichment or good faith—Politicians, egos and sycophancy

(See Forte (ed.), *Good Faith in Contract and Property Law*: MacQueen at pp. 22–33 and Blackie at pp. 153–155.)

This case is as important, and as full of puzzles, as it is briefly reported. It takes up just one page in the law reports for the year 1822–1823. Short reports lack good background stories. But this story can found in the papers of the case in the Advocates' Library in Edinburgh.

We have the Battle of Trafalgar to thank for it. One consequence of that victory at sea was the rash of phallic monuments that began sprouting up all over Britain. The one in Trafalgar Square in London is

185 feet high. Scotland was actually first in the field, with an obelisk in Glasgow. Edinburgh followed on later with an upturned giant stone telescope, and also with the monument that gave rise to this case. This one, though nearly as high as the one in Trafalgar Square, does not have Nelson, who commanded the ships, standing on the top of it. Rather, it has the government minister who got them built. His name was Viscount Melville. He died of natural causes.

The defenders in this case were a group of naval officers. They were paying for the monument. They wanted a site for it that would enable it, or at least the man on the top of it, to be seen from the sea. The point was to remind sailors to think with gratitude of the man who provided the ships. The pursuer was another naval officer. He made available for nothing a site that had the desired characteristics. It was in the middle of a speculative housing development he was creating on his land. He, in fact, changed his development to make a reasonably impressive space for it. (Melville Crescent is still there, a cross-roads between Melville Street, named after the Viscount and Walker Street, named after the pursuer). Building this square meant he built rather less housing there than he had originally planned, and so lost out on the profit he would have made from that further housing. He let the defenders start to prepare the site. But they suddenly decided not to go on with the project there and Mr Walker sued them. The thing was, this was their fourth choice of site. All of a sudden their third choice site had become available, after all. First choice of site had been one of the hills in Edinburgh. (The one with the upturned stone telescope on it). That was no good, though, as such a tall monument would get in the site lines of the real telescope of the astronomical observatory that was also up there. Second choice had been a bit of ground on the way up from Princes Street Gardens to the Castle. But that was no good either, because very tall monuments are very heavy. The ground there is an artificial pile of earth. Although the monument would have been visible from the sea for a while, in course of time it would gradually have sunk below nautical sight into the bowels of the City of Edinburgh. The third choice, in the middle of another square (named after Scotland's Patron Saint), was originally not a runner as some of the owners of the ground there, rather unpatriotically, did not want it. They had now changed their minds. It can be seen there to this day—and, believe it or not, from the sea, too.

In these circumstances the Court held that the pursuer was entitled to "indemnification for any actual loss and damage that he may have sustained, and for the expences (*sic*) incurred in consequence of the alteration of the site of the monument." The puzzle is this: what was the ground in law for this finding. The difficulty is one which all legal systems are faced with: If someone suffers loss in a situation where it was anticipated that there would later have been a contract, or some other legally binding relationship (*e.g.* marriage), but that anticipated legally binding relationship never comes about, can that person claim anything from the other party, who causes that never to happen? The result of this case strongly suggests that as a matter of justice the pursuer should be entitled to something. But then it might be commented that the whole point of negotiations is that people do and should take the risk of the possibility of their negotiations not resulting in the anticipated binding legal relationship. It is a basic fact of commercial life, for example, that businesses daily spend money hoping to get business, but don't. It would not be sound policy if they could routinely recover from other people with whom they hoped in vain to enter into contracts.

One idea might be that there would only be liability to the disappointed party if there was already some sort of temporary contract, perhaps a contract to contract. But that was definitely not the basis of the Court's decision. The Court confirmed the finding of the first instance judge that "no binding contract had been completed". That was inevitable since for a contract in connection with land to be valid it had to be in certain forms of written documentation.

The case is often thought of as a case based on some principle within the law of unjustified enrichment. In a way the defenders were enriched. They did have the benefit of thinking they could put the monument there, and of arranging their affairs on that basis for a while. However, being benefited in that manner is not what is typically required as a necessary ingredient in a case of unjustified enrichment. A benefit that can be valued in economic terms is required, for that is the limit of liability in an unjustified enrichment case. In this case about the monument it was never suggested that a monetary figure could be put on the extent that the defenders had benefited. Moreover, what they were held liable for was expressed not in terms of the value of their benefit but of the losses to the pursuer: they were required to cover the pursuer's "actual loss and damage" and "expences (*sic*)".

If it is not contract and not unjustified enrichment, might it be delict? Delict is a set of rules compensating for losses irrespective of whether there is or is not contractual liability. So it might at first sight be thought that the liability was based on the rules of that area of law. Yet it is not clear what bit of the law of delict could cover this case. The defenders were not negligent. Nor did they intend to cause the losses to the pursuer. However, in the Scots law of delict intention means intention to cause harm, not simply intention to do something. Further, the pursuer's loss in not building houses was a pure economic one. They certainly did not intend to cause him that sort of harm. Even if they had, it is not clear what part of the law of intentionally causing pure economic losses ('the economic delicts") would cover it.

Some legal systems in Europe deal with this type of claim with a specific set of rules founded on the concept of good faith. Perhaps this case shows that Scots law is one of these. In these legal systems in certain types of context a lack of good faith on the part of a party negotiating can result in liability. Such rules are sometimes referred to by writers on law as a doctrine of *culpa in contrahendo*. However, the difficulty of finding an agreed translation for the word *culpa*—some say wrongdoing, some say, here, lack of good faith, some say fault—shows how difficult it is for the law to find a clear set of rules even if this idea is part of the law. One Scottish rationalisation in a later case is that what a lack of good faith here means is confined to situations that would give rise to delictual claims (fraud and so on) and also to a situation where there is an "implied assurance" by the party who finally refused to go ahead that there was a contract between them even though in law and in fact there was not.

In Australia in a famous case the same result was reached by extending the idea of "estoppel" found in legal systems deriving from English law. The rules of that area of Anglo-American law are pretty open-ended and unclear. But one of the ideas is leading people on. In the present case we have leading the other side on with respect to the anticipated contract. However, the rules of that area of law are normally thought of as ones that in appropriate contexts prevent someone from asserting a right he or she has already acquired on some other legal basis, rather than giving a person a right based solely on this ground. In the present case it was not held that the defenders were prevented from asserting that there was no contract. On the other hand the background papers of the case show that the pursuer did partly argue drawing on ideas that seem to come from the Scottish equivalent area of law about leading people on, in Scotland called "personal bar". When all is said and done, however, maybe those acting for the pursuers were just as puzzled as anybody what the legal basis for the claim was. When lawyers have right on their client's side, but no clear legal ground, they fire off at the other side and at the judges all the legal ideas that seem sort of relevant (the "Buckshot Tactic"). They hope at least one of them will inspire the Court, even if the Court does not understand it clearly.

The pursuer never got the monument on his land. But to Scots lawyers at least, the consolation prize, a case of monumental interest, is much more famous than the monument that is now on the third choice site. As for the pursuer, he not only got some money (how much is not revealed in the case as reported or in the background papers), but some decades later he (or his successors) actually got a monument erected on the site. It is of Viscount Melville's son. He was in his day a significant politician like his father. But no-one remembers him now at all. Suitably it is quite a wee monument compared to that that was originally meant to be there to his father. Nevertheless, it is a big enough monument to have meant that in the event it was a good idea after all that the pursuer had left room for it, by not building so much housing. Does that mean, with hindsight, that the pursuer was unjustifiably enriched himself, if the court did award him compensation in respect of the pure economic loss he sustained through consequentially making less money on his housing development than he otherwise would have?

THE TRUE STORY OF BURKE AND HARE

Case 4: Hare v. Wilson (1829) Syme 373
(High Court of Justiciary, Scotland)

Criminal law—Murder—King's evidence—Establishment cover-up

(See Ian Rankin, *The Falls* (2001))

Myth and legend surround the story of these two whisky-drinking Irish immigrants. Their legendary status as grave-robbers was far from the truth, which is that they killed at least 16 people during 1827–28. The background to the case is Auld Reekie herself, a Jeckyl and Hyde in stone. On the one hand, the city was then basking in the international repute of its philosophers, lawyers and surgeons developed during the Scottish Enlightenment. On the other hand it was a city of dank closes and dark deeds. Both sides came together in this very Scottish tale of the macabre.

Surgical techniques at the time were surprisingly far advanced, and the Medical School at Edinburgh University forged ahead, at least partly due to the popular lectures given by Dr Knox, in which he dissected corpses in order to explore and illustrate the workings of the human body. Corpses, however, were not necessarily easy to come by, even for those working in an early nineteenth century infirmary before anti-septic methods of surgery had been developed. So Dr Knox would pay for corpses, and a lucrative "resurrectionist" trade developed in and around Edinburgh.

The Hares owned a house in the West Port area of Edinburgh, near the Grassmarket. They were owed rent by one of their lodgers, but he died before his pension quarterly day. Hare, with his friend Burke, decided that, all being fair in debt and death, the sale of the body would pay off the debt due by the deceased. So they delivered the body to Dr Knox, at his establishment in Surgeon's Square. Surprised and pleased at how much they got, and realising (perhaps from something the good Doctor said) the shortage of bodies, they resolved to contribute to the advancement of science. But they could not wait for the luck of another lodger dying unexpectedly. Much quicker to obtain corpses by turning living bodies into dead ones.

The first victim was smothered with a pillow and taken to Knox, who asked no questions, but thereafter 'Burking' was invented: placing the thumb under the chin and putting the first two fingers firmly over the nose, thereby blocking the air supply and keeping the mouth shut.

Various other victims were induced or seduced to their lodgings where they got drunk and strangled. It is revealing that Knox encouraged the delivery of fresh bodies and paid £10 in the winter and £8 in the summer. Burke and Hare normally killed nomads, growing wealthy by trading on the bodies of fellow Irish immigrants, but they attracted the attention of the better classes when they killed a prostitute and an "idiot"—Daft Jamie. Legend has it that when Burke told Daft Jamie that he was going to be killed, he responded "If you kill me I'll tell ma mither"! Posterity does not record whether he did so. Eventually, the authorities closed in, and Burke and Hare were arrested.

Burke and his mistress, Helen McDougal, were tried. Hare wasn't. He testified against Burke, was given immunity and got off scot-free. The trial was started on Christmas Eve, and the tradition then was for criminal trials to continue until completion. At 9.30 on Christmas morning, the jury returned a verdict of guilty for William Burke and not proven for Helen McDougal. A mob of 25,000 turned up at Burke's execution, which took place on January 28, 1829. Helen McDougal was released, but was mobbed wherever she went. Hare, who had turned King's Evidence, was granted immunity but he was detained under a warrant issued by a sheriff, at the behest of Daft Jamie's family. They raised a private prosecution against him and, in line with the tradition at the Scottish Bar, the "pauper's brief" had the best counsel in the land. Hare appealed to the High Court for liberation, which is the case reported here.

The first issue considered in this case concerned the existence of the right to private prosecution in Scotland, independent of the public prosecutor. The issue was not decided then but, 150 years later, in *X v. Sweeney*, 1982 S.C.C.R. 161 it was confirmed that private prosecution was possible under Scots law. In that case, which referred to *Hare v. Wilson*, the victim of rape and assault was allowed to proceed with a private prosecution where the Crown did not proceed with the indictment due to concerns over the complainer's fitness to give evidence. The second point in this case concerned the immunity of a *socius criminis*. The Court decided, by a majority, that Hare was immune from prosecution although the judgments are unclear as to whether he should be immune in respect of all crimes or restricted to the three crimes on the indictment, even although he only gave evidence in relation to one of those and he did not, even then, incriminate himself. The modern view appears to be that a *socius criminis* cannot be prosecuted for matters covered by the libel in the indictment: see *McGinley & Dowds v. MacLeod*, 1963 J.C. 11. Hare was released from Calton jail and given money and transit. However a mob of about 8,000 formed at Dumfries and tried to lynch him. He was smuggled out by police and was last heard of walking towards Newcastle.

The authorities were so afraid of the mob reaction to the testimony of Hare at Burke's trial that they attempted to cover up the story. Burke had left confessions which were not published until the authorities had helped to smuggle Hare away from Edinburgh. Hare's own confessions were mysteriously, perhaps conveniently, misplaced by the Lord Advocate. An inquiry committee was later set up and concluded that there was no evidence that Knox or his assistants knew that murder was committed in procuring the bodies he received. The Report was wary of changing the impression that Burke and Hare's activities were unique. Knox may well have been a popular teacher but if he was as innocent as he protested his knowledge of forensic pathology left much to be desired. The suspicion remains that there were too many familial links between the medical profession and the Crown and that the Edinburgh establishment feared a mob riot over the resurrections.

One final, macabre, point. Burke's brain was dissected by the great professional enemy of Knox, Dr Monro. On January 29 & 30, 1829, 30,000 people came to view his body and it is still in the Anatomy Museum of Edinburgh University. Various distinguished Edinburgh society members also received a piece of his skin.

THE BONNY BURDEN O' BON ACCORD

Case 5: Incorporation of Tailors of Aberdeen v. Coutts (1837) 2 Sh & Macl 609 (HL) and (1840) 1 Rob 296 (House of Lords, Scotland)

Heritable property—Burgage tenure—Real burdens—Rules of constitution

(See Reid, "What is a Real Burden?" (1984) 29 J.L.S.S. 9 and "Defining Real Conditions", 1989 J.R. 69.)

Today virtually every property in Scotland is encumbered by real burdens. These are the obligations that either prohibit you from carrying out certain activities in your own house or garden (*e.g.* a prohibition on keeping pigs in your back garden), or impose obligations on you to do things (*e.g.* a requirement that you and your neighbours maintain a common roof). Until recently Scotland was unusual in the world in allowing both types of obligation to be imposed on land. It was the present case that confirmed this was possible.

The Tailors of Aberdeen were a merchant body that owned land in Aberdeen. They proposed to develop Bon Accord Square in Aberdeen and in 1822 employed Adam Coutts, a local solicitor, to do the paperwork. The Tailors thought that certain conditions should apply to each property that was sold, to make sure that the development proceeded in an orderly way (this was over a century before planning permission from a local council became necessary). These conditions or real burdens were set out by Coutts with the traditional prolixity of the conveyancer and can be read in full at pages 609–617 of the 1837 report. They include obligations to put up and maintain metal railings, specifications as to how the houses and pavements were to be built (only "well-dressed granite stone" was permitted for the houses and "well-hewn hill stone" for the pavements); and then a lengthy list of prohibitions, such as no outward opening window shutters, and the almost poetic (but in a William Carlos Williams way) prohibition on the "tanning of leather, making of candle, soap, or glue, slaughtering of cattle, erecting of glass-works, distilleries, or iron-foundries, making of bricks or tiles".

In 1824 the Tailors sold a plot of land to a local builder, George Nicol. To aid his purchase of properties in the area Nicol needed finance and he borrowed in total £1,100 from the same Adam Coutts who had drafted the burdens. A disposition in favour of Nicol was granted and recorded and he acquired ownership. Unfortunately, just one year later he became insolvent. To satisfy the debt it was decided that the plot should be transferred to his principal creditor, Coutts. A disposition was granted in favour of Coutts, but this disposition failed to refer to the many burdens imposed on the property in the earlier disposition. The question was, was he bound by them? Did the burdens attach to the land (so binding whoever owned the land, *i.e.* the "singular successors") or were they enforceable only against a person who accepts them in dispositions in their own favour? Were they, in other words, real or personal burdens? The case lasted many years, and eventually reached the House of Lords in 1837.

The initial stages of the court proceedings were dominated by a suggestion that Coutts had been fraudulent. This argument was dropped just before the case reached the House of Lords. However, this caused a problem. Because so much time had been taken up considering the nature of Mr Coutts's character in the Court of Session there was no consideration of the substantive question. The House of Lords did not want to deal with the case unless they had the view of the Court of Session judges on that question, so they referred the case back to the lower court. Thirteen Court of Session judges were consulted. In the course of their opinions the most important judgment was that of Lord Corehouse, who provided a number of rules as to how to create real burdens, that is burdens that will run with the land and bind even those singular successors whose disposition (*i.e.* title to the land) does not refer to them. These rules are still treated authoritatively today. They provide (among other provisions) that the burden must appear in full in the title of the burdened property, that it must be precise, and must not be contrary to public policy.

Real burdens providing restrictions on use, and imposing positive obligations, had little legal support prior to this judgment. Lord Corehouse was therefore creating a new legal concept. However, despite this innovation he provided a detailed series of rules still used today. So where did these detailed rules come from? Had Lord Corehouse a flash of inspiration? Professor Reid has shown how Lord Corehouse actually borrowed the rules from a quite different concept. In Scots law there are two categories of real burden. The term today is mainly used to describe the conditions that encumber ownership of land. However, in 1840 the term mainly described what are referred to today as pecuniary real burdens (rights in security created over land). Lord Corehouse lifted the rules of constitution from pecuniary real burdens and, as they fell into disuse, so real burdens (in the modern sense) thrived.

In 1840 (11 years after starting) the case went back to the House of Lords where Lord Corehouse's rules of constitution were approved. As the urbanisation of Scotland continued throughout the nineteenth and twentieth centuries, real burdens were used in virtually every building development, commercial and residential—each burden having to satisfy Lord Corehouse's test of validity. And with the Scottish Law Commission's recommended codification of the law (see *Report on Real Burdens*, (Scot Law Com No. 181, 2000)) the effect of *Tailors of Aberdeen v. Coutts* will last long into the next century.

One final peculiarity. Contrary to common perception (caused at least in part by some loose comments by Lord Brougham in the House of Lords—see also the problems he caused in another area of the law **Case 89**) this case did not involve any speciality of the feudal system of landownership. Bon Accord Square was and is situated within the Royal Burgh of Aberdeen and as such was held on what is called Burgage Tenure, the principle feature of which is that feuing is not permitted. Originally the Tailors had feued the ground to Nicol but the mistake was rectified a year later and a disposition granted in his favour. It was this disposition that contained the burdens and was recorded in the General Register of Sasines.

WHERE PARLIAMENT FEARS TO TREAD

Case 6: H.M. Advocate v. Greenhuff (1838) 2 Swin. 236 (High Court of Justiciary, Scotland)

Criminal Law—Declaratory power of the High Court—Human rights—Art. 7, ECHR

(See Jones, "Common Law and Criminal Law: The Scottish Example", 1990 Crim. L.R. 292; Capoddi, *"Nulla Poena Sine Lege* and Scots Law: A Continental Perspective", 1998 J.R. 73)

Thou shalt dae nae wrang. The criminal law of Scotland is based on this general proposition and is, unlike English law, by and large common law rather than statutory. It follows that the Crown in bringing charges has quite a high level of discretion, and the court can hold criminal acts which have never before been charged as criminal offences. There really is no such thing in Scots law as nominate crimes, at least in the sense that the prosecutor does not need to name a specified crime, so long as he or she alleges sufficient facts to indicate to an accused the action which is alleged to be worthy of punishment (see Criminal Procedure (Scotland) Act 1995, Sched. 3, para. 2). Sometimes the prosecutor alleges facts that have never before been held to amount to a criminal offence: the question arises of whether the court can convict. And sometimes the court really, really wants to convict. Usually, it will say that the act always was criminal but has just never been charged before; sometimes it says that it is simply a new method of committing an existing crime; very occasionally the court has declared that the action never was before a crime but, because it is today recognised as being so obviously wrong, it now is. This last is the court exercising what is called the Declaratory Power of the High Court. It was in the present case that this alleged power was first explicitly accepted and exercised.

Bernard Greenhuff had access to the house of a friend, Mrs Cameron in High Terrace, Edinburgh. He decided to make some money by inviting other friends to this house where cards and other games of chance might be played, for money. The friends told other friends. The door was left open, and people who were friends or acquaintances of neither Mr Greenhuff nor Mrs Cameron were made welcome, so long as they played the game. Mr Greenhuff made lots of money, for the banker always wins. The players included doctors and lawyers. Perhaps a lawyer was one of the losers, for lawyers know how to turn tables. We will never now know who shopped Mr Greenhuff but, like the prophet Zachariah, he was wounded in the house of his friends. He was reported to the authorities, and was indicted and brought before the court.

The prosecutor, however, had a problem. The statute under which Greenhuff was originally charged was discovered to apply only to England and there was no equivalent statute for Scotland, except one of 1621 which, because it prohibited the running of gaming establishments only in public houses, did not apply to the present case where the establishment was in Mrs Cameron's private address. So he changed the indictment to charge Greenhuff under common law, but was then immediately faced with another problem. There was no precedent for such a charge, actions such as Greenhuff's never before having been found to be criminal. But in the early 1800s, courts were not reticent in applying their own notions of morality when it came to interpreting the criminal law (things are different now—see how morality was dealt with in *R. v. Brown*, **Case 87**). Lord Justice-Clerk Boyle held that gaming in a house in the centre of Edinburgh was such an affront to public morality that the charge was clearly competent. He quoted Baron Hume, whose works on criminal law are regarded as Institutional, and who had asserted that unlike the English the Scottish Supreme Criminal Court had an inherent power to punish every act of an "obvious criminal nature". It follows, said the Lord Justice-Clerk, that "this Court has a power to declare any thing that has a tendency to corrupt public morals, and injure the interests of society, an indictable offence". Most of the other judges agreed, with only Lord Cockburn, who said he "cared nothing for the theory, or the doctrine, of any modern institutional writer", dissenting on the ground that only Parliament, failing which long usage of the court, could render actions criminal, otherwise the lieges might be at risk of prosecution for acting in a manner they believed to be lawful because they had been given no indication otherwise.

Greenhuff served two months in the Jail of Edinburgh.

Due to the substantial doubts as to whether the High Court retains this power in the modern era, the Court is today much more likely to say that the act is a new method of committing an old crime, and there is no case in the law reports of the twentieth century in which the High Court of Justiciary has explicitly stated that it was in fact exercising its declaratory power. The nearest that they got was in *Khaliq v. H.M. Advocate*, **Case 71**. In *Grant v. Allan*, 1988 S.L.T. 11 the Court affirmed that the power existed, but declined to exercise it there.

The "declaratory power", in the sense of the power of a court to declare criminal conduct which was innocuous before the declaration, is unlikely to have survived (if, in truth, it ever existed) the implementation of the European Convention on Human Rights, for Article 7 thereof provides that no one shall be held guilty of any criminal offence on account of any act or omission which did not constitute a criminal offence at the time when it was committed (see *S. v. H.M. Advocate*, **Case 78**). The Declaratory Power, by its very nature, operates retrospectively and, for reasons such as those given by Lord Cockburn all these years ago, it is likely that Article 7 will prevent the power ever being used again.

PRYDE AND PREJUDICE IN A PLACE OF PLENTY

Case 7: Elspeth Pryde or Duncan v. The Heritors and Kirk-Session of Ceres (1843) 5 D. 552
(Inner House, Court of Session, Scotland)

Administrative law—Judicial review—Poor law

William Duncan was a weaver in Ceres. When he died in 1840 he left behind a pregnant widow (Elspeth Pryde or Duncan) and a family of seven children. The family sought the assistance of relatives. The second daughter was taken in by William Duncan's brother. The eldest daughter, aged 13, resided with her mother and other family earning between two and three shillings a week from weaving. Elspeth herself earned between 1s and 1s 6d winding bobbins. Elspeth applied for parochial relief to the body responsible for dealing with the poor, the property owners (or heritors) and Kirk-Session of her local parish, Ceres. The family was awarded an allowance of 3s 6d a week.

Elspeth sought to have this sum increased and she took her case to the Court of Session using the process known as advocation—the traditional Scots law term for review. The issue was simple. Did the Court possess the power to review the proceedings of the bodies with the responsibility to provide for the support of paupers? If they did have such a power, what were its limits?

The Lord Ordinary was concerned that if the allowance were to be reviewed favourably it would lead to cases on the same lines from every district in Scotland and would result in the most interminable and ruinous litigation. The Court, however, had to make sure that the heritors did not evade their obligations. His Lordship noted, from reports to Parliament on the condition of the handloom weavers, that many thousands of families in Scotland in that meritorious class of artisans had no more than five or six shillings for their subsistence. So Elspeth's plight was not unusual. The Kirk-Session for their part pointed out that the eldest daughter could earn up to three shillings a week and that Elspeth was in good health and could earn two shillings per week. They also pointed out that Elspeth's own father lived next door to her and could relieve her of at least one of her children and a brother in

Edinburgh could relieve her of another. On the basis of this the Lord Ordinary accepted that the Kirk-Session had acted reasonably and he rejected the plea for more money. Elspeth Duncan appealed.

The Whole Court looked at three questions: is it competent to review the decisions of those responsible for fixing allowances for the poor? Where specific sums were fixed could there be review in terms of the adequacy of the amount fixed? Finally, could the Court fix the amount which they regarded as appropriate as an allowance for the poor?

There was precedent which seemed to show that in the past the Court had exercised a supervisory jurisdiction where an applicant had been denied relief merely on the grounds of prejudice, such as being Irish (*Higgins v. Heritors and Kirk-Session of the Barony Parish of Glasgow* (1824) 3 S. 168), but there was no precedent for the Court being asked to substitute its own sum for that offered by a Kirk-Session. The majority in the present case were clear that they had jurisdiction to supervise the work of the heritors and Kirk-Session, though Lord Moncreiff took the more limited view that review was only available where there was refusal to implement the legislation or in extreme instances. He was of the view that this included reviewing awards which were illusory and amounted to a manifest evasion of the statutory duty.

As to the question of whether or not an award could be reviewed by the court the Lord President thought, like Pollyanna, that the need for intervention would be limited since the heritors and Kirk-Session would surely focus their minds on the interests of the parochial poor rather than on their own pockets. He seems to have forgotten all those cases in *Morison* in which one parish tries to ensure another parish is the one liable for the support of indigents (see *Morison's Dictionary*, 10551– 10595). Taking a slightly more technical view, Lord Mackenzie noted that the obligation under the legislation of 1579 did not actually involve discretion. It required them to take care of the needful sustenation of those who were forced to live by alms. This established the level which had to be achieved. Where it was not achieved then there was a remedy. That remedy allowed the Court to fix the level of support. Lord Jeffrey noted that the statutory right was one to needful sustenation—nothing more, nothing less. He could not see that there could be any discretion by which a man might be starved who is entitled to needful sustenation. The fact that there had been few cases was accounted for by unsuccessful applicants resorting to begging. Their practical remedy, paradoxically, was to do what the statute forbade.

As to the amount which the Court was prepared to substitute for the inadequate 3s 6d, a small addition was made for the posthumous child. The wages of the second daughter were to be applied for her needs since, as the Lord President noted, a girl of her age must be decently clothed and fed to be able to earn such wages as she did. The amount to be awarded should be able to secure the family from the cravings of hunger and the risk of loss of health from an inadequate supply of food.

Six shillings a week was his Lordship's view, with this being lowered as the children's surplus earnings came into play. His colleagues, however, were less willing to nominate a sum and the matter was left with the Heritors and Kirk Session to come up with a more appropriate sum than they had previously done.

This case is the bedrock of modern-day judicial review of bodies with discretion and all this because the richer citizens of the pretty Fife village of Ceres wanted to save a few shillings at the expense of a widow and her children. When one reads the powerful opinions of the minority judges it is quite clear that this is a classic "principle" which could quite as easily have gone the other way.

MCNAGHTEN'S CASE

Case 8: Daniel McNaghten's Case [1843] 10 Cl. & Fin. 200; R. v. McNaghten [1843] 4 St. Tr. NS 847 (House of Lords, England)

Criminal law—Murder—Insanity—Proper test— "McNaghten Rules"

(See R. Moran, *Knowing Right From Wrong: The Insanity Defence of Daniel McNaghten* (London, 1981))

Daniel McNaghten was a Scottish actor turned wood-turner and political radical in the Glasgow of the 1830s. Although the Reform Act of 1832 had extended the franchise to large sections of the middle class, Chartists, Socialists and other radicals supported the People's Charter which advocated *inter alia* universal male suffrage, abolition of property requirements, annual Parliaments and voting by secret ballot. In September 1841 McNaghten made a complaint to the Glasgow Commissioner of Police that he was being persecuted by the Tories because of how he had voted in an election and complained generally that he was being followed and harassed by police spies. In late 1842 he left Glasgow and in January 1843 turned up in London, where he announced himself to the authorities by shooting and killing Edmund Drummond, the private secretary of Sir Robert Peel, the Prime Minister. When arrested, he said that he had been forced to kill Peel because of the persecution he had suffered at the hands of the Tories. At his trial the defence mounted on his behalf was that he had killed Drummond, mistaking him for Peel, while legally insane. Though otherwise of sound mind, the defence argued, he suffered from a morbid delusion which left him unable to perceive right from wrong in relation to the delusion. The prosecution accepted that he suffered from the delusion but did not accept that a partial insanity such as this could justify an acquittal. Interestingly they did not argue that his crime was sanely and politically motivated and it has been suggested that this was to avoid revealing the undoubted network of police spies and informers which operated in Britain generally and in Glasgow in particular on behalf of Peel and his Government and Party. Nine doctors gave evidence for the defence, evidence which the prosecution accepted.

Lord Chief Justice Tindal charged the jury that if they believed that McNaghten was incapable of distinguishing right from wrong in relation to the act charged, then they should acquit him. Unsurprisingly since the prosecution had not opposed the finding of insanity, the jury found McNaghten not guilty by reason of insanity. Public and press reaction to the acquittal and a consequent fear of assassination (said to affect both Peel and Queen Victoria) led to the House of Lords asking for the opinion of the English judges on the law in relation to insanity and crime. The judges attended at the Lords and delivered their opinion on June 19, 1843. This was an unusual but not unique procedure. It was not the first occasion on which the judges had been required to answer an abstract question of law. In formal terms their opinion was not a binding expression of law. Nevertheless the opinion delivered by them, known thereafter as *"The McNaghten Rules"*, was accepted by the House of Lords then and has been accepted since in English courts as the definition of legal insanity and applied as law. It remains the basis for the English approach to insanity in modern criminal law (*Sullivan* [1984] A.C. 156). It has been influential throughout English speaking jurisdictions and is still a basis for many current approaches. While the Rules were applied in Scotland for a period in the nineteenth century (*James Gibson* (1844) 2 Broun 332), it is now accepted that, though influential, they are not part of Scots criminal law (*H.M. Advocate v. Sharp*, 1927 J.C. 66). While modern Scots law emphasises the necessity of proving "total alienation of reason in relation to the act charged as a result of mental illness, mental disease or defect or unsoundness of mind" (*Brennan v. H.M. Advocate*, 1977 J.C. 38), there is a strong tradition of incorporating a broader approach which can include inability to resist impulse caused by mental illness etc. (*H.M. Advocate v. Sharp*).

The judges answered five questions put to them. The central definition came in the answers to the second and third questions which dealt with the proper questions to be left to the jury and the terms in which they should be put. The answers were: "... that the jurors ought to be told in all cases that every man is to be presumed to be sane, and to possess a sufficient degree of reason to be responsible for his crimes, until the contrary be proved to their satisfaction; and that to establish a defence on the ground of insanity, it must be clearly proved that, at the time of the committing of the act, the party accused was labouring under such a defect of reason, from disease of the mind, as not to know the nature and quality of the act he was doing; or, if he did know it, that he did not know he was doing what was wrong'. Colloquially this has been summarised as "did he know right from wrong?' It is an essential part of the insanity defence that the accused's inability to tell right from wrong is due to a defect of reason caused by a disease of the mind.

The *Rules* have also been criticised because they adopt only one approach to insanity, that is a reason-based approach. They do not cover the situation in which the accused knows that what he or she is doing is wrong but is unable to stop him- or herself from committing the act because of mental illness. A number of other approaches have been proposed. In 1924 a committee proposed extending the definition to the person who had no power to resist an impulse because of mental disease (*Report of the Committee on Insanity and Crime* Cmd. 2005). In 1975 the Butler Report strongly criticised the *Rules* for being based on the "obsolete belief of the pre-eminent role of reason in controlling social behaviour" (*Report of the Committee on Mentally Abnormal Offenders* Cmd. 6244). Based on their recommendations the Law Commission's Draft Criminal Code would introduce a "mental disorder verdict" where it was proved that the accused was at the time suffering from "severe mental illness or severe mental handicap", unless the jury finds that the illness did not cause the offence (*Draft Criminal Code Bill 1989*, cl.35: Law Com. No. 177). None of these proposals has been implemented.

Daniel McNaghten was detained in Bethlem Royal Hospital until transferred to Broadmoor in 1864 where he died a year later. Peel had died in 1850. Secret ballots were introduced in Britain by the Reform Act 1872. No-one now knows the extent to which McNaghten's feelings of persecution had any foundation in reality.

ENGINE, ENGINE, BURNING BRIGHT

Case 9: Allan v. Barclay (1864) 2 M. 873
(Inner House, Court of Session, Scotland)

Delict—Damages—Remoteness   of   damage—Economic   loss—Consequential losses

(See Wilkinson and Forte, "Economic Loss: A Scottish Perspective", 1985 J.R. 1.)

On September 23, 1863 a mechanical vehicle belonging to the defender broke down on the public road, blocking passage. The driver failed to move the obstruction, but left it on the road, and darkness fell. Light from the engine was clearly visible, marking the machine as an obstruction.

Late that night William Hill, a carter in the employ of John Allan, a brewer from Airdrie, was driving his cart and horse along the road. Unfortunately, the horse, coming across the obstruction, took fright at the burning engine and shied, tumbling itself, the cart and William Hill into the ditch at the side of the road. Hill was injured, and both the horse and cart were damaged. Hill's employer, Allan, wanted to seek compensation for his losses, but he faced a problem. His property, the damaged horse and the cart were valued at a mere £20, which was below the financial limit for raising an action in the Court of Session. So he sued also for recovery of his economic losses suffered through the injuries to his employee, Hill. Allan alleged that William Hill was instrumental to his business and that any substitute would not have the same knowledge of his business and customers and that consequently he, Allan, would suffer economic loss of at least £30. This brought his total claim up to £50, which was then the jurisdictional limit for the Court of Session to hear the case.

Unfortunately for Allan, while Hill's injuries were, of course, physical his own losses were both consequential upon these physical injuries and, in effect, purely economic. The law has for long (starting with this case) set its face against the easy claiming of pure economic losses and the competency of claiming for loss of an employee's services was here rejected. Since that knocked £30 off the value of the claim the whole claim fell and it was dismissed as incompetent. The law of economic loss has substantially developed since, particularly through *Hedley Byrne v. Heller & Partners,* **Case 46)** and its progeny, and the decision in the present case on the facts was repeated in *Reavis v. Clan Line Steamers* **(Case 23).**

Though this case is, perhaps, best known as an early example of the rejection of claims for pure economic loss, its other importance lies in how it dealt with consequential losses, that is to say, losses consequential upon direct losses. Allan's economic loss was caused by Hill's physical loss, which was caused by the (alleged) negligence. Had Allan's loss of Hill's services not been economic the question of how losses caused by losses, perhaps themselves caused by other losses, would have arisen. The Lord Ordinary, Lord Kinloch, addressed this issue, though it was not part of the Inner House's reasoning. He laid down what has come to be called "the grand rule": "The grand rule on the subject of damages is, that none can be claimed except such as naturally and directly arise out of the wrong done; and such, therefore, as may reasonably be supposed to have been in the view of the wrongdoer". Though it has come in for much criticism, this test for distinguishing between direct (and therefore recoverable) and indirect (and therefore irrecoverable) losses is as good as any, balancing as it does the concepts of directness, reasonableness and foreseeability. The test is clearly designed to be a unitary one but much judicial time has subsequently been wasted trying to separate "directness" from "reasonableness" in attempts to award or to withhold damages in particular cases (see in particular *Re Polemis* [1921] 3 K.B. 560 and *Wagon Mound* [1961] A.C. 388).

It may, incidentally, be noted that Hill subsequently raised his own action for personal injuries, and the action, being unencumbered by issues of economic loss or consequential loss, was held relevant. Whether he succeeded in proving that the abandonment of the engine was an act of negligence for which damages could be awarded (and if so how much he got) is not recorded in the law reports.

LEGAL IMPERIALISM

Case 10: Brand's Trustees v. Brand's Trustees
(1876) 3 R. (HL) 16
(House of Lords, Scotland)

Property—Land law—Fixtures—Acquisition by accession and occupation—Legal process

(See Reid, "The Lord Chancellor's Fixtures", 1983 J.L.S.S. 49)

This case concerns the law of fixtures in Scotland. Prior to this case the law was relatively straightforward and simple. All land is heritable, and if anything is permanently attached to the land, it in turn becomes heritable, by the process of accession. Everything else is moveable. Thus a pile of bricks is moveable, but when they are built into a wall, they become heritable. Conversely when that wall is demolished, the bricks revert to moveable status. Erskine provided two further requirements— the article should be to some extent "fixed or united", and the attachment should be for the perpetual use of the heritage. Of course these are matters of fact about which there may be argument in any particular case. There was, for example, a series of cases in the Court of Session concerning mining machinery in which the question was always the same—was it or was it not fixed to or united with the land. The practical importance of the question arose starkly when the land was owned by one person but used (under the terms of a lease) by another person: if the machinery became part of the land, it fell into the landlord's ownership and the tenant could not remove it at the end of the lease. The results in this series of cases were predominantly in favour of such machinery being treated as moveable property, and as such it could be taken away at the end of a lease of the ground. This was the decision principally in the case of *Fisher v. Dixon* (1843) 5 D. 775, and it was considered to be a sound statement of Scots law on the subject.

That was until the House of Lords decision in the present case, another mining machinery case. The House of Lords was and is the final Court of Appeal for English, Scottish and Irish cases, and the Court was and is composed of judges from these jurisdictions. The significant difference between then and now is that today at least two Scottish Lords of Appeal normally listen to Scottish appeals; but in *Brand's Trustees*, a Scottish case, the appeal was heard by three English judges (the Lord Chancellor, Lord Cairns, Lords Chelmsford and Selborne) and one Irish judge (Lord O'Hagan). The Lord Chancellor, giving the leading speech, said:

"I would remind your Lordships that there are with regard to matters of this kind, which are included under the comprehensive term of 'fixtures', two general rules, a correct appreciation of which will, as it seems to me, go far to solve the whole difficulty in this case. My Lords, one of these rules is the general well known rule that whatever is fixed to the freehold (*sic*) becomes part of the freehold or inheritance. The other is quite a different and separate rule. Whatever once becomes part of the inheritance cannot be severed by a limited owner ... These, my Lords, are two rules—not one by way of exception to the other, but two rules standing consistently together. My Lords, an exception indeed, and a very important exception indeed, has been made, not to the first of these rules, but to the second ... That exception has been established in favour of the fixtures which have been attached to the inheritance for the purpose of trade...."

As Professor (as he then wasn't) Kenneth Reid pointed out in his article cited above this is nothing but a restatement of the English law of trade fixtures, according to which the mining machinery on the death of the tenant, unless previously severed, became the property of the landlord. The House of Lords was unanimous on this point, and thus the decision became a statement of Scots Law under the doctrine of *stare decisis*. It has remained so, and will remain until it is changed by an Act of Parliament, or until the House of Lords reconsiders its verdict. A reminder of this fact was provided by the case of *Scottish Discount v. Blin and Others*, 1986 S.L.T. 123 where *Brand's Trustees* was affirmed and followed, but no appeal made.

Professor Reid calls the decision in *Brand's Trustees* "as blatant an example of anglicisation as any in our history". The whole topic of legal imperialism is summed up here, the imposition of the law of a much larger jurisdiction upon the law of a smaller, defenceless, jurisdiction. Thankfully, we in Scotland have never been guilty of imposing our law upon a weaker jurisdiction. That at least is what we like to think. But it is not true.

The Shetland Islands are a group of islands lying well to the north of the Scottish mainland. They are on a comparable latitude to Bergen, and are much nearer that city than they are to Edinburgh. The whole atmosphere of the islands is Norwegian, which is not surprising, as they were originally part of Norway. (On how they came to be part of Scotland, see *Lord Advocate v. University of Aberdeen and Budge*, **Case 47**) These islands were governed by a Norse form of law, known as udal law. A brief summary of the differences between Scots and Udal Law is that in matters of landownership, there was no concept of the feudal superior, such as was the case in Scotland; in udal succession law, the property was divided among all the children, and not given to the eldest male child; a payment of scat was made, which was a form of land tax; weights and measures were totally different; the law of the foreshore, seabed and territorial sea and fishings were different; and the law of treasure trove and abandoned moveables was totally different.

In the case of *Bruce v. Smith* (1890) 17 R. 1000 ("the Hoswick Whale case") the first traces of the overlaying of udal law by Scots law are seen. Where a whale was actively pursued and beached, its carcass belonged, under udal or customary law, one third to the hunter, one third to the landowner and one third to the Crown, who was not in the practice of claiming this right. In *Bruce* it was narrated that a shoal of small whales, known as caaing whales, was driven from some miles at sea, into Hoswick Bay, Shetland. The whales were stranded on the beach and killed below the low water mark by 314 men and boys who waded into the water waist deep. The carcasses were then dragged onto the beach, flenched, and sold by auction for some £450. There was, of course, no Greenpeace then. The landowner then claimed one third of the free proceeds, in accordance with the local custom, which claim was resisted. It was held by the court that the custom was not just or reasonable, and did not have the force of law, and the whole proceeds were therefore payable to the captors. This is an application of the Scots law of acquisition by *occupatio*, derived from the Roman law and irrelevant to Norse law. Scottish legal imperialism was again on display in *Lord Advocate v. University of Aberdeen and Budge*, **Case 47**).

CANNIBALISM AND THE CABIN BOY

Case 11: R. v. Dudley and Stephens (1884) 14 Q.B.D. 273 (Queen's Bench Division, High Court, England)

Criminal law—Murder and Cannibalism—Necessity

(See A.W.B. Simpson, *Cannibalism and the Common Law* (The Hambledon Press, London, 1994))

'Twas a dark and stormy night, the night the *Mignonette* went down. On its way to Sydney, Australia the yacht left Tollesbury Port, Essex, in late spring 1884, just in time to hit the rigours of the southern winter in the South Atlantic. The 17-year-old yacht was not in good shape and it had been sold, cheaply, to a lawyer in Australia, who employed a four-man crew to deliver it to him. It was in no condition to undertake such a long and arduous voyage.

It had all started out so well. A 17-year-old boy, Richard Parker, signed up in May 1884 as the fourth and youngest member of the crew of the *Mignonette*. This was to be his first long ocean voyage and he was filled with excitement. The other three members of the crew were Thomas Dudley, the captain, Edwin ('Edward", to the law reporters) Stephens, the mate and Edmund Brooks, all experienced professional sailors. But they could not prevent the *Mignonette* sinking, 1,600 miles north west of the Cape of Good Hope, and 680 miles south of the nearest land, the island of St Helena (where Napoleon had been exiled after Waterloo). All four crew survived the sinking of the yacht and were cast away in a dinghy, but they were only able to carry with them two tins of turnip and no drinking water. On the fourth day adrift they caught a small turtle which they made last for eight days. After that they had nothing. For water they had to catch the rain as it fell, and eventually forced themselves to drink their own urine. After the turtle there was nothing to eat for eight days, and the condition of all the men deteriorated rapidly. Richard Parker's condition was the most extreme and he started to slip into unconsciousness. The fittest was Edmund Brooks. With no sign of rescue and no provisions, Dudley proposed that they should follow a custom long known and accepted by sailors: one of them should die in order to allow the others to survive by eating him and who this was to be should be decided by lots. Stephens agreed, but Brooks did not. However much this custom was accepted by the sailing community, it was not sanctioned by the law. To kill another person is the crime of murder.

After twenty days adrift in total, Dudley and Stephens agreed that it was necessary, if any of them were to survive, that one must die and that Richard Parker, as the weakest and looking likely to die soon, was the obvious choice. Dudley killed Richard and all three, including Brooks, drank his blood and then ate his flesh. Four days later they were picked up by the *Moctezuma* and taken back to the Port of Falmouth. Neither Dudley nor Stephens attempted to conceal what they had done. When they were arrested and put on trial for the murder of Richard Parker they attracted great public support, and a public defence fund was set up to pay for their legal expenses. So great was the support that there was a surplus in the fund, and there is an unconfirmed suggestion that the surplus was used to pay for the schooling of Richard Parker's young sister Emily (who received an education above the level of the rest of the family).

Dudley and Stephens were tried at the Exeter Assizes, the judge being Baron Huddleston. Because of public sympathy there was a strong likelihood that the jury would not convict. But such a verdict would legitimise the unofficial custom of drawing lots and eating human flesh. Baron Huddleston informally let the jury know that whatever the verdict the men would not hang. Dudley and Stephens pled not guilty. They made no attempt to argue that the charge should be reduced to manslaughter because of the circumstances in which they found themselves. The choice was between conviction of murder or acquittal because they acted under necessity. Under the direction of Baron Huddleston the jury returned a special verdict, which even at that time had become obsolete in English law. Under this special verdict the jury recounted the facts as they found them to be proved and asked the Court to determine whether in these circumstances Dudley and Stephens were guilty of murder. The Court was adjourned to the Queen's Bench Division of the High Court where a bench of five judges, presided over by Lord Coleridge and including Baron Huddleston, returned a verdict of guilty of murder and sentenced Dudley and Stephens to be hanged. They were, as the jury had been assured, reprieved and a sentence of six months imprisonment, without hard labour, substituted.

The importance of the case is the rejection by the Court of the defence of necessity put forward on behalf of Dudley and Stephens. It was simply not the law "that a man may save his life by killing, if necessary, an innocent and unoffending neighbour". The two major grounds for rejecting the defence of necessity were, first, the moral proposition that "to preserve one's life is generally speaking a duty, but it may be the plainest and the highest duty to sacrifice it" and, secondly, considerations of public policy: "Who is to be the judge of this sort of necessity? By what measure is the comparative value of lives to be measured?" While this rhetoric expresses an admirable moral code, it is a code easier to comply with within the safety of a court room than adrift without food and water for twenty days in the South Atlantic Ocean. Instead of recognising the reality of the life-or-death dilemma faced by the men and others like them, and trying to provide a solution, the Court adopted an impossibly absolute standard in its judgment. But the rhetoric was accompanied by a pragmatic recognition of the reality, in pardoning the two men and imposing the relatively trivial sentence of six months. In effect the law said one thing and did another.

Although this case was concerned with necessity as a defence to murder, its absolute terms left the very existence of that defence in English law in doubt for many years until it was all but reinstated in the guise of "duress of circumstances", a specific defence conceptually linked to and with a similar definition to duress by threats (*R. v. Pommell* [1995] 2 Cr. App. R. 607). However, neither duress by threats nor duress by circumstances is available in relation to a charge of murder, either as an acquittal defence, or to reduce the charge to culpable homicide (manslaughter, in English law).

Scottish courts fought shy of the defence for many years. It has never arisen in such a dramatic context as the trial of Dudley and Stephens, but it has appeared in a number of cases involving road traffic offences where a driver claimed he or she had had to drive in breach of the law (for example, while disqualified) because of the necessity of the circumstances, whether to escape attack or to drive someone to hospital in an emergency. Hume had given no support to the defence of necessity. He had indeed rejected the traditional Scottish plea of Burthensack (by which a person who was starving might carry off as much meat as he could carry on his back) as a plea which would mitigate the capital punishment for theft. But in *Moss v. Howdle*, 1997 J.C. 123 the High Court of Justiciary did finally acknowledge the existence of the defence of necessity in Scots law (in a road traffic case). The Court defined the defence as equivalent to the Scottish defence of coercion (*Thomson v. H.M. Advocate*, 1983 S.C.C.R. 368). Thus it is only available, whatever the crime charged, where there is immediate danger of death or great bodily harm to the accused or others and there is no alternative for the accused but to act as he or she did. An influential case in forming the approach of the High Court was the Canadian case of *Perka v. The Queen* [1984] 2 S.C.R. 232 in which different theoretical approaches to the possible defence were discussed at length. The Supreme Court of Canada rejected the approach of comparing the good achieved by the commission of the crime with the harm it causes. This was on similar grounds to that of Lord Coleridge— who is to decide? Instead the basis of the defence was seen as moral involuntariness (where a person was compelled to act by extreme circumstances forcing him or her to do so).

None of the modern cases has involved the crime of murder. It seems clear that in England, while the defence of duress of circumstances may be available generally it is not available for murder. In Scotland, it seems likely that the defence would not be available as an acquittal defence but there is no reason in principle why necessity should not be available in Scotland, unlike England, to reduce the crime from one of murder to one of culpable homicide. This in effect, if not in formal law, is what happened to Thomas Dudley and Edwin Stephens.

REALITY AS FICTION

Case 12: Bank of England v. Vagliano Brothers
[1891] A.C. 107
(House of Lords, England)

Bills of exchange—Fraud—Statutory interpretation—Reality as a legal fiction

Anthony Isidor Glyka worked as a clerk for merchant bankers, Vagliano Brothers. His dealings in high finance no doubt encouraged him to consider ways of getting rich quick, and he started to speculate enormously on the Stock Exchange. The problem was that, on a clerk's salary his own money was not enough to finance these deals. So he devised an elaborate system of fraud. Glyka knew that a Mr Vucina in Odessa had previously drawn up bills of exchange payable to C Petridi & Co. These bills were to be paid by Vagliano Brothers. Glyka forged 43 bills purportedly drawn by Vucina, to be paid by Vagliano Brothers to C Petridi & Co. He persuaded Vagliano Brothers to accept these bills. Vagliano Brothers instructed the Bank of England to pay out on the bills and, by forging the signature of C Petridi & Co, Glyka himself received payment of the large sum of £71,500. Unfortunately for him, the fraud was discovered. He was arrested, pleaded guilty to forgery and was sentenced to 10 years penal servitude. But on whom was the loss to fall?

Vagliano Brothers (who did not want the loss to fall on them) raised an action for a declaration that the Bank of England should not have paid out on the forged bills and accordingly that the Bank should not have debited the Vagliano Brothers' account with the sum of £71,500. The loss, they argued, should fall on the bank. Vagliano Brothers won the case at first instance and at the Court of Appeal by 5 judges to 1. Like Caesar the day he overcame the Nervii, Vagliano Brothers doubtless felt peaceful satisfaction at this outcome. But if so it was not to last. The House of Lords divided 6–2 in favour of the Bank.

The main point of the case was the interpretation of a provision in the Bills of Exchange Act 1882. The right to receive payment under a bill of exchange can be transferred by means of the payee "endorsing" (*i.e.* adding his signature) in favour of another party who becomes in effect the new payee. However a transfer is not effective where the endorsement is forged. Some bills do not have any named payee. These are known as bearer bills, and the right to payment lies with the person in possession of the bill.

The issue was whether the Bank of England had acted correctly when it paid over to Glyka the sums under the bills made payable to"C Petridi & Co" which had forged endorsements of that party. The Bank argued that it had, and their main reason was to be found in section 7(3) of the 1882 Act, which states: "where the payee is a fictitious or non-existing person, the bill may be treated as payable to the bearer." The Bank contended that in this case C Petridi & Co were a fictitious payee; therefore the bills were bearer bills; therefore the Bank had correctly made payment to the person in possession of them, namely Glyka.

The difficulty with this argument was that C Petridi & Co did exist. How could they at the same time be fictitious? This point was the stumbling block for the majority judges in the Court of Appeal and the dissenting judges in the House of Lords, Lords Bramwell and Field. Lord Bramwell said that the Bank's argument meant treating C Petridi & Co as "at the same time real and unreal, they are that which is said to be an impossibility, being and not being at the same time." Lord Field made the stark point that Glyka's fraud would not have worked if he had invented a name for the payee. Glyka was more likely to get away with his scheme if he used the name of an actual person known to Vagliano Brothers.

The majority of the House of Lords saw no difficulty in accepting the seemingly illogical conclusion that C Petridi & Co were both a real existing person and fictitious. Lord Halsbury pointed out that many of the characters in the novels of Sir Walter Scott are based on real, historical people but in the novels they are fictitious characters. Lord Macnaghten interpreted fictitious to mean feigned or counterfeit. All the characters in the bills forged by Glyka were feigned or counterfeit persons and they were not "the less fictitious because there were in existence real persons for whom these names were intended to pass muster". Lord Hershell drew an analogy with a fictitious entry in a book of accounts. This does not mean that the entry has no real existence but only that it purports to be something which it is not.

Vagliano Brothers was not the last word on the mystery of the fictitious payee, and in later cases the courts have arrived at different conclusions on facts broadly similar to those here. It is not easy to reconcile all the decisions.

Vagliano Brothers does contain two further points of interest for anyone pondering on the reality of fictitious persons. The first is that the plaintiff is referred to as the Vagliano Brothers, yet it is clear that the plaintiff is one and no more than one individual person. So where were the other Vagliano Brothers? The answer was that Mr Vagliano was indeed a sole trader but he had continued to use the name of a partnership he had previously entered into with his brothers. The second point concerns a key witness in the civil action, a man who held a high-ranking position in the Bank of England. The name of the witness? Mr Disney!

A QUESTION OF TRUST

Case 13: Heritable Reversionary Company Ltd
v. Millar (McKay's Trustee)
(1891) 18 R. 1166 (IH) reversed by (1892) 19 R. (HL) 43;
[1892] A.C. 598
(House of Lords, Scotland)

Heritable property—Latent trust—Vesting of property in trustee in sequestration

(See Goudy, "Bankruptcy—Trust" (1891) 3 J.R. 365; "John Inglis" (1891) 7 Scottish Law Review 265; (1891) 3 J.R. 344; Editorial (1891) 35 Journal of Jurisprudence 449; McLaren, "Lord President Inglis" (1892) 4 J.R. 14.)

One of the most important judicial figures of the nineteenth century was Lord President Inglis. A son of the manse, John Inglis had been an MP, Solicitor General, and Lord Advocate, before being elected as Dean of the Faculty of Advocates. He was appointed Lord Justice-Clerk in 1858, and eight years later Lord President of the Court of Session. He held that office for quarter of a century until his death in 1891. In the obituaries it was stated that "Since Lord Stair died Scotland has not lost so able a jurist as the late Lord President Inglis." (Journal of Jurisprudence); and "as a jurist and a judge he is undeniably the most venerated Scotsman of his time". (Scottish Law Review). Inglis dominated Scottish legal life in the second half of the nineteenth century. His opinion in the Inner House in the present case was his last important judgment.

The facts were straightforward. Daniel McKay was manager of Heritable Reversionary Co. In 1882 he bought tenements in Edinburgh on behalf of the company and recorded title to them in the General Register of Sasines (GRS). However, the title did not narrate that McKay held the tenements as trustee for the company. In 1886 McKay signed a formal declaration of trust in favour of the company, but this was not recorded in the GRS. In 1890 McKay was declared bankrupt and Robert Millar was appointed as his trustee in sequestration. Both Millar and the company asserted a right to the tenements and they agreed to put a special case to the court. The question for Lord President Inglis and his colleagues was whether the tenements formed part of McKay's sequestrated estate, available for his creditors, or whether the company was entitled to exercise its right to them. They held that the tenements formed part of McKay's estate.

Lord President Inglis, and Lords Adam and Kinnear, founded upon the principle of allowing third parties (including creditors and therefore the trustee in sequestration) to rely on the "faith of the register". This meant that if there was no indication of any right affecting ownership apparent from examining GRS a third party should be allowed to assume that there were no hidden rights affecting ownership. In their judgments Lords Adam and Kinnear relied on the seventh edition of George Joseph Bell's *Commentaries on the Law of Scotland*, edited by their colleague on the bench Lord McLaren.

However, Lord McLaren himself dissented and, modestly referring to an earlier edition of Bell's work (the fifth), criticised Bell's analysis. Lord McLaren was also the author of the leading textbook on trusts and he argued that the beneficiary in the trust should prevail. He pointed out that ordinary creditors did not check GRS before extending credit to an individual. In his view the argument based on the "faith of the register" was irrelevant.

The decision of the majority caused some commercial concern, brought to public notice by Henry Goudy, an advocate and Professor of civil law at Edinburgh University ((1891) 3 J.R. 365). At that time a large number of securities over land (mortgages) were constituted using a right of reversion, which in effect was a quasi-trust. The debtor transferred ownership of their house to the lender and the lender agreed to hold the house "in security" for them. Professor Goudy perceived that the effect of the decision, coming soon after the collapse of the City of Glasgow Bank, was that if a lender became insolvent the debtor could lose his home.

The case was appealed to the House of Lords and Heritable Reversionary Co. used Professor Goudy as one of their counsel. His arguments prevailed, and the decision of the Inner House was reversed. Foreshadowing the case of *Sharp v. Thomson* (**Case 94**), over a century later, the House of Lords did not concentrate on the careful consideration of the principles of property law by the then late Lord President and his colleagues but instead focused on statutory interpretation. Section 102 of the Bankruptcy (Scotland) Act 1856 provided that the trustee in sequestration had right to "the whole property of the debtor". The Court held that these words did not include property held by the debtor on trust for a third party, even if that trust was latent, *i.e.* not apparent from examination of titles in GRS. This principle survives today, although the rule is now in statutory form. Section 33(1)(b) of the Bankruptcy (Scotland) Act 1985 provides that property held in trust for another is expressly excluded from vesting in the trustee in sequestration.

The reasoning behind the decision in the House of Lords has not faired as well. Throughout their speeches the Law Lords talk of the beneficiary having "true" or "beneficial" ownership (*per* Lord Watson at pp. 46 and 47, Lord Field at p. 54, and Lord Herschell at p. 43). The trustee is described as having "apparent" ownership (*per* Lord Field at p. 54, and per Lord Watson at p. 46). This is English terminology, reflecting the fact that in English trust law both the trustee and the beneficiary have real rights, although of different natures. Later case law has made clear that, in Scotland, the beneficiary has only a personal right—a right to sue the trustee—as opposed to a right of ownership. Ownership of trust property rests only with the trustee.

GET FLU AND MONEY'S DUE

Case 14: Carlill v. Carbolic Smoke Ball Company
[1893] 1 Q.B. 256
(Court of Appeal, England)

Contract— Offer and acceptance— Unilateral contract— Promise

(See Simpson, "Quackery and Contract Law: The Case of the Carbolic Smoke Ball" (1985) 14 Journal of Legal Studies 345).

If you get ill, or there is a lot of some disease going about, you have three options: do nothing, use the official healthcare services or use alternative therapies. None of these is guaranteed to work for the cure or prevention of all illnesses. None does much for flu even today. It was the same in the 1890s. There was lots of flu about. The son of the Prince of Wales died of it. So did lots of other people. Mrs Louisa Carlill, a lady (as the law reporters emphasised), was determined to protect herself from that danger. She saw an advertisement in the *Pall Mall Gazette* for an alternative therapy by the Carbolic Smokeball Company. It was for a small flexible ball containing powdered carbolic acid, a fierce disinfectant. She bought one from a chemist's shop. She followed the instructions religiously, puffing the powder up her nose at precisely the same times three times a day for two weeks and, it is thought, had a good involuntary sneeze each time from the irritation to her nasal passages. But she got the flu after all. She remembered the manufacturers' advertisement that she had seen. It said they would pay £100 (perhaps £10,000 in today's money) to anyone who did this but still got the flu (or a number of other diseases). They seemed serious enough as the advertisement said they had deposited ten times that sum with a bank to pay any claims. Moreover their advertisement referred to letters saying how good it was from all sorts of important people, including important doctors.

So she got her husband (who had practised as a lawyer) to write and claim the money for her. He got the brush off. She raised an action. Now, unlike Scots law, English law does not recognise that one-sided seriously intended promises are legally enforceable as such. So she had to show that there was a contract between the manufacturers and herself with regard to her being entitled to this payment. The chemist's shop of course had contracted with her. That was a simple sale. But they had not agreed to pay any money if the remedy did not work. The manufacturers had never met her. She had never met them. How could there be a contract with them? Every law student knows a simple rule: A contract exists when an offer is met in its terms by an acceptance communicated to the offeror. But Mrs Carlill had never communicated anything to the offeror. However, both the judge at first instance and the Court of Appeal were unanimously of the opinion that there was a contract for all that. Of course they had to take this line. As a scholar who has examined the background of the case in depth puts it: they were clear in their own minds that "the defendants had not behaved as gentlemen, and that was essentially that".

So why was there a contract here? There was not much case law to help the judges establish clear reasons. There was a case some sixty years before where an advertised reward to someone who produced information was held to be a contract that was enforceable by a person who did produce that information. But that could be easily fitted into an offer and acceptance analysis. The acceptance was communicated in the communicating of the information to the person who offered the reward. So, absent any really useful case law, the Court relied on theory. And it was to a trendy new German theory that they turned. German theorists were riding high at the time, not just in law, but in everything from medicine to theology by way of mythology, philosophy and linguistics. An enormously famous German legal scholar, Karl von Savigny, had said that contracts arose where the will of both parties was to enter into enforceable legal relations. That was obvious here. But often the more obvious something is the more difficult it is to give supporting legal reasons. So the reasoning was: (i) the terms of the advertisement were obviously a serious expression of a will to pay the £100, and (ii) Mrs Carlill's act in buying and using the remedy exactly according to its instructions was clearly evidence of her exercising a will to enter on a serious course. She had seen the advertisement so that entailed her committing herself also to a legal relationship with the manufacturer. A further special English law difficulty, that there must be"consideration", was got round by saying that consideration was there in the "inconvenience" caused to Mrs Carlill in having to do all that puffing of the powder up her nose. This way there was a contract with them. It was a one-sided contract or, as it is normally put by English lawyers, a "unilateral" contract. It was a contract under which she was not obliged to do anything. But if she did, as she did, then there was a contract. Or perhaps there were actually two contracts. Either a contract came into existence at the time that she started using the remedy, or it came into existence at the end of the period which the instructions said it was to be used for, or there were both of these contracts. If the first view was correct there was a problem as to what were the terms of the contract if she did not go on with the use of the remedy. This might have been of practical importance, for example, if she had started using the remedy and had good grounds for believing the defendants were going to take the money out of the bank they had deposited it in. If there was already a contract before she had completed the course and got flu, it might be argued that she could raise an action to require them to keep the money there. The Court thought that the contract did not come into existence until she had completed the course. But then does that mean that the defendants could have avoided liability if they had in some way withdrawn their offer before that time?

Some legal systems have different ways of analysing these sorts of relationships. One is Scotland. That has not stopped Scottish courts following *Carlill*. Indeed, the Court of Session jumped at the opportunity in a case a year or so later. But it should not have done so. In Scots law, rather than having to look to see if there is a contract in unilateral relationships, the law has another tool available. It asks, was there a seriously intended promise to be bound if the conditions of the promise were met? That seems nice and simple. The person who fulfils the terms of the seriously intended promise does not even need to have heard of the promise before he or she can be said to have met its terms. So if someone like Mrs Carlill had bought the remedy without seeing the advertisement and had followed the instructions he or she could still claim. But it is not quite as simple as that. First, legal systems that do recognise the enforceability of seriously intended one-sided promises typically have some further requirements, such as how to prove the existence of the promise. Secondly, since 1995 in Scotland a further requirement applies in cases where the person making the promise is not doing so in the course of business. In those cases for a promise to be enforceable *either* (i) it has to have been made in a signed writing *or* (ii) the person meeting its terms has done so knowing of the promise and that is known to the promisor when the former is acting to meet its terms. In the latter case the promisor would be barred from denying that the promise exists, *i.e.* barred by "personal bar" (roughly equivalent to what English lawyers call estoppel). So if, for example, a private person made a promise to pay a reward for bringing back a lost cat, and someone found the cat and returned it, never having heard of or seen the reward notice, the promise of a reward would not be legally enforceable (unless it had been made in a signed writing), up to the moment that the promisor becomes aware that someone is acting to fulfil its terms, *i.e.* when that person arrives with the cat. One commentator thinks that this is not the law because the Requirements of Writing (Scotland) Act 1995 refers to the need for a signed writing where there is a *"gratuitous unilateral obligation"* and doing something (like catching and then bringing back a cat) is not gratuitous as something is done by the beneficiary of the promise (just as Mrs Carlill's actions amounted to "consideration" in English law). They are not getting something for nothing (as Mrs Carlill did not). On that view the statutory enforceability of promises only applies to promises such as to pay a certain sum if someone reaches a given age. But other commentators convincingly point to the fact that the phrase must have been meant to apply to all "unilateral" obligations, *i.e.* those of a take it or leave it sort. These are gratuitous (and so statutorily enforceable) in the sense that the only person who can be forced into doing anything is the promisor.

Mrs Carlill died at the age of 96. Cause of death: flu (amongst other things).

GETTING IT RIGHT IN THE HOUSE OF LORDS

Case 15: London Street Tramways v. London County Council [1898] A.C. 375 (House of Lords, England)

Legal process—Precedent—Overruling the House of Lords—The 1966 Practice Statement

This is one of those cases in which the facts and how they were resolved are entirely irrelevant to the point of law for which the case is important—here the House of Lords set down the rule of precedent that it was unable to reverse its own previous decisions. The Lord Chancellor (Lord Halsbury) stated that it had been established for some centuries that a decision of the House on a point of law is conclusive and binding on the House in later cases. Only an Act of Parliament could set right a decision of the House of Lords which is thought to be wrong. His Lordship accepted that this approach might bring about hardship in an individual case but countered this point by saying "what is that occasional interference with what is perhaps abstract justice as compared with the inconvenience—the disastrous inconvenience—of having each question subject to being re-argued and the dealings of mankind rendered doubtful by reason of different decisions, so that in truth and in fact there would be no real final Court of Appeal?'

The decision in *London Street Tramways* was much debated in subsequent years. There was an attempt to argue that the rule established in the case applied only to English law but not to Scots law. It is difficult to see what substance there was to this point. None of the reasons which Lord Halsbury gave for the rule turned on any point unique to English law or inapplicable to the Scottish legal system. Furthermore *London Street Tramways* was primarily concerned with whether the House would overrule a decision on the same point of law made in 1894. The 1894 decision was made in two cases which were heard together: the first (also *London Street Tramways v. London County Council*) was an English appeal but the second, *Edinburgh Street Tramways Co v. Magistrates of Edinburgh*, was an appeal from the Court of Session: [1894] A.C. 456. A second and conceptually weightier issue was what if the rule in *London Street Tramways* was itself wrong? Did the rule apply to the *London Street Tramways* decision which formulated it? Even if the rule was correct when it was made in *London Street Tramways*, what if it was decided later to change it? How could this be done? The *London Street Tramways* decision said that only an Act of Parliament could alter an erroneous decision of the House of Lords.

In the event the *London Street Tramways* rule was changed but the method of doing so was surprising. The judges in the House of Lords, after deep reflection and discussion, simply announced that as a matter of practice the House would modify its approach to precedent. Although normally its previous decisions would still be treated as binding on the House in later cases, the House would depart from a previous decision when it appeared right to do so (*Practice Statement (Judicial Precedent)* [1966] 1 W.L.R. 1234).

This announcement at least made clear how the House was going to approach precedent but the question still remained whether it had followed the correct method of freeing itself from the *London Street Tramways* rule. In *Davis v. Johnston* [1979] A.C. 264, Viscount Dilhorne justified its method by pointing out that the House of Lords was part of a legally illimitable Parliament which could not bind itself for the future. The 1966 Practice Statement, he argued, was simply a reminder that the *London Street Tramways* rule was subject to this general principle. This explanation of the Practice Statement is far from convincing, as many lawyers, especially in Scotland, have long doubted whether Parliament is without legal limits (see **Cases 37 and 100**).

A second explanation is that the Practice Statement was a constitutional convention. It had never been objected to in Parliament and as it had been announced by the Lord Chancellor, it had to be assumed that the Statement had been approved by the Executive (*R. v. Knuller, etc.* [1973] A.C. 435, 485). However the notion of a constitutional convention is itself uncertain and does not much help in trying to understand the basis of the Practice Statement.

Perhaps there is no real answer to this question. In *Broome v. Cassell & Co* [1972] A.C. 1027, 1038 counsel in argument before the House of Lords raised the point that one cannot get rid of doctrines of judicial precedent by means of a practice statement. Realising that this was not a point to press too far he added: "But, if the House of Lords wishes to do something, no one can stop it being done." These words recall a phrase used by the famous legal philosopher H.L.A. Hart when discussing the ways in which courts decide difficult issues in constitutional law: "Here all that succeeds is success" (*The Concept of Law*, p. 149). Today, the Human Rights Act 1998 requires all courts to decide cases consistently with the jurisprudence of the European Court, even when inconsistent with earlier precedent. This could be argued to be an implicit statutory endorsement of the Practice Statement.

There is one final error to note about the *London Street Tramways* case. This is that despite what appears in the *Appeal Cases* reports, this is not the case's correct name. An Errata page at the beginning of the volume informs the reader that the name "London Street Tramways" is a mistake and should be "London Tramways."

THE CORONATION CASES

Case 16: Krell v. Henry [1903] 2 K.B. 740
(Court of Appeal, England)

Contract—Frustration of contract—Damages

The death of the old Queen in 1901 caused more inconvenience than merely the necessity of issuing new stamps and coins. In addition, a coronation of the new monarch required to be organised. Even with Royalty, however, the vicissitudes of the common cold can interfere with great and complicated plans. King Edward VII, on the day of his coronation, was feeling unwell and the ceremony was postponed. This was doubtless a disappointment to the crowds who had gathered in London to watch the coronation procession; it was even more of a disappointment to those who had spent good money on securing an advantageous viewpoint from which to watch the proceedings. One such was Mr C.S. Henry, who had hired a flat at 56A Pall Mall for the two days during which the festivities were to take place, the highlight being the procession of the newly crowned monarch. He had paid £25 as a deposit for the total of £75 that the owner of the flat, Mr Paul Krell, was charging. When the coronation was cancelled, Krell sued Henry for the balance and Henry sued Krell for the return of his deposit.

Though the terms of the contract did not refer to the coronation, the Court of Appeal held that both parties had understood the coronation to be the foundation of the contract and that when that foundation no longer existed the contract too no longer existed. Though the form of the contract could be carried out (*i.e.* the rooms could be occupied and the view over Pall Mall could still be enjoyed), its true purpose had been frustrated and as a result the terms of the contract could no longer be enforced. Vaughan Williams L.J. said (at p. 754) "I myself am clearly of opinion that in this case, where we have to ask ourselves whether the object of the contract was frustrated by the non-happening of the coronation and its procession on the days proclaimed, parole evidence is admissible to shew that the subject of the contract was rooms to view the coronation procession, and was so to the knowledge of both parties. Once this is established, I see no difficulty whatever in the case". However, he was careful to point out that each case had to be judged by its own circumstances—a sure judicial sign that consistency in applying the stated principle in later cases was not necessarily to be expected.

This is shown in a judgment of the same court (constituted by the same judges) a few days earlier, *Herne Bay Steam Boat Co. v. Hutton* [1903] 2 K.B. 683. The defendants had contracted to hire a steamship from the plaintiffs for the purpose of viewing the naval review to be held as part of the coronation celebrations at Spithead, and to cruise around the fleet. A deposit was paid but on the cancellation of the naval review due to the King's illness the defendant failed to pay the remainder and the contract was repudiated. The plaintiff then sued for the remainder and in this case was successful. The Court held that the contract had not been frustrated since the viewing of the naval review was not the sole basis of the contract. It remained possible for the defendant to enjoy a sail around the harbour, so that there had not been a total failure of the basis of the contract nor a total destruction of the subject-matter of the contract.

The other Coronation Cases include *The Civil Service Co-Operative Society Ltd v. The General Steam Navigation Company* [1903] 2 K.B. 756, in which the plaintiffs who had agreed to hire a boat to watch the naval review at Spithead was held not entitled to recover the moneys paid, and *Elliott v. Crutchley* [1903] 2 K.B. 476 in which caterers were held not entitled to recover expenses which they had laid out in anticipation of the naval review.

THE ART OF FOLLY

**Case 17: McCaig v. University of Glasgow, 1907 S.C. 231;
McCaig's Trustees v. Kirk Session of the United Free
Church of Lismore, 1915 S.C. 426
(Inner House, Court of Session, Scotland)**

Wills and succession—Trust provision—Public policy—Extravagance and waste—Judge as art critic

(See www.lawscot.org.uk/whatis/famous_cases.html)

Mr John Stuart McCaig was a wealthy landowner in Argyllshire. He came from a large family, his beloved parents having had nine children, but on his death his only surviving relative was a sister. She, of course, expected to inherit. John McCaig, however, had other plans. In his trust disposition and settlement he provided that his estate was to be used for the building and maintenance of what he described as "artistic towers" to be placed on prominent positions throughout his land, and for statues of his parents and their nine children to be placed on top of these towers. One such tower was built during his life, on a prominent hill overlooking the town of Oban, and there it remains to be seen today. Now, while property ownership gives the owner the entitlement to be as extravagant and wasteful as he or she wishes during life, the law does not lend its good offices to extravagance and waste on death. It follows that a will or trust which disinherits an heir on intestacy will be struck down if there is no person who benefits from its provisions in place of the heir, or if its provisions are so wasteful as to be contrary to public policy. Miss Catherine McCaig, the surviving sister, challenged her brother's will on this basis. In the first *McCaig* case the Court of Session struck the will down, though it was careful not to venture into the unchartered territory of public policy. Rather, the judges held that there were no beneficiaries to John McCaig's will and therefore the heirs were not disinherited. The court was not impressed with the argument put forward by the trustees (Glasgow University, the Court of Session itself having turned down the office when McCaig had presumptuously offered it to them) that there were beneficiaries, in the form of the workmen and artists who were to build the towers and carve the statues—that benefit, they held, was too remote from the will and wills, to be valid, had to confer a direct benefit on a direct beneficiary. John McCaig's will being struck down, the estate fell into intestacy and Catherine McCaig inherited as the nearest heir.

Miss McCaig died seven years later, probably having spent the intervening years wracked with guilt for having denied her brother's last wishes. But she hoped to buy eternal forgiveness with the terms of her own will. She stipulated that not stone but bronze statues of her parents and their children were to be placed within the circular tower at Oban, which was then to be sealed up and entry forbidden to the public. The remainder of her estate was to be used for the care and maintenance of this cloistered and undisturbed vale of death, for all time coming. Miss McCaig had no heirs to disinherit, so the displacement rule applied in the first *McCaig* case could not apply here. But again the Court of Session had little hesitation in striking down the will. This time, however, they founded directly on the notion of public policy. It was contrary to public policy, they held, for the law to enforce a provision that was extravagant and wasteful in the sense that it benefited no-one and used up large amounts of money in doing so.

There have been other cases since in which provisions in trusts and wills have similarly been held invalid for this reason. One is reminded of *Aitken's Trs v. Aitken*, 1927 S.C. 374, in which the testator had achieved during his life the great honour of being elected champion of the Riding of the Marches at Musselburgh, not once but twice. When making his will he wanted this noble achievement to be suitably commemorated, and so made provision for the creation of a large bronze equestrian statue to be erected in the middle of the town, some of his own property being demolished to make room for it. Not only was this wasteful but, according to the judges, it would merely open the man to ridicule rather than enhance his memory. Lord Blackburn pointed out that the will had stated that the statue had to show artistic merit, but with gratuitous malice added, "judging from a photograph which was exhibited to us of the testator ... it would, I think, be impossible for any sculptor with such a subject to produce a statue which faithfully represented the subject and at the same time was of 'artistic merit'".

Poor Miss Sutherland, on the other hand, might elicit rather more sympathy than Messrs Aitken and McCaig, when she similarly had her will struck down on the ground of gross waste. She had wanted to leave her art collection to the public and left her estate for the establishment of a small art gallery in St Andrews. Lord Justice-Clerk Grant was not impressed with the collection: he described it as a "heterogeneous conglomeration" of no real interest and that therefore to set up a gallery to show it would be extravagant and wasteful (*Sutherland's Trs v. Verschoyle*, 1968 S.L.T. 43). A similar, but more extreme, English case is *Re Pinion (dec'd)* [1965] Ch. 85 where the testator, Arthur Pinion, fancied himself as both artist and patron. He left his studio and his collections to be turned into a museum of his own work. Harman L.J. was not impressed with the quality, describing the testator's paintings as "atrociously bad" and holding that there was "no useful object to be served in foisting upon the public this mass of junk".

All these cases show that judges are, in the public interest, judges not only of fact and law, but also of artistic merit. Thank god we trust their taste.

A COW CASE

Case 18: Morrisson v. Robertson, 1908 S.C. 332
(Inner House, Court of Session, Scotland)

Property—Contract—Error in essentials—Good faith—Rogue—Cow

(See Wilson, "999 for Recision" (1966) 29 MLR 442)

There are other cow cases in the Scottish law reports, such as that of the cow in the closey and the shock it caused (*Gilligan v. Robb*, 1910 S.C. 395), or of the cow in the ironmonger's shop (*Cameron v. Hamilton's Auction Marts*, 1955 S.L.T. (Sh. Ct) 74, or of Evolvira, the disappearing cow ("What happened to Evolvira is wrapt in the same sort of mystery as surrounds the 'Marie Celeste'", said Lord Justice-Clerk Thomson in *Islip Pedigree Breeding Centre v. Abercromby*, 1959 S.L.T. 161, or of the headbutting bull who knew where the nettles were (*Foskett v. McClymont*, 1998 Rep. L.R. 13). The present case involved two cows who were (or were they?) sold to a rogue who sold them on. This raises an issue which can arise in a variety of ways: two innocent parties duped by a rogue who disappears, one of whom has to suffer the loss, but which one?

Mr Robert Morrisson, a dairyman from Kirkaldy, took his cows to market. The market was slow that day, and no-one offered him the price he was asking. After the auction mart, as Mr Morrisson was preparing to return home, he was approached by one Alexander Telford, a rogue, as Mr Morrisson did not then know but was soon to find out. Telford claimed that he was the son of Mr Wilson, a dairyman from Bonnyrigg, who wished to purchase two of Mr Morrisson's cows. Mr Morrisson was acquainted with Mr Wilson, and knew him to be a man of good credit, so he agreed to sell the cows, and permitted the rogue to take them away on terms of normal trade credit. The rogue Telford then sold the cows on to Mr Robertson, who purchased them in unquestioned good faith. The rogue disappeared with the money. Mr Morrisson sought recovery of the cows from Mr Robertson. Who was to bear the loss? Both Morrisson and Robertson had been duped by the rogue; but Robertson had possession. It is sometimes said that possession is nine tenths of the law, but that is stuff and nonsense. It is ownership that is nine tenths of the law (the other tenth being when an owner can be deprived of property by various means, such as that illustrated in *International Banking Corp v. Ferguson Shaw*, **Case 20**); and it is legal analysis that determines ownership.

One of the basic (though not quite absolute) principles of property law is *nemo dat quod non habet*: you cannot give what you do not have. The most obvious application of this rule is when a thief steals your property—if he "sells" your property to a third party then the property is still yours, because a thief does not take good title to your property and as such he cannot pass on good title. This is not affected by the fact that the purchaser was acting in good faith—the loss falls on him. But in the present case it is not at all clear that the rogue was a thief. After all, Mr Morrisson had agreed to him removing the cows. Telford was certainly a fraudster, but if a contract (*e.g.* a contract of sale) is entered into fraudulently the contract is not necessarily void—it may simply be voidable (*i.e.* valid until reduced). The Inner House held that on the facts of the present case there was no contract. Mr Morrisson thought he was contracting with Mr Wilson, through the agency of the latter's son. But Mr Wilson knew nothing of this and his son (if he had one) was not at the auction mart that day as his father's agent. Mr Morrisson had no intention of contracting with the person called Telford and so never did sell his cows to Telford. As such Telford never had title to the cows and could not pass on title to Robertson. So the end result was that Robertson was in possession of cows which were not his, and he had to return them to Morrisson. Robertson did, of course, have an action for redress against the rogue but the rogue, unsurprisingly, had disappeared.

The matter would have been different had Telford fraudulently induced Morrison to contract with him by claiming that he himself was a man of credit—for in that case Morrisson would be contracting with Telford, and the contract would be valid, though voidable due to the fraud, with the result that the rogue could pass on title (which he had acquired through the valid contract) to an innocent third party, the loss falling on Morrisson. This in fact is what happened in *Macleod v. Kerr*, 1965 S.L.T. 358, where a rogue bought a car using a stolen cheque, and then sold on the car to an innocent third party. The court held that there was a valid, though voidable, contract because the seller had intended to sell to the rogue—the result was that the third party got to keep the car while the original owner had a (worthless) right of redress against the now-vanished rogue.

Morrisson v. Robertson is one of these cases in which the judges themselves declared it an easy one to decide but with which, by doing so, a puzzle has been created which has exercised commentators ever since. What did the case really decide? What branch of law is really involved? The criminal law writer, Sheriff Gordon, sees the case as one of theft (with the result that the rogue could never pass on good title). Contract lawyers focus in, as the court did, on the validity of the contract. Property lawyers, such as Professor Reid, suspect that the case is wrong and in his book *Property* (at para. 610) he points out that passing of ownership is not dependent in itself on the validity of a contract. He implies that the case might have been decided differently by applying a property law analysis. In the end, the Court was attempting to find the justice of the case. The real problem was that the justice lay equally between Morrisson and Robertson. The law is not sufficiently blunt to say that they should therefore get one cow each. King Solomon once suggested a similar solution. It wouldn't have worked then, either.

FOR THE LOVE OF LANDLORDS

Case 19: Davidson v. Sprengel, 1909 S.C. 566; 1909 1 S.L.T. 78 (p. 220) (Inner House, Court of Session, Scotland)

Landlord and Tenant—Damages—Safety in tenancies

In 1906 Mary Davidson was almost three years old. She went for sweets in Rose Street in Edinburgh. She burned to death. Her father sued the landlord since she had gone up in flames as a result of the gas lighting on the stair catching her dress. Her father's claim was unsuccessful because of a new principle introduced into the common law by the Court of Session.

The Davidsons, like some 90 per cent of the population in Britain at that time, lived in accommodation rented from private landlords. The concept of local authority housing had hardly developed at all and amounted to less than three per cent of the housing stock. The period from 1890 saw two quite distinct trends in the rights of tenants to enjoy safe and healthy houses. On the one hand there appeared a range of statutory protections designed to ensure that tenants have the opportunity to secure for themselves, in return for their rent, decent accommodation. Most important was the requirement for all houses let on short leases to be "fit for human habitation", which was introduced in the Housing of the Working Classes Act 1890. Sir John Rankine opined that this was not really necessary because the common law of Scotland required landlords to provide accommodation which was "tenantable and habitable". Slightly less obvious but of major practical assistance was the imposition of a statutory duty on local authorities to act on the community's behalf against public nuisances. The concept of public nuisance included houses which were unhealthy or dangerous either in themselves or in their access. In addition, there was the Public Health (Scotland) Act 1897. So on paper things looked rosy for the poor in Scotland, with a benign state looking after their interests. The reality was (unsurprisingly) somewhat different, as an examination of the proceedings of the Society of Public Health Inspectors and their Sanitary

Journal during the nineteenth and early twentieth centuries reveals. What seem now extraordinarily high levels of density of occupation were found throughout Britain generally, and particularly in Scotland. The proportion of families living in single rooms in Scotland at the turn of the last century was 25 per cent, with further 35 per cent living in two rooms. The average room occupancy level was 5.6 persons per room.

While Parliament was making some (if largely ineffectual) efforts to ameliorate the living conditions of the poor, the interests of the landlords were being vigorously protected by the courts, particularly in a series of cases from about 1890 to 1914, of which the present case is a representative example. Others include *Webster v. Brown* (1892) 19 R. 675, in which a nurse failed in an action against her landlord for damages after she had fallen on the steps leading to her house in Glasgow. She claimed that she had informed the factor. In a startling decision covering only one page the Court of Session introduced, apparently out of the blue, a new concept for limiting such claims. They adopted the Roman law notion from the field of delict of the voluntary acceptance of risk, or *volenti non fit injuria*. Their Lordships made clear where responsibility lay and what should be done. Landlords did indeed have an obligation to their tenants to provide tenantable property: if they did not do so they were liable. If, however, the landlord did nothing to repair a defect that had been brought to his attention the remedy for the tenant was to leave the defective property and seek damages from the landlord, otherwise the tenant would be in *volenti* and not able to complain if the defect caused him or his family damage. Given the availability of alternative housing at the time this might seem an unrealistic counsel.

The doctrine was refined in a number of subsequent cases so that it did not apply where the tenant had been assured there was no danger and this was not a matter of common sense; it was applicable where the danger was obvious to the non-expert; if the landlord promised to carry out the repairs but this was not done and there was injury then this did not amount to the tenant voluntarily accepting the risk—*Shields v. Dalziel* (1894) 24 R. 849, *Caldwell v. McCallum* (1901) 4 F. 371; *McManus v. Armour* (1901) 3 F. 1078.

In *Davidson* the Court of Session introduced the concept of a "defect obvious at the time of commencement of the lease" which would render the tenant *volenti* (and give the landlord a defence to any action based on the injury the defect caused). So in the space of 15 years tenants were required to decamp to fresh accommodation the moment that they feared that their current dwelling was insanitary as well as reject any property offered in which there was a defect. Against the background of the writings and speeches of the new army of Sanitary Inspectors the judiciary appeared to have taken refuge in a pure model of equal contracting parties which bore little relation to reality.

In 1907 a year after Mary Davidson's early demise young Robert Mechan had an accident on the common stair where he resided in Glasgow. He slipped and fell through a gap between the stair railing and the tenement wall and sustained injuries. He was luckier in that he did not die. His claim for damages (*Mechan v. Watson*, 1907 S.C. 25) was, however, no more successful than had been that of Mary Davidson. Commenting on these cases in 1961 Professor T.B. Smith doubted whether they were sound law any longer—but within 12 months of the publication of his *Short Commentary*, Lord Mackintosh in *Proctor v. Cowlairs Co-Operative Society Ltd*, 1961 S.L.T. 434, whilst noting that the doctrine of voluntary acceptance of risk might seem "socially unrealistic", felt constrained by precedent to follow the decision in *Webster* and refuse the claim of the widow of a tenant killed upon a dangerous stair. The defect had been reported to the landlords but no remedial action had been taken—until after the death of the tenant.

WHAT THE ROMANS HAVE DONE FOR US

Case 20: International Banking Corporation v. Ferguson, Shaw & Sons, 1910 S.C. 182 (Inner House, Court of Session, Scotland)

Property—Contract—Specification—Unjustified enrichment

What do you do when things go wrong but there is no-one to blame? The law is limited in its ability to put things right. Sometimes there are factual limitations—if you break a leg, the law cannot mend it. Sometimes there are legal limitations. The law of contract, for example, is of no use unless there is a contract or at least a potential contract. The law of delict can be of no help (generally speaking) in the absence of any fault. The law of property is more absolutist than either contract or delict and is seldom of use in helping to balance the equities of a situation, for Scots property law (again generally speaking) operates independently of equity. But sometimes it can be of use. And sometimes justice is achieved by combining different areas of the law, which is thus revealed as a seamless web in which categorisation is the artificial means by which lawyers keep control and students learn to understand. The Romans knew this. Doctrines from the Roman law can still be borrowed and applied to Scots law today, as illustrated in the present case.

International Banking Corporation was an American banking organisation which owned some cotton-seed oil. They arranged with shippers for the oil to be shipped to Scotland, where it was to be sold.

Due to an unexplained mix-up for which no-one could be held responsible, the oil was delivered to the wrong party in Glasgow, who, believing the oil to be his, sold it to the defenders. The defenders made lard with the oil, sold the lard and made profit. The law of contract might have been used by the pursuers to recoup their losses—the shippers were in breach of contract in delivering the oil to the wrong person. Instead, the pursuers sued the defenders direct, seeking the return of their oil or, alternatively, its value. The value of the oil when it reached Glasgow was £156; the profit made by the defenders when they made lard with it and sold the lard amounted to £6. When the pursuers sought the return of their oil, the defenders offered the £6. Unsurprisingly, the pursuers did not think this sufficient and they took their claim to the court.

The pursuers argued that since the party to whom the oil had been delivered never took title to the oil (even although they thought, mistakenly, that they had) they could not pass on title to the defenders—*nemo dat quod non habet*—even when both were acting in good faith. Thus, the defenders were obliged to return the property to the rightful owner. The flaw in this argument, of course, was that the property no longer existed, though something made of the property (lard) did. As a subsidiary claim, though without specifying the basis upon which it was made, the pursuers sought the value of the oil. The defenders pleaded that as they were at all times in *bona fide* they had no obligation to pay the value of the oil to the pursuers. The Court decided the matter on a ground not raised in the pleadings of either party.

The Inner House held that though the oil no longer existed, a new entity (lard) had been created out of it and the first question was who owned that new entity. The Roman law doctrine of *specificatio* provides that if A uses B's raw material to make new goods, the newly manufactured items belong to A rather than B so long as this is done in good faith and so long as the manufactured items cannot be reduced back down to their component parts. Though this doctrine had never been applied in the Inner House before, it was stated in all the Institutional writings to be a doctrine from the Roman law received into Scots law, and the judges in the present case were content to apply it to the facts at hand. So the lard belonged to the defenders, as manufacturers. But the doctrine also contains an equitable compensation component so that the pursuers had to be recompensed for what they had lost, which was the value of the oil rather than, which might be greater, the value of the lard. So the pursuers recovered their £156.

Specificatio is not to be confused with the other Roman law doctrines of *commixio* or *confusio*, whereby materials of two or more persons are mixed together in a way that makes it impossible to separate them out, such as grain from two different farmers, or malts from two different distilleries, being accidentally mixed. In these cases, the combined whole is owned by both, even if one party was the one doing the mixing. Property law solves the problem alone, without the need to call upon the law of unjustified enrichment. But *specificatio* trumps these other doctrines so that if the mixing creates a new type of property, it is the mixer who owns the whole, subject to the requirement for equitable compensation.

THE CASE OF ARTEMUS JONES

Case 21: Hulton v. Jones [1910] A.C. 20
(House of Lords, England)

Delict—Defamation—Innocent defamation—Malice

(See Mitchell, "Malice in Defamation" (1998) 114 L.Q.R. 639; Mitchell, "Artemus Jones and the Press Club" (1999) 20 J. Leg. Hist. 64).

> "Upon the terrace marches the world, attracted by the motor races—a world immensely pleased with itself, and minded to draw a wealth of inspiration—and incidentally, of golden cocktails—from any scheme to speed the passing hour. 'Whist! there is Artemus Jones with a woman who is not his wife, who must be —you know—the other thing!' whispers a fair neighbour of mine, excitedly, into her bosom friend's ear. 'Really; is it not surprising how certain of our fellow countrymen behave when they come abroad? Who would suppose, by his goings-on, that he was a churchwarden at Peckham?'
>
> "No one, indeed, would assume that Jones, in the atmosphere of London, could take on so austere a job as the duties of a churchwarden. Here, in the atmosphere of Dieppe, on the French side of the Channel, he is the life and soul of a gay little band that haunts the Casino and turns day into night, besides betraying a most unholy delight in the society of female butterflies."

This slight piece was published by the defendants in the *Sunday Chronicle*, on July 12, 1908. When he read it, Mr Artemus Jones, a bachelor who did not live in Peckham and who was not a church warden—but who was a barrister—decided to take offence and he sued the newspaper for defamation. His friends testified that they had read the article and assumed that it referred to him. The Jury awarded what was then the substantial sum of £1,750 and the defendants appealed on the ground that since they did not know of the existence of Mr Artemus Jones and had intended the article to be a frivolous and fictitious piece, they could not be said to have had the malice that is the foundation of defamation. Both the Court of Appeal and the House of Lords dismissed the appeal. The House of Lords held that the tort of libel "consists in using language which others knowing the circumstances would reasonably think to be defamatory of the person complaining of and injured by it. A person charged with libel cannot defend himself by shewing that he intended in his own breast not to defame, or that he intended not to defame the plaintiff, if in fact he did both'. The malice that the law purports to require is inferred from the words used and not from the fact that they are directed towards a particular individual. The question is whether the reasonable reader would assume that the use of a name was intended to refer to a real individual rather than a fictitious character.

In fact, this case gives the lie to the proposition that defamation is an intentional delict based on malice. If the words complained of are defamatory then malice is presumed in the pursuer's favour, rebuttably in a case of qualified privilege and irrebuttably in any other case. Lord Shaw of Dunfermline pointed out that this principle, for which the case has since become famous, was not new. He cited two English cases; in addition the early Scottish case of *Finlay v. Ruddiman* (1763) Mor. 3436 comes to the same conclusion.

The large jury award requires, perhaps, explaining. It has been suggested (Mitchell, above) that the jury simply did not believe the defence that the newspaper were entirely unaware of the existence of Mr Artemus Jones. He had himself worked with that same newspaper some 14 years prior to the action. In addition, the journalist who wrote the piece was a member of the Press Club, whose members included Artemus Jones and between whom and the Paris Correspondent of the Sunday Chronical there was some "bad blood" in relation to the payment of subscriptions to the Club. Thus it is that a jury's assessment of the facts can apparently lead to a legal proposition unsupported by these facts.

THE SACRED AND THE PROFANE

Case 22: Smith v. Oliver, 1911 S.C. 103
(Inner House, Court of Session, Scotland)

Wills and succession—Promise—Rei interventus

To be powerful and wealthy does not always make one good, even when one uses one's power for religious or charitable purposes. Mrs Julia Oliver was wealthy, and she used her wealth to get her own way, even with her church. In the early 1890s, the Roman Catholic Archdiocese of

St Andrews and Edinburgh decided to build a church to serve the parish of Dalry, in Edinburgh. Mrs Oliver was, through her wealth and her personality, a powerful presence in that parish. When she heard that the building of a church was planned, she called upon Father Forsyth, the priest in charge of the project, to exhibit the plans to her. Meekly, as was appropriate for one who (as events proved) would inherit nothing on this earth, the priest took the plans to the redoubtable Mrs Oliver. Sadly, she disapproved of the modest scale of the plans that the Archdiocese had drawn up. But the parish was not wealthy, and could afford no other. No matter, declared Mrs Oliver, build the church grandly, with decoration and beauty and ostentation, and I myself will bear the extra expense. So the plans were altered to suit this (apparently) generous benefactress.

Mrs Oliver paid to the church £150 per year, extracting in the process meliorations to the plans that cost substantially more than this. Shortly before the church was completed Mrs Oliver promised Father Forsyth that on her death she would leave between £6,000 and £7,000 to the Archdiocese and she changed her will accordingly. On the strength of this promise, the plans were once more altered, and (one hopes) Mrs Oliver eventually got the church she wanted. She lived another 10 years, eventually expiring in 1908. There was only one problem. Five days before her death, she had altered her will, leaving her whole estate to her nephew, Edward. Father Forsyth probably swore. The Archdiocese, more commercially hard-headed, sued.

One of the major differences between Scots and English law is that in Scotland a unilateral promise is legally enforceable, while in England only contracts under which both sides undertake obligations can be enforced in a court of law. So the first claim that Archbishop Smith made in his action against Edward Oliver was that Mrs Oliver had promised to leave the money in her will to the Archdiocese and that she had broken this promise. That claim would have been relevant, but for the unfortunate circumstance that the promise could not be proved. For to be enforceable in Scots law the promise required then to be proved by either writ or oath, that is to say either by some writing of the alleged promisor, or a statement from the witness box in response to the question (which must, of course, be answered truthfully):"did you make this promise?" (This requirement was abolished by section 11 of the Requirements of Writing (Scotland) Act 1995). Proof by oath was impossible, since Mrs Oliver was now dead and proof by writ was impossible, since Mrs Oliver, canny woman, had put nothing in writing. So however much the court wanted to believe Father Forsyth, the claim based on promise was doomed to failure.

The second claim made by Archbishop Smith also failed. He argued that the Archdiocese's actions in acceding to Mrs Oliver's continual demands for alterations and elaborations to the church plans, which involved a substantial increase in the expenditure that would otherwise have been needed, amounted to *rei interventus*. This is a doctrine which converts an incomplete contract into a complete contract if the party wishing to escape from it has allowed the other to act to his or her detriment on the understanding that the contract is valid. However, that argument failed in the present case also since it is limited to saving the validity of potentially invalid contracts: it had long been held that the doctrine could not convert a promise into a contract. (The common law doctrine of *rei interventus* has now, it should be noted, been converted into a statutory rule: see sections 1(3)–(5) of the Requirements of Writing (Scotland) Act 1995).

This case may be compared with the slightly earlier decision in *Morton's Trs v. The Aged Christian Friend Society of Scotland* (1899) 2 F. 82. Here, Mr Morton wrote to a charity offering to pay them £1,000 over ten years if they accepted certain conditions. The charity accepted the conditions, carried them out, and Mr Morton paid for the first eight years. Then he died, and his executors refused to pay any more. The court held that there was a contract between Mr Morton and the charity, which the executors were obliged to fulfil. So it is possible to bind oneself contractually in a way which requires payment after one's death, which is a way around the normal rule that a will is always revocable before death.

One hopes that Mrs Oliver's nephew religiously attended the services at the church which his Aunt had designed, but got for next to nothing. One also hopes (in vain, probably) that the poor of the parish of Dalry did not suffer from the church being put to expense that it could ill afford to please the whim of a demanding old woman who had never herself been poor.

LOST AT HIGH C

Case 23: Reavis v. Clan Line Steamers, 1925 S.C. 725; 1925 S.L.T. 538
(Inner House, Court of Session, Scotland)

Delict—Secondary economic loss—Loss of services

Hattie Reavis was an entrepreneurial soul, an early version of Stock, Aitken and Waterman in the U.K. music business. Long before rock and pop bands went on world tours, long before the Black and White Minstrel show on television, she could spot a certain type of musical talent and market it. She formed an orchestra in 1918 in the United States of America, with the aim of providing a "novel and unique type of musical entertainment". For this purpose she recruited "the coloured people" of the United States and the West Indies, choosing individuals because of their talent at "rendering negro melodies". The orchestra was an immediate success in America and early in 1919 her orchestra was booked for an extended period in London. She was earning large profits—no mention is made anywhere of how much she was paying her performers—from their performances and from the sale of her music and copyright. Sharp woman, she realised that she could make even more with a world tour, and started to make plans for one.

However, in October 1921 Hattie Reavis' future plans for musical world domination were more or less put to an end. She had set sail for Dublin from Glasgow with her orchestra (her "profit-yielding asset", as it was described in the pleadings, of which she claimed to be "sole proprietrix") in the steamship *The Rowan* but unfortunately the boat was involved in a collision with the steamship *West Camak*. Undeterred, *The Rowan* continued her journey but, in an era when the seas were obviously more heavily congested than the roads, shortly afterwards she was involved in a more fateful collision with the *Clan Malcolm* owned by Clan Line Steamers. *The Rowan* sank, with the loss of many lives.

Hattie Reavis raised an action for damages against the owners of the *Clan Malcolm*. Interestingly the first parts of her claim related to her poor distressed self. The crisis had given her "bruises on her body" requiring medical attention as well as a "severe nervous shock" requiring, she alleged, a consultation with a specialist in Vienna. She also claimed to have lost £465 cash on board the steamer—a considerable wad to carry around in those days—professional property belonging to her, and in addition she claimed for her future earnings as a professional performer, as she could no longer continue in that line. The Lord Ordinary, Lord Constable, accepted that she had a relevant claim for all these losses and this matter was not in dispute before the Inner House.

However, she also made a substantial claim for damages for the loss of her "profit-yielding asset"—her orchestra. Eight orchestra members had been drowned, whilst a number of other members were incapacitated and no longer able to perform. Indeed, only eighteen of the original thirty-one were able to carry on, and even some of those "were not fit to perform efficiently". This was a sad state of affairs for the performers, but more crucial for Hattie Reavis were the lost profits she would have earned on her world tour with her performers. Could she not simply replace them and recruit new members? This was allegedly impossible due to the unique type of performance given by her singers, the orchestra's phenomenal success and the distant sources from which she would have to fill the vacancies. As the Lord Ordinary noted, the pursuer's averments "contain a good deal of somewhat inaccurate phraseology". They were notably insensitive and assumed that the pursuer owned the orchestra. Lord Constable disparagingly made the analogy between the pursuer's claim and a claim that she might have owned a group of performing animals. He rejected this part of her claim and Mrs Reavis appealed to the Inner House of the Court of Session. The leading judgment was given by the first Lord President Clyde who pointed out that the legal issue was whether a third party incurred liability to a master (old-fashioned terminology for an employee) for injuries caused to his servant (old-fashioned terminology for an employee). The Inner House affirmed Lord Constable's judgment and rejected Hattie Reavis' claim. The Court approved earlier authority and held that one cannot have a property right in the services provided by another nor can one claim damages for another person's fault which causes injury beyond injury to your own person, business or other capabilities and health or own property (see *Allan v. Barclay*, **Case 9**).

This case is authority for the proposition that secondary economic loss, *i.e.* loss as a result of injury to another person, is not recoverable. Indeed the principle confirmed in this case has also been extended in recent years to disallow the recovery of financial losses which are derived from damage to the property of a third party as opposed to their person (*Dynamco v. Holland & Hannen & Cubbits Ltd*, 1971 S.C. 257). This is now an established rule against recovery of secondary economic loss, perhaps because it was recognised even in the last century that such rights may give rise to "rights of action which in modern communities, where every complexity of mutual relation is daily created by contract, might be both numerous and novel' (*per* Lord Penzance in *Simpson & Co. v. Thomson* (1877) 5 R. (H.L.) 40). Nonetheless, it should be noted that where initial damage to property of a third party subsequently results in property damage to a pursuer, damages are recoverable in respect of such losses. In some Commonwealth jurisdictions, claims have been allowed for losses incurred, for example, by railway companies where a bridge, not owned by them, was damaged by the negligence of a third party, and they have been unable thereby to transport freight (see *e.g.* the Canadian case of *Norsk Pacific Steamship Co. Ltd v. Canadian National Ry* (1992) 91 D.L.R. (4th) 289.) It is sometimes suggested that this approach should be adopted by Scots law and that, on the satisfaction of normal delictual principles, recovery should be allowed for such secondary economic losses. Should Scots law allow recovery for secondary economic losses, any claims arising would make the sums sued for by Hattie Reavis seem like a drop in the ocean.

DUMB AND DUMBER

Case 24: Buck v. Bell (1927) 274 U.S. 200; 71 L. Ed. 1000 (Supreme Court, United States of America)

Forced sterilisation—Eugenics—US Constitutional law—Human rights

(See Lombardo, "Three Generations, No Imbeciles: New Light on *Buck v. Bell* (1985) N.Y.L.R. 30.)

Emma Buck, a widowed mother who had three small children, supported her family through prostitution and with the help of charity. But her children were taken away from her when she was committed to the Virginia Colony for Epileptics and Feebleminded in Lynchburg, Virginia. Her daughter Carrie was sent to live with the Dobbs family and attended school until she was withdrawn from education in order to take on more of the Dobbs' housework duties. Carrie became pregnant: as a result, she claimed, of being raped by the Dobbs' son. She was brought before the same man who had committed her mother to the Colony in Lynchburg. The superintendent of the colony, Dr Albert Priddy, was an advocate of eugenics, the belief that the stock of the nation could be improved by limiting the reproduction of those with physical and mental deficiencies. This movement had many adherents in the inter-war years in both America and Europe. The American Eugenics Society provided a model statute which was adopted in various states and the Society regarded compulsory sterilisation to be "the practical application of those fundamental biological and social principles which determine the racial endowments and the racial health—physical, mental and spiritual—of future generations". The first legislative expression of this movement was in Indiana in 1907 where legislation permitted the compulsory sterilisation of "confirmed idiots, imbeciles and rapists" in state institutions. This legislation had spread to 24 more states (including Virginia in 1924) by the time *Buck v. Bell* reached the Supreme Court.

In early 1925, Dr Priddy sought a declaration that Carrie was feebleminded and suitable for compulsory sterilisation. Carrie scored a mental age of nine on the Binet-Simon test. In evidence before the Circuit Court of Amherst County a social worker testified that if Carrie was discharged from the Colony she was likely to have illegitimate children. She also suggested that Carrie's daughter, Vivian, who was by then eight months old, was "not quite a normal baby". Carrie, in defence, challenged the constitutionality of the Virginia legislation under which Dr Priddy sought to have her sterilised. The Colony Board allocated an attorney, Irving Whitehead, to act on her behalf. He was a former Board member and a personal friend of both Dr Priddy and his attorney. He called no witnesses to challenge the Board's evidence of Carrie's feeble-mindedness. He made no effort to present strong arguments on her behalf and the suspicion remains that he was hoping to lose in order to present the Board with a judgment validating what they were doing. The Circuit Court rejected Carrie's challenge and ordered that she be sterilised. The appeals court upheld this decision and the matter went to the Supreme Court. By the time the case reached the Supreme Court Dr Priddy had died and his place in the process was taken by his successor Dr John H. Bell.

On May 2, 1927, a week after hearing argument, the Supreme Court rejected Carrie's appeal on an eight to one majority. They noted the facts of the case and the background to the legislation. Their discussion of the merits runs to less than 500 words. The bench was composed of several major jurists, including Louis D. Brandeis and William N. Taft. The ruling of the Court was delivered by perhaps the most eminent of them all, the poet's son, Oliver Wendell Holmes.

Holmes recalled the Great War and called upon Carrie to make a sacrifice for the nation: "the public welfare may call upon the best citizens for their lives. It would be strange if it could not call upon those who already sap the strength of the state for these lesser sacrifices, often not felt to be such by those concerned, in order to prevent our being swamped with incompetence." He presented the relationship between crime and mental impairment starkly: "It is better for all the world, if instead of waiting to execute degenerate off-spring for crime, or to let them starve for their imbecility, society can prevent those who are manifestly unfit from continuing their kind." He concluded with the infamous declaration: "Three generations of imbeciles are enough".

Carrie Buck was sterilised without her consent on October 19, 1927.

The State of Virginia itself sterilised over 7,500 men and women between 1924 and 1972 including Carrie's sister, Doris. 50,000 people were sterilised throughout the United States. The operations were performed mainly in mental-health facilities upon people considered feeble-minded and anti-social, including "unwed mothers, prostitutes, petty criminals and children with disciplinary problems".

Across the seas the eugenic sterilisation laws were adopted in Denmark (1929), Norway and Sweden (1935), Finland (1935), Estonia (1936) and Iceland (1938). The Swedes were particularly active, and sterilised 62,888 of their fellow-citizens between 1935 and 1975. These were principally recorded as "voluntary", though in reality they were usually a precondition to release from institutions or to access to welfare benefits or to permission to keep their existing children. Unsurprisingly, the most enthusiastic proponents and practitioners were the Nazis in Germany who under the 1934 "race hygiene" programme sterilised over two million people. The American author of the original model

Sterilisation Act was awarded an Honorary degree from Heidelberg University in 1936. The defence team in the *Nuremberg Trial* (Case 32) pointed out that such laws had been declared constitutionally acceptable in *Buck v. Bell*.

The practice of sterilising developmentally disabled young women has diminished substantially, but it still occurs. The House of Lords accepted that sterilisation was in the best interests of a 17-year-old patient in *Re B (a Minor) (Sterilisation)* [1987] 2 W.L.R. 1213; the Supreme Court of Canada disallowed a sterilisation in similar circumstances because it was unclear whether it really was in the girl's interests (*Re Eve* (1986) 31 D.L.R. (46) 1). Though eugenics itself is no longer regarded as acceptable, efforts to improve the race continue to form a major part of medical work. Genetic counselling, tapping into the knowledge gained by mapping the human genome, and abortion of disabled foetuses all have the same aim as the Court in *Buck v. Bell*, though they are presented in more benign terms.

Doris Buck (Carrie's sister) was told that the operation which she underwent was for an appendix and rupture and she spent her married years consulting physicians who failed to notice that her fallopian tubes had been severed. She only discovered the cause of her lifelong sadness in 1980. Carrie was paroled from the colony shortly after being sterilised and went on to marry twice. The evidence from her letters and recollections of those who knew both Carrie and Doris suggest that neither would be considered mentally deficient by today's standards. *Buck v. Bell* has never been overruled.

A GLASGOW HARD CASE

Case 25: Ramsay v. Liverpool Royal Infirmary and others
1930 S.C. (H.L.) 83; [1930] A.C. 588
(House of Lords, Scotland)

Wills and succession—Validity of will—International private law—Domicile

This case concerned a dispute over the validity of a will. The key legal debate was whether the testator was domiciled in Scotland or England. The determination of a person's domicile may be important for tax reasons and is also crucial in international private law: the law of the country where a person is domiciled will determine many matters of personal law, such as whether that person has capacity to marry, the devolution of property on intestacy and, as here, the validity of a will.

In this case, George Bowie, the testator, left a holograph will (*i.e.* one written and signed by him) which was valid by the law of Scotland but invalid by the law of England. It became important to know where he was domiciled since the law of the domicile at that time governed the validity of a will and so George Bowie's will would be valid if he were domiciled in Scotland and invalid if he were domiciled in England. In the will, he left a number of bequests to three Glasgow infirmaries and one Liverpool infirmary. In this action, those beneficiaries sought a declaration that he was domiciled in Scotland at the date of his death. If they were successful they would be entitled to the bequests, failing which the English rules of intestacy would govern and his niece would be entitled to his estate. The law for determining domicile is fairly convoluted, but a starting point is that every person has a domicile of origin, and in Bowie's case, that was clearly Scotland, where he had been born and brought up. However, one can subsequently acquire a domicile of choice in another country. (For this purpose England counts as another country due to its separate legal system.) To do so one has to reside in the other country and also intend to reside there permanently. The intention aspect is the more difficult and was in contention here. The basic rule is that in order to have the requisite intention the person must intend to make that country their home for the indefinite future. This is a matter for the courts to ascertain from the facts surrounding the person's life and the case therefore revolved around the background of Bowie's life.

Bowie had lived mainly in Glasgow until, at the age of 37, he gave up work. Ten years later, he moved to Liverpool, not to find work but to be close to other members of his family. He stayed there until he died 35 years later, and stayed in the same lodgings for over 20 years. During this time he only left Liverpool twice to make a short visit to the United States and a holiday trip to the Isle of Man. It was noted that he was "not a successful searcher after work" and that "until 1912 he was dependent on his brother's bounty". He never returned to Glasgow at all but told people he was proud to be a Glasgow man and received a Glasgow weekly newspaper. In his will, he directed that his bequests to the four infirmaries should be given anonymously as from a "Glasgow man". But was he still domiciled there? It was held unanimously by the House of Lords that there was insufficient evidence of an intention on Bowie's part to change his domicile from his original Scottish one. This meant that Scots law governed the validity of his will and so the bequests contained therein were valid. One judge opined that there was "slender evidence of intention" on his part while Lord Thankerton clearly considered that his general apathy was such as to preclude any intention and definitely not one to reside indefinitely in England.

A similar case is that of *Winans v. Attorney General* [1910] A.C. 27. Here, a US citizen dedicated the later part of his life to various projects, including one involving boats designed like cigars, to destroy the naval supremacy of the U.K. and give the US that position. He hated Britain. All the more galling, therefore, that as a result of illness, and for climate reasons, he needed to spend each winter and then all his life in Brighton, on the south coast of England. He kept apart from locals and his intention was to return to the United States although this was clearly unlikely to happen and in the last 47 years of his life he did not visit the States even once. It was held that he had not acquired an English domicile of choice at death as the necessary intention had to be a positive one but he had no fixed or settled purpose to remain in England and therefore retained his domicile of origin in the US.

Both these cases demonstrate a particularly strict standard to satisfy the intention test for the acquisition of a new domicile of choice. It could be argued that the courts have confused sentiment with intention and also that in these instances they were sceptical of such "undesirables" "benefiting" from an English domicile. However, the primary purpose of the use of domicile as the appropriate "personal law" is to determine a range of legal issues by the legal system with which the person is most closely connected. The rules for determining a domicile of choice do not necessarily achieve this aim, as exemplified by these two cases.

THE MOOROV CASE

Case 26: Moorov v. H.M. Advocate, 1930 J.C. 68 (High Court of Justiciary, Scotland)

Evidence— Criminal law— Corroboration— Similar fact evidence

Mr Samuel Moorov ran a drapery business from a shop in Argyle Street, Glasgow but, unlike most drapers, he was not a nice man. His employees, all female, never stayed long with him. In interviewing young women who applied for jobs in his shop, or shortly after they started working for him, he would suggest that they submit to his sexual advances. If they refused, he would ignore that refusal, and press his advances regardless. The girls left in distress. They did not complain about their treatment: the early 1930s was not a good time to be unemployed and, in any case, who would believe a shop-worker over her respectable employer?

Eventually, however, one woman did speak out. She went to the police. They investigated and, eventually, more women from the past started to come forward with similar stories. Then some more. In May 1930 Moorov was put on trial before a High Court Jury to face 21 separate counts of assault, indecent assault and attempts to ravish. But the prosecutor faced one huge problem. None of the assaults had been witnessed, having taken place in the drapery premises when no-one but Moorov and his current victim were present. It was Moorov's word against the girl's. The jury had little difficulty in believing the girls' word but that is insufficient in Scots criminal law to secure a conviction. For it is one of the fundamental protections granted by the law of Scotland to those charged with criminal offences that there must be at least two independent pieces of evidence pointing to guilt of any charge: this is the requirement for "corroboration". The problem in the present case was that each charge related to a different woman, who herself could provide one piece of evidence (her own testimony) but could provide nothing else.

Nevertheless, the jury found the evidence of all the victims overwhelming and convicted Moorov. He appealed on the ground of lack of corroboration. A Full Bench of seven judges upheld most of the convictions, and the importance of the case lies in how they dealt with the issue of corroboration.

They found corroboration from the fact that all the allegations were similar in fact, in circumstance and in time, with the result that each witness, giving direct evidence of her own experience, also provided corroboration (if she was credible) for the evidence provided by each of the other witnesses. The victims, in other words, were mutually corroborative.

Now, this is a dangerous doctrine and it needs to be applied with care. It really only works if the facts show some underlying unity of purpose which makes all the events part of a single course of action. The High Court limited it in the present case to those offences which were similar not only in circumstances (such as an employer ravishing employees) and in place (the back shop of the drapery store) but in time as well. So they allowed Moorov's appeal in relation to one of the convictions because the assault had occurred more than four years before any of the others.

What has come to be called "the Moorov Doctrine" has been applied in a variety of circumstances since, including in *H.M. Advocate v. McQuade*, 1951 J.C. 143 to corroborate a series of knife attacks (six within four months) within a limited geographical area and in *McCudden v. H.M. Advocate*, 1952 J.C. 86 when the accused attempted to bribe, separately, two football players to lose matches. On the other hand, in *Tudhope v. Hazelton*, 1984 S.C.C.R. 455 the Moorov Doctrine was not applied when a policeman was charged with assaulting prisoners in a police cell, because the offences were separated by 15 months. In *H.M. Advocate v. Cox*, 1962 J.C. 27 evidence of sodomy did not corroborate the very different offence of incest; but where both victims were young children evidence of rape of one was held to corroborate evidence of sodomy against the other: *P. v. H.M. Advocate*, 1991 S.C.C.R. 933.

THE MOST FAMOUS CASE OF ALL

Case 27: Donoghue v. Stevenson
1932 S.C. (H.L.) 31; [1932] A.C. 532
(House of Lords, Scotland)

Snail in bottle—Paisley in August—Birth, marriage, divorce, death (life, in other words)—Delict—Duty of care

(See Rodger, "Mrs Donoghue and Alfenus Varus", 1988 C.L.P. 1; McBryde, "*Donoghue v. Stevenson*" in *Obligations in Context* (Gamble ed., 1990) pp. 13–32; Rodger, "Lord Macmillan's Speech in *Donoghue v. Stevenson*" (1992) 108 L.Q.R. 236).

Once upon a time (and some 2000 years after Luke's lawyer first asked the question, "and who is my neighbour?") there was, or at least might have been, a snail in a bottle of ginger beer. The rest is history.

Mrs May McAllister or Donoghue is a true icon of the twentieth Century, rather like Marilyn Monroe and Princess Diana. She was a Cambuslang lassie, the daughter, sister and sometime wife of steelworkers. She was poor all her life, and though she was never idle, she did have more than her share of unhappiness. Born in 1898, she married at age 17 by declaration *de praesenti*; after the birth of a healthy son, she gave birth to three premature babies in succession, none of whom survived more than a few days. Twelve years into her marriage, she separated from her husband and, at about the same time, she and a friend visited Minghella's Café in Paisley for some summer refreshment. It is from such domestic trivia that great events sometimes emerge, and so it was on that August evening in 1928. What would be the state of the law if, as would be more normal, the weather in Paisley had been cool and rainy and Mrs Donoghue had ordered a pot of tea and a fairy cake instead of a ginger beer and an ice cream? But it was not and she did not and the law is as we know it today.

The narrow legal issue was whether the manufacturer of goods (the ginger beer) could be liable in delict to the ultimate consumer thereof (Mrs Donoghue) in the absence of a contractual relationship such as existed between the manufacturer and the retailer (the café) and between the retailer and the purchaser (Mrs Donoghue's friend). The wide legal issue was what was the test to determine the existence of a duty of care, breach of which leads to liability in delict? The answer to the narrow issue, which seems obvious today but was novel then, was Yes. Consumers are now protected by the Consumer Protection Act 1978.

The answer to the wide issue was that you owe a duty of care to your "neighbours", that is to say those persons who you ought to have in contemplation as being likely to suffer harm as a result of your acts or omissions. This is the "foreseeability" test for determining the existence of a duty of care and it applies in all cases of physical injury to the person (but not, at least not unqualifiedly, to other forms of harm). The case was sent back to the Outer House to give Mrs Donoghue the chance to prove the facts and to persuade the judge that her injuries, which she alleged had been caused by the defective ginger beer, ought to have been foreseeable to the manufacturer. But the action was settled before any proof was held and Mrs Donoghue, having restructured much of the law of delict for the whole of what was then the British Empire, retreated into (almost) anonymous obscurity.

But the affection in which this case has been held by generations of lawyers throughout the English-speaking world meant that Mrs Donoghue's life-story was followed. Her estranged husband acquired a new woman, who presented him with two living sons, and in 1945 Mrs Donoghue divorced her husband and she became, once again, May McAllister. In 1958, at the age of 59, she expired of a heart attack, while resident in a mental hospital in Glasgow. Hers had not been an unusual life for one of her economic background at that time—more a slipping-down life than dinner at the homesick restaurant. Yet her famous trip to Paisley does leave some questions unanswered. Who, for example, was the friend with whom she shared the trip? Professor Norrie refers to the friend as "the third murderer of the common law" (*Stair Memorial Encyclopaedia of the Laws of Scotland*, Vol. 15, para. 258). There is no evidence of a liaison of which society then would have disapproved but of which today we would simply have hoped would bring this modest lady some happiness. Lord Macmillan refers to the friend as "she" (1932 S.C. (H.L.) at 61). More interesting is the fact that while everyone knows that there might not have been a snail in any case, rather less well-known is the fact that it might not have been ginger beer. The doubt arises from the unquestioned truth that ginger beer and ice cream do not mix and from the fact that the word "ginger" was then, as now, applied by the poorer folk of Glasgow as a generic term to all fizzy, sugary drinks (just as in other parts of the country fizzy, sugary drinks are referred to as lemonade whether or not they have any trace of lemon). In other words, a lapse in taste by the Glaswegian Mrs Donoghue might be considered to be less likely than a misunderstanding of what she was saying by these grand and dusty lawyers from Edinburgh. However (and, frankly, rather disappointingly) Professor McBryde puts paid to that particular myth. After some practical historical research he was able to reveal that in the 1920s ginger beer was always sold in dark bottles in the Glasgow area, while the fizzy sugary drinks were sold in clear bottles. As all the world knows, the drink purchased by Mrs Donoghue's friend was contained in a dark bottle.

Legally, however, the real mystery of the case is why Lord Atkin gets all the credit. Lord Macmillan's speech, however watered-down (see Rodger, above) is just as important and his has the merit, lacking in Lord Atkin's, of being original. For as Professor Evans-Jones points out for us, Lord Atkin's famous neighbourhood passage, apart from the biblical accretion, is a clear lift from Erskine. This is so obvious once you are told so.

A NATIONAL DELICACY

Case 28: Cuthbert v. Linklater, 1935 S.L.T. 94
(Inner House, Court of Session, Scotland)

Delict—Defamation—Unintentional defamation—Fictitious character

Gwendoline Cuthbert took such offence at a novel written by Eric Linklater that she sued for defamation. Cuthbert, an extrovert and fervent Scottish nationalist, had been associated with the Scottish nationalist movement since 1913. She was known publicly under the pseudonym Wendy Wood and was chairperson of the Democratic Self-Government Organisation which had been founded in 1932. The background to the litigation is interesting and demonstrates that claims for defamation are commonly based on long-standing personal disputes as opposed to chance derogatory comments (see also *Hulton v. Jones*, **Case 21**). Linklater had stood in the nationalist cause as a Parliamentary candidate for Fife in 1933 but Wendy Wood had refused a request to assist him on the basis that she considered his policy on self-government to be too weak. The dynamics of Scottish nationalist politics at that time are in many ways similar to current debates in the Scottish nationalist movement in the wake of the Scotland Act 1998 and the establishment of the Scottish Parliament. Was Linklater taking a literary revenge? Cuthbert thought he was, and was determined that she would get the last laugh.

In order to understand the legal case one needs to be aware of two parallel stories, one set in reality and the other fictional. In reality, the factual backdrop to the case took place during the celebration of the anniversary of the Battle of Bannockburn when Gwendoline Cuthbert (aka Wendy Wood) visited Stirling Castle with a group of friends. The party removed the Union Flag from the flagstaff, rolled it up and threw it at the guard at the Castle. This event subsequently received fairly widespread publicity and Wendy Wood was closely associated in the public mind with the incident. The fictional story is found in Eric Linklater's novel, *Magnus Merriman*, a fairly languid account of nationalist politics. The principal character in the book, Magnus Merriman, was contesting a parliamentary by-election as a nationalist and the novel detailed how during this period he met a young woman who was described as looking like Joan of Arc. This character in the novel was called Beaty Bracken who "had recently achieved fame by removing a Union Flag from the Castle and placing it in a public urinal'.

Wendy Wood sued for defamation on the basis that the author, Linklater, invented the story about the placing of the Union Flag in the public urinal without any belief in its truth. Inventing stories is, of course, what novelists get paid for, but Wendy Wood claimed that the passage represented her as Beaty Bracken, supported by her contention that there had also been prior public comparisons between herself and Joan of Arc. She claimed that the depiction of her in the novel held her up to public hatred, ridicule and contempt by "being immodest and indecent, and a woman of low and depraved mentality, without natural and proper womanly delicacy of mind or action, and unworthy of respect as a woman".

As well as claiming that Beaty Bracken was not Wendy Wood, the defender claimed that the action was irrelevant and there was no legal injury to the pursuer. After debate Lord Moncrieff considered that the passage complained about in the novel indicated clearly that by placing the flag in the public urinal she must have entered the public urinal, a term which had "only one single application", and the implication of entering such a place was without doubt an attack upon a woman's modesty. The issue was appealed to the Inner House where their Lordships unanimously agreed that the passage "contains an imputation of indelicacy of a gross kind against a woman and that this was an actionable wrong", *i.e.* it could give rise to an action of damages for defamation. The Court said that despite her personal views she ought not to be deprived of the Courts' protection, though one judge stated that he did not have the slightest sympathy with the action being brought. Of course the pursuer, Wendy Wood, would still require to satisfy the jury at trial that she was the person referred to as Beaty Bracken in the novel. Unfortunately for legal historians the case was later settled out of court.

This case highlights some interesting points under the law of defamation. First, the obvious point is that the creation of "fictional" characters in novels may be defamatory where they closely resemble real people and their lives. The crucial issue was that this case confirmed for the first time that imputations or allegations of indelicacy or immodesty against women can be actionable under defamation. In an earlier case of *A.B. v. William Blackwood & Sons*, 1902 5 F. 25 a magazine had contained an article entitled "Among the Fife Miners'" which described life in a Fife fishing village. One passage depicted a 17-year-old girl undressing for bed in mixed company and that she was thereby lacking in "delicacy". The judge considered that this would not necessarily be slanderous. Nonetheless, the present case clarified that women should be treated on a parallel with men if they are "accused of what is universally considered to be an immoral act or if it imputes conduct which is contrary to the generally accepted standard of honour or propriety amongst gentlemen" (*per* Lord McLaren in *Macfarlane v. Black & Co.* (1887) 14 R. 870 at 873). The dilemma in seeking to raise a similar action of defamation nowadays is that generally accepted standards change as society develops and, for instance, allegations against a woman regarding entering male toilets are unlikely still to be sufficient to constitute allegations of immodesty or indelicacy.

In a final twist to this tale of urinal immorality, and bearing in editorial mind the important rule that you can not defame the dead, there have been unsubstantiated suggestions in recent years that Wendy Wood, like Major Boothby, was in fact a British spy infiltrating the nationalist movement. The feud goes on beyond the grave.

MADAM AND EDITH

Case 29: Sim v. Stretch
[1936] 2 All E.R. 1237, (1936) 52 T.L.R. 669
(House of Lords, England)

Delict—Defamation—Correct test for defamatoriness—Petty dispute

(See (1936) 52 L.Q.R. 453)

Sometimes, in the Law Reports, one comes across a case that contains an important legal principle and at the same time provides a revealing snapshot of the life and times of the protagonists. Historians may not be interested in the technicalities of the law, but they would appreciate the feeling for period that comes out of some cases. Often, it is the language of the judges. Sometimes it is the facts themselves. A perfect example of the latter is found in the perfect little case of *Sim v. Stretch*, decided in the 1930s and located in a very particular section of society, which will be instantly recognisable by anyone familiar with the works of that great dame, Agatha Christie. While reading the case one remains vaguely surprised at the lack of a baronet found dead in the library locked from the inside with an oriental dagger sticking out of his neck and a group of relatives, all enemies with ambiguous alibis, outside the door.

The story centres around Edith Saville, a young housemaid in the employ of Mrs Sim at a house owned by Mr Sim, "Old Barton", in the quintessentially home counties village of Cookham Dean. Edith had previously been employed in a neighbouring property, "The Twigs". In early 1934, new owners moved into "The Twigs", a Mr and Mrs Stretch. Shortly thereafter Mrs Stretch persuaded Edith to hand in her notice at "Old Barton" and come to work for her at "The Twigs". Mrs Sim was not amused. She wanted her housemaid back, reliable help being so hard to come by these days. She waited until the Stretches were away from home, went to "The Twigs" and talked to Edith. Whatever blandishments were held out to Edith we will never know. But the fact of the matter is that that day Edith walked back to "Old Barton" with Mrs Sim, and when the Stretches returned to "The Twigs" they found their house deserted. Bluntly, the housemaid had been poached and then counter-poached; and this led to as furious a dispute between Mrs Stretch and Mrs Sim as any that had been seen in English village life since that supreme Chef, Anatole, was lured away from Mrs Bingo Little (aka the novelist of mushy sentimentality, Rosie M. Banks) by Mrs Dahlia Travers, Bertie Wooster's good and deserving (though utterly ruthless) aunt.

Now, sometime before she was persuaded back to "Old Barton" by Mrs Sim, Edith's wages from Mrs Stretch had fallen due, but Mrs Stretch had persuaded Edith to open a Post Office Savings Account with the wages, and she offered to take the money to the bank in Maidenhead to open the account for her. It was while Mr and Mrs Stretch were in Maidenhead that Edith was lured away. Later that same day, Mr Sim telegraphed Mr Stretch to inform him that Edith had returned again to "Old Barton", but the telegram contained also the words: "Please send her possessions and the money you borrowed also her wages to Old Barton". Mr Stretch was outraged at the suggestion that he had borrowed money from a domestic servant and, deciding to take offence, he sued Mr Sim for defamation.

This petty dispute went all the way to the House of Lords, on the narrow but important issue of how the law is to define a defamatory statement. For it is an important principle that a statement is not defamatory merely because it causes offence to the subject of the statement, nor because it causes hurt or outrage, even when false. The law requires something more objective than personal affront. Until this case, the test in English law was pretty well settled that the words complained of had to be such as would expose the plaintiff to hatred, ridicule and contempt. But their Lordships were agreed that this test was too narrow. Instead, Lord Atkin proposed to his brethren (who agreed) the following test: "Would the words tend to lower the plaintiff in the estimation of right-thinking members of society generally?" This has been the test that has been applied in England and Scotland since. It is an objective test, in that the court must assess not what people think but what "right-thinking" people think. Judges are, axiomatically, right-thinking people.

Was Mr Stretch defamed on this test? Lord Atkin was "at a loss to understand why a person's character should be lowered in anyone's estimation if he or she has borrowed from a domestic servant'. As such there was no defamation. "The truth of this case" said Lord Atkin, who had a knack for seeing reality, "is that the whole matter is a trumpery affair and that the alleged libel would probably never have been heard of but for the wounded feelings caused by the improper enticement'. But Mr Stretch did not leave court empty-handed. Mrs Sim had induced Edith to break her contract with Mr Stretch, and for that Mr Sim had to pay damages of £25.

AN ISLAND YARN

Case 30: Crofter Hand Woven Harris Tweed Co Ltd v. Veitch, 1941 S.C. (H.L.) 1, 1943 S.L.T. 1 (House of Lords, Scotland)

Conspiracy – Lawful means conspiracy – Intent to injure

(See Elias and Ewing, "Economic Torts and Labour Law: Old Principles and New Liabilities" [1982] C.L.J. 321, and Thomson, "An Island Legacy: The Delict of Conspiracy" in Carey Miller and Meyers, *Comparative and Historical Essays in Scots Law*).

Harris Tweed, manufactured on the islands of Lewis and Harris in the Outer Hebrides, is recognized throughout the world for its method of manufacture and the quality of its product. The cloth is woven by hand by crofters from wool taken exclusively from island sheep. (A history of the trade can be found in another case arising from attempts to protect the good name of "Harris Tweed": *Argyllshire Weavers Ltd v. A. Macauley (Tweeds) Ltd*, 1965 S.L.T. 21). However, as a result of industrial action in support of the island product an important legal battle had to be fought to protect the indigenous weaving industry and to prevent others from taking advantage of the Harris Tweed label and good name.

The case arose because unlike the majority of mill owners who only used island yarn the Crofter Hand Woven Harris Tweed Co sought to import yarn from the mainland and use that wool in its weaving process. Other local mill owners took exception to this practice as did the Transport and General Workers Union. It had been trying to negotiate with the mill owners for better terms and conditions for its members and to gain agreement for a closed shop. The mill owners' association told the union that a reduction in wages was more likely because of "cutthroat" competition from independent producers like the pursuers. Thus the union became concerned that increased competition from a company which was seeking to use non-island wool would affect the job prospects and the terms and conditions of the spinners employed in the mills and the weavers in their crofts. So Veitch, the national official of the TGWU in Scotland and Mackenzie, the local branch official, instructed the dockers, working in Stornoway harbour, who were all TGWU members, to boycott both the pursuers' yarn which was being imported from the mainland and their cloth which was being exported back there. The dockers were able to carry out this industrial action without breaking their contracts of employment.

The boycott worked, and created a substantial negative impact on the business of Crofter Hand Woven Harris Tweed Co. So they sought an interdict to bring the embargo to an end. They argued that the two union officials (and a representative of the mill owners as well) were involved in a conspiracy to injure their business. A major problem for the pursuers was that the combination did not involve any unlawful act since the dockers were not breaking their contracts when they imposed the boycott. However, it was argued that the action became unlawful because the union officials (and the mill owners' representative) were intent on damaging the company's business.

At first glance, it may seem odd that a pursuer can have a cause of action when two or more people combine to injure him or her but do so by lawful means. However, it was established as a result of a trilogy of cases in the House of Lords that whereas a lawful act done by one person does not become unlawful by the intent to injure another, such an act if done by two or more persons in combination is unlawful if done with the intent to injure that other (*Mogul Steamship Co v. McGregor Gow & Co* [1892] A.C. 25, *Allen v. Flood* [1898] A.C. 1, *Quinn v. Leathem* [1901] A.C. 495. Thus motive and purpose become relevant when a group of people are combining together. This has been justified on the basis that the coercive pressure of a group is greater than that of an individual acting alone.

The essential elements of this wrong are (a) that there is an agreement between the conspirators, (b) which is to give effect to an unlawful purpose and (c) it results in damage to the pursuer. In the present case there was no doubt that (a) and (c) were established since the two union officials had conspired together to organise the boycott. Moreover, there was indisputable evidence that the pursuers' business had been damaged by the embargo. The critical question for the pursuers was (b): was the purpose of the combination unlawful?

In answering this question, the House of Lords made a distinction between those cases where the combination seeks wilfully to injure the pursuer and those where the real purpose of the combination is not to injure but to forward or defend the conspirators' trade interests. Only the former type of conspiracy was unlawful. In the present case, the Court concluded that the conspiracy was not unlawful because the predominant purpose of the combiners was to benefit their trade union members by preventing under-cutting and regulated competition and so help secure the economic stability of the island industry. So the interdict was not granted.

The case is important because the judges in the House of Lords were able to reassess the common law rules which establish liability for a lawful means conspiracy. They concluded that the pursuit of union objectives as the predominant purpose could constitute a justification for the action and remove any liability for the conspiracy. The House of Lords made it clear that, no matter how unethical or even wrong-headed the industrial action was, an intention to protect the interest of the union members provided as much of a defence to trade unionists as it had for traders. The case has remained the bedrock for lawful means conspiracy ever since.

FOR THOSE IN PERIL DRINKING TEA

Case 31: Muir v. Glasgow Corporation
1943 S.C. (H.L.) 3, 1944 S.L.T. 60
(House of Lords, Scotland)

Delict—Negligence—Standard of care

The misfortunes and tragedies of children have contributed disproportionately to the development of the law of negligence. Here it was six children. The reports of the case only give the name of one of them. A superficial glance at its name might suggest it was a boy. But in fact it was a girl, Eleanor Muir. The pursuer was her father, who sued for her. Eleanor's misfortune was to be badly scalded by hot tea as she stood sheltering from the weather at the sweetie counter of a shop run by the local authority for the City of Glasgow in the King's Park on the south side of that dear green place. The shop was part of the ground floor of an old house there. To get to the tearoom you had to walk in through double doors from the park outside, turn left and then walk through the shop down a narrowing space past the sweetie counter. Eleanor and her friends, a small group from a party of around 900 people from the nearby burgh of Rutherglen, who were in the park that day, were there in the shop spending money on things bad for their teeth. Mrs Emily Alexander, the manageress of the shop and tearoom, was there too, with her back to the door.

The event of Eleanor's accident was a picnic in the first June of the Second World War. There would be no picnics there for years after that.

The next year the sweetie shop would be occupied by the military. However, this was before Dunkirk and the park was alive with the sound of other children on picnic, too. These included a much smaller group from a Free Church of Scotland from Milton, another wee place close by. These children were not just on a picnic, but on a Sunday School Picnic. These still happen, although they were a bigger thing then. Buses would set off from cities, towns and villages all over Scotland with long paper streamers flying behind them in the slipstream and held by excited childish hands. Usually it rains. On this occasion it started out fine but, as one judge put it, "it had come on very wet in the afternoon". But there was a shelter in the park, where, for a small fee, boiling water for making tea to fortify the visitors against the weather was available.

The adults in charge of the Sunday School Picnic availed themselves of this facility to the extent of filling up an urn with boiling water. But as the shelter was already bursting at the seams with lots of people from Rutherglen, they got permission from Mrs Alexander for their own group to come down to the house to use the tearoom on payment of a total fee of 12 shillings and sixpence (63p). Mr McDonald, the Church Officer of the church from which the group came, carried the urn by its handle on the one side; one of the Sunday School boys took the handle of the urn on the other side. This boy handed over to another boy, who, on the way down hill from the shelter, had had the less onerous task of carrying the cakes. Perhaps because he was fresh to the job, there was nothing wrong with his urn carrying. But Mr McDonald let the urn fall and tilted his side just after they had turned into the narrow space near the sweetie counter en route for the tearoom in the house. Eleanor Muir and her friends were scalded. Why Mr McDonald failed properly to control his side of the urn has remained unexplained to this day. One of the judges speculated that it might have been some "unexpected physical failure" (or as another put it, "a temporary muscular failure") on his part; another speculated he might have stumbled. Perhaps they thought in this way, because Mr McDonald was a Church Officer of a Presbyterian church in Scotland. It would be within Scottish judicial knowledge that Church Officers are expected to be good at carrying heavy things reliably. One of the duties of that office is, with a steady and stately bearing, to carry the large pulpit bible into the church in front of the minister at the start of a service. Lord Macmillan, whose judgment is the one for which this case will be forever remembered, would have been especially well aware of that. His father was a Free Church minister in Greenock.

This may explain, too, why the apparently natural course of suing Mr McDonald for negligent failure properly to control a tea urn in a confined space full of children was not adopted. Or it may be that he was not insured while Mrs Alexander's employers, the defenders, Glasgow Corporation, were, and would not attract any human sympathy. If she were shown to be negligent in allowing the urn of near boiling water to be brought into the shop area, then they would on ordinary principles be vicariously liable (see *Williams v. A & W Hemphill Ltd,* **Case 49**) to compensate for the harm caused by her negligence. But the House of Lords held unanimously that she was not negligent. In the process a test for the "standard of care" for what is or is not negligence was crystallised out of former decisions. That test has ever since resounded (explicitly or implicitly) through all reported decisions on the matter.

Lord Macmillan here famously states and elaborates the nature of the test. It is based on whether a person did or did not act "reasonably" in the circumstances. To ascertain that, it is necessary to ask what is the nature of "the reasonable man" (gender-neutral language being then unknown in the law). It is necessary after that then to ask further what such a person would or would not have done "in the circumstances of the particular case". The first of these two questions focuses on whether the reasonable man would foresee an adverse outcome of doing something. The reference point is not the individual, personal standards and abilities of the person who actually caused the harm. People come in different versions when it comes to their perception that there may be an adverse outcome from doing or not doing something. So Lord Macmillan's objective "reasonable man" is an artificial construct as someone "presumed to be free both from over-apprehension and from over-confidence". He lies at the middle of a continuum: somewhere, in Lord Macmillan's words, between those who "imagine every path beset by lions" and those of "a more robust temperament," who "fail to foresee or nonchalantly disregard even the most obvious dangers". The second question allows "room for diversity of view" by providing a "subjective element" in the sense that the individual judge has to decide "in the circumstances of the particular case what the reasonable man would have had in contemplation, and what, accordingly, the party sought to be made liable ought to have foreseen".

It follows from this that judges or juries may differ as to the conclusion they come to in applying the test to the facts. Yet their different views may be equally correct as a matter of law. That is part of the necessary uncertainty that arises from having a law of negligence.It follows, too, that regrets after the event, such as those of Mrs Alexander who said that she should not have let Mr McDonald and the boy and the tea urn come in, tell us nothing of use as to whether a person did or did not at the time of the event themselves behave as a reasonable person.

The case is a trap for the unwary in at least two respects, arising from Lord Macmillan's focus on the foreseeability question. The first trap is that foreseeability is not the only matter that is relevant to whether a person did or did not behave reasonably. Other cases show that other aspects have to be weighed in the balance, for example, whether a reasonable person would go ahead even though there was a foreseeable risk, and the practice, if any, of others in the context in which the events happened. The second trap is that Lord Macmillan did not keep his duty of care questions clearly separate from his standard of care questions, as all students of law are enjoined to do today. His main authority was another judgment of his own in the case of the pregnant fishwife (*Bourhill v. Young*, 1943 S.C. (H.L.) 78), a case about when is a duty of care capable of arising in respect of secondary nervous shock (on which issue, see *Alcock v. Chief Constable of West Yorkshire Police*, **Case 82**).

POWER BOWS TO REASON

Case 32: The Nuremberg Trial
November 20, 1945–October 1, 1946
(International Military Tribunal)

International law—International military tribunal—Conspiracy to wage war—Crimes against humanity—War crimes

(See www.nizkor.org/hweb/imt/tgmwc/)

The evil and horror unleashed upon the world by the Nazi regime are notorious and require no rehearsing here. Its defeat in May 1945 was a triumph for justice. But military victory and defeat are a brutalist form of justice. A more rationalist justice can only come from the cold rule of law. This was achieved through the establishment, under the London Agreement (signed in August 1945 by the four main Allies), of the International Military Tribunal (IMT). The purpose of this Tribunal was to try, according to law, the leading surviving figures of the Nazi regime.

The defendants included Grand Admiral Doenitz, Hitler's successor as Fuerer; Frank, the Governor General of Poland and Hitler's legal adviser; Reichmarschall Goering; Hess, who had been Hitler's deputy until his flight to Scotland in 1941; von Papen, Hitler's vice-chancellor and the man who ensured that Hitler came to power in 1933; Seyss-Inquart, Austria's Quisling and Reich Kommissar of Holland, personally responsible for the deaths of 80 per cent of that country's Jews; and Speer, the architect and slave-trader. The charges included crimes against the peace, commission of war crimes and crimes against humanity, and conspiracy to commit such crimes. The trial opened, in Nuremberg, on November 20, 1945, before eight judges, two each from the U.K., the US, the Soviet Union and France. In his opening speech, the US Counsel captured the zeitgeist of the occasion: "That four great nations flushed with victory and stung with injury stay the hand of vengeance and voluntarily submit their captive enemies to the judgment of the law is one of the most significant tributes that Power has ever paid to Reason".

Some people, of course, considered that the trial was nothing more than a show-trial, victor's justice, at which a finding of guilt was inevitable. Certainly the Soviets were of the view that there should be no chance of an acquittal for the defendants and the Soviet judge, Nikitchenko indicated that the purpose of the Tribunal was merely to pronounce "just punishment for the offences which have been committed". Nevertheless, majority verdicts were acceptable and no single judge had a veto on any decision. That the trial was a trial conducted under the Rule of Law is clear from the fact that it dealt with a number of difficult legal issues, and that three defendants, including von Papen, were acquitted.

The first legal issue arose from the fact that several Nazi organisations were put on trial as well as the individual defendants. The problem was to separate institutions from members, for the Nazi Party itself had many millions of members—were all these members liable to be tried? The IMT thought not, mere membership being insufficient to fix guilt. Thus persons excluded were those who had no knowledge of the criminal purposes or acts of the organisation and those who were drafted by the State for membership (unless they had been personally implicated in acts condemned by Article 6 as members of the organisation). A variety of organisations were indicted: the SA, the General Staff and High Command of the German Armed Forces, the SS, the SD/Gestapo, the Reich Cabinet and the leadership corps of the Nazi Party. The SS, SD/Gestapo and leadership corps were adjudged to be criminal.

Secondly, the legal basis for the charges was open to challenge. In particular, the notion of a common plan or conspiracy, which was the basis for counts one and two of the indictment, caused difficulty. Conspiracy is not a crime in French or Soviet law (or even for that matter in German law) and its definition is very unclear in the Anglo-American legal systems. The Tribunal decided that actions of persons which conspired to wage aggressive and unprovoked war were sufficient. But who did that cover? The Prosecution had argued that any participation in the affairs of the Nazi Party or Government was sufficient evidence of a participation in a criminal conspiracy, but this was resisted by the IMT. The Tribunal felt that the conspiracy must not be too far removed from the time of decision or action and that criminal planning demanded more than the mere declaration of a party programme. However, it was the view of the IMT that the evidence established the common planning to prepare and wage war by certain of the defendants, including Goering and Hess.

Thirdly, there was the issue of the nature of the third count against the defendants, which was committing war crimes. What was the difference between waging war (as the Allies had done) and committing "war crimes". Was, for example, the Allied invasion of Norway any different from the Nazi invasion of Poland? War crimes were defined within the IMT Charter as "Violations of the laws or customs of war. Such violations shall include, but not be limited to, murder, ill-treatment or deportation to slave labor or for any other purpose of civilian population of or in occupied territory, murder or ill-treatment of prisoners of war or persons on the seas, killing of hostages, plunder of public or private property, wanton destruction of cities, towns or villages, or devastation not justified by military necessity". The Tribunal had no difficulty in finding that the actions of the German armies fell within that definition; nor did it have difficulty in finding the defendants charged with this count (except Hess) guilty of war crimes. Another legal problem was the claim that the Tribunal was creating new crimes retrospectively (which would be contrary to the rules of natural justice). The IMT was very clear that the actions defined as war crimes had been criminalised before 1939 and recognised as crimes under international law. Reference was made to provisions of the 1907 Hague Convention and the Geneva Convention of 1929.

Fourthly, one of the most significant legal innovations of the Nuremberg Trial was the creation of the notion of "crimes against humanity". These were defined within Article 6 of the Nuremberg Charter as: "Murder, extermination, enslavement, deportation, and other inhumane acts committed against any civilian population, before or during the war, or persecutions on political, racial, or religious grounds in execution of or in connection with any crime within the jurisdiction of the Tribunal whether or not in violation of the domestic law of the country where they were perpetrated." A difficult legal issue in respect of crimes against humanity was the fact that many of the atrocities committed by the Nazis had been perpetrated prior to the beginning of the war in 1939. Were such acts "within the jurisdiction of the Tribunal"? The Tribunal took the view that the Nazi policies of repression before the outbreak of war did not have a sufficient link with crimes against peace or war crimes, and as a result actions before the outbreak of war could not be tried by the IMT.

Fifthly, there was the "superior orders" defence raised by the defendants. They said "I should not be punished for what I did, because I was only following orders". This claim was preposterous given the high rank of the defendants and amounted to a claim that no one in Germany, alone or together, could physically defy, control or stop Hitler. This cut little ice with the IMT. Following the domestic jurisprudence of most countries, they held that "superior orders" cannot free a person from personal responsibility, but might be used in mitigation of punishment.

Another issue less often highlighted revolved around the indictment of Gustav Krupp, who did not in the end stand trial. The main running of the Krupp Weapons Works in Essen, which used the slave-labourers supplied by Speer, had been the responsibility of Gustav's son, Alfried. The indictment against Gustav seems to have been a drafting error as earlier lists of defendants had named Alfried and a large amount of evidence pointed to his involvement in war crimes in respect of slave labour and the use of prisoners-of-war in Krupp factories. By the time of the trial Gustav was seriously ill and an attempt was made, sponsored by the Americans, to substitute Alfried as a defendant for Gustav. This was witheringly dismissed by Sir Hartley Shawcross thus:"This is a court of justice, not a game in which you can play a substitute if one member of the team falls sick". The proceedings against Gustav were suspended, due to his senility, which in itself proves the Trial was tempering justice with mercy.

In the end the convictions were inevitable, not because the Trial was a farce but because of the deeds of the defendants. Von Papen was acquitted (and though later sentenced by a German denazification court he served little time in prison). Hess received a life sentence (dying at the age of 92 in Spandau Prison in 1987); Speer received 20 years, Doenitz 10. Goering poisoned himself hours before his execution. Frank and Seys-Inquart were hung on October 19, 1946, and it is believe that their bodies, together with the others sentenced to death, were burned at Dachau and their ashes thrown in a river.

THE *WEDNESBURY* CASE

Case 33: Associated Provincial Picture Houses Ltd v. Wednesbury Corporation
[1948] K.B. 228; [1947] 2 All E.R. 680
(Court of Appeal, England)

Administrative law—Judicial review—Unreasonableness

Parliament often allows other bodies, such as local authorities, to make decisions. While no-one can challenge the decisions Parliament itself makes (if expressed in statute) it is sometimes possible to challenge those of other decision-makers. This is so even when Parliament appears to confer a wide, unlimited, discretion to decide however the decision-maker wants to decide. But the courts keep control in the sense that they maintain a power to review the decisions of those whom they have decided to allow to decide. This was seen in *Pryde v. Heritors of Ceres*, **Case 7.** But what is the limit of that power? That is the question that the present case was concerned with.

In the 1940s, local authorities had the statutory power to allow licensed cinemas to open on Sundays, "subject to such conditions as the authority think fit to impose". That seemed a very wide discretion conferred by Parliament. But its exercise was open to challenge. Wednesbury Corporation granted AP Picture Houses Ltd a licence for Sunday performances in the Gaumont Cinema subject to the condition that no children under the age of 15 years were to be admitted with or without an adult. APPH brought an action seeking a declaration that the condition was *ultra vires* and unreasonable. The action was dismissed at first instance and APPH appealed.

The Court of Appeal dismissed the appeal, holding that Wednesbury Corporation had not contravened the law and had not acted in excess of their statutory powers. They had properly taken into account the moral and physical health of local children. The importance of the case lies not in this result but in the *dicta* of the Master of the Rolls, Lord Greene, as to what constitutes unreasonableness in decision-making. He attempted to distinguish two types of unreasonableness, one of which might be described as "ordinary unreasonableness", while the other is now described as "Wednesbury unreasonableness".

In Lord Greene's view, when discretion is granted to a decision-making body, such as a local authority, provided that the discretion is exercised within the four corners of certain principles recognised by the courts, the discretion is absolute and cannot be questioned in any court of law. Lord Greene makes it clear that in judicial review the role of the court is not that of a court of appeal and the court is not entitled to substitute its own opinion for that of the decision-maker. This principle applies as well in appeals from discretionary decisions such as, for example, appeals in child residence and contact disputes (see *Britton v. Central Regional Council*, 1986 S.L.T. 207). The principles he referred to include directing oneself properly in law, taking relevant considerations into account and disregarding irrelevant considerations. If a decision-maker does not obey these rules, he may be said to be acting unreasonably. This may be described as unreasonableness in the ordinary sense.

However, Lord Greene identified another type of unreasonableness. He quoted Warrington L.J. who, in the case of *Short v. Poole Corporation* [1926] Ch. 66, had given the example of the teacher who was dismissed because she had red hair. This would be taking an irrelevant matter into consideration. It can also be described as doing something so absurd that no sensible person could ever dream that it lay within the powers of the decision-maker. So if the decision-maker has kept within the four corners of the matters which he ought to consider but has nevertheless come to a conclusion which is so unreasonable that no reasonable authority could ever have come to it, the court can then interfere, not as an appellate court but as a judicial authority concerned to see whether the decision-maker has contravened the law by acting in excess of the powers conferred by Parliament. In Lord Greene's view this would require "something overwhelming". This type of unreasonableness has, since this case, been described as "Wednesbury unreasonableness".

This standard of unreasonableness would seem to be pitched very high but in decided cases the judges tend to lower the threshold of unreasonableness to match in with their own ideas of administrative good behaviour. This brings the judges quite close to doing what Lord Greene said that they should not do in judicial review, that is to substitute their view of the merits of the decision for that of the original decision-maker. But then judges have always been good at not appearing to do that which they are not supposed to do.

THE LIFT THAT MOVED OF ITS OWN ACCORD

Case 34: Millar v. Galashiels Gas Co.
1949 S.C. (H.L.) 31; 1949 S.L.T. 223
(House of Lords, Scotland)

Health and safety at work—Breach of statutory duty—Statutory interpretation—Strict liability

Factories and other workplaces together with the activities that go on in them can be very dangerous places. This fact of life has been recognised in statutes since the start of the nineteenth century. Legislation has sought to regulate employees' health and safety in ways which are much more focused and extensive than the common law. In this regard, statute has placed higher standards on employers than that demanded by the common law duty to take reasonable care. Today's modern health and safety legislation is a network of statutory provisions which apply both generally and to specific activities and which create obligations consistent with the risks and dangers associated with the activity. The standard ranges from liability based upon reasonable practicability to one that is strict or even absolute. Strict liability can lead to liability even though the employer has sought to take appropriate precautions.

This is best illustrated by what happened to Mr Millar when he was trying to unload some coke from a bogie when working for the Galashiels Gas Co. This task required him to push the bogie into a lift, to ascend to the first floor and then to empty the bogie. He was then required to push the bogie back on to the lift and to return to the ground floor. On one occasion, whilst he was emptying the coke from the bogie, the lift managed to move upwards in the shaft without the gates to the first floor actually closing. Mr Millar did not see this and ran the bogie into the lift shaft. Since there was no lift there, both he and the bogie fell to the bottom of the shaft where Mr Millar was fatally injured.

His widow sued the company in damages for breach of statutory duty under the now repealed Factories Act 1937, s.22(1). The company argued that they could not be liable because the lift had never been known to fail on any occasion. No satisfactory explanation for the isolated incident was ever found. There was no doubt that the employers had taken every practical step to ensure that the mechanism worked properly and that the lift was safe to use. They were not, in other words, at fault. Nevertheless, the company was held liable for Mr Millar's death.

The case turned on the construction that the House of Lords placed upon the relevant statutory provision. The Factories Act required that every lift or hoist had to be of good mechanical construction, sound material and adequate strength and be properly maintained. The Act defined "maintained" as "maintained in an efficient state, efficient working order and in good repair". On the basis of this definition, the House of Lords held that liability could be established without proof of fault. As Lord Reid put it "if the duty is proper maintenance and maintenance is defined as maintenance in efficient working order, then, once it is established that the duty goes beyond a duty to exercise care, the fact that on a particular occasion the mechanism was not in efficient working order shows that there had not been proper maintenance". Essentially, the judges regarded the provision as creating a strict duty upon the employers and considered that neither intention nor lack of care needed to be shown in order to prove a breach of it. It must be remembered, of course, that even where a court construes a statutory provision as imposing strict liability it is still necessary for the pursuer to show that his or her injury was *caused* by a breach of that duty.

Even although this case was decided under old and now repealed legislation *Millar* is still vitally important today and should not be regarded as some sort of historical curiosity. It set an important benchmark for the level of responsibility that might be placed upon employers whose employees are engaged on particularly dangerous activities. It is cited frequently in the courts and remains an authoritative guide to some aspects of modern health and safety legislation. For example, Lord Bonomy applied the *Millar* formulae in *Johnston v. JT Inglis & Sons Ltd* (December 14, 1999) when interpreting regulation 6 of the Provision and Use of Work Equipment Regulations 1992. This provision declares that every employer must ensure that work equipment is in an efficient state, in efficient working order and in good repair. The language is identical to the provision regarding lifts and hoists in the Factories Act but encompasses a much broader category of machinery. Following *Millar*, Lord Bonomy held that all that the pursuer has to aver in a case of failure to comply with the duty under reg. 6 is that the machine did not work properly.

TO CATCH A THIEF

Case 35: Lawrie v. Muir, 1950 J.C. 19
(High Court of Justiciary, Scotland)

Criminal law—Evidence—Improperly obtained evidence— "Fairness" and judicial discretion

Just because a person commits a crime does not mean that they should be convicted thereof. For one thing, as is well-known, a person is innocent until proven guilty beyond reasonable doubt. If there is reasonable doubt then the person cannot be convicted—even if, as sometimes happens, a civil court finds on the balance of probabilities that the person did indeed commit the crime, for an example, see the O.J. Simpson trial. Similarly, a person who commits a crime might be entitled to an acquittal if the evidence presented against him or her was improperly obtained. It is the question of what "improperly obtained" means that the present case is concerned with.

Milk used to come in glass bottles. The milkman would take full bottles from the dairy and deliver them to doorsteps, retrieving the empty bottles which the householder had left there for that purpose. The bottles, being of strong glass, were relatively valuable and certainly not disposable. Each dairy owned their own bottles though there was no requirement on consumers to return the bottles to the correct dairy. Replacements were expensive. So a company was set up by statute to collect and restore to the correct dairies bottles that went astray. The company were given enforcement powers and, in all contracts between the Scottish Milk Marketing Board and the dairies they supplied, the latter were obliged to allow the company inspectors access to their premises to check that they were not using other dairies' bottles. It was made an offence under milk marketing regulations for one dairy to use the bottles of another without the other's consent.

Jeanie Lawrie was a dairy keeper in Portobello, Edinburgh. In September 1948 two company inspectors called at her dairy, produced their warrant cards and requested to inspect her premises. Believing she had no choice, Mrs Lawrie allowed them in, and they found 116 bottles, of which 31 belonged to other dairies. She was charged under the regulations and convicted. She appealed and raised an issue of law which was of such importance and of such wide significance that the High Court of Justiciary referred the case on to a Full Bench of Seven Judges. For Mrs Lawrie had had no contract with the Scottish Milk Marketing Board; this meant that the inspectors had no right to enter her dairy—in other words, the evidence of the inspectors was unlawfully obtained. The point of law was this: in what, if any, circumstances is evidence admissible that has been unlawfully obtained?

This is a matter of great legal and practical importance, out of all proportion (as is not unusual) to the petty facts of the case. The police and other investigators must act within the law—they cannot themselves become criminals in order to enforce the law. But, being human, they will sometimes overstep the mark, sometimes deliberately and sometimes (as here) accidentally. The evidence they obtain will be tainted, but does that make it inadmissible? Mrs Muir went for broke and argued that in no circumstances is improperly obtained evidence admissible in a criminal court. Lord Justice-General Cooper gave the Opinion of the Court and he rejected this absolutist proposition.

Lord Cooper pointed out that there were two highly important interests which conflict here: the interest of the citizen to be protected from illegal or irregular invasions of his or her liberty, and the interests of the state to secure that evidence necessary to enable justice to be done is available to courts of law. He seemed to suggest that the latter interest is the more important, for in his view the reason why citizens should be protected from illegal or irregular invasions of liberty is to protect the innocent from undue interference and not to protect the guilty from overzealous prosecutors. The correct balance is achieved, he said, by expressing the rule thus: "an irregularity in the obtaining of evidence does not *necessarily* make that evidence inadmissible". It might do so, but it does not necessarily do so. The correct issue is one of "fairness", balancing the nature of the irregularity with the circumstances in which it was committed, in order to determine whether the irregularity can be excused. It would be unfair to allow evidence where the departure from the strict procedure for obtaining evidence had been adopted deliberately with a view to securing the admission of evidence obtained by an unfair trick; on the other hand it would usually be wrong to exclude some highly incriminating production in a murder trial merely because it was found by a police officer in the course of a search authorised for a different purpose or before a proper warrant had been obtained.

So the test is highly discretionary, dependent upon the court's view of fairness, balancing the investigator's intent with the seriousness of the crime and the seriousness of the departure from proper investigatory practice. Where did justice lie in Jeanie Lawrie's case? The Full Bench held that the balance was very fine in the present case but, because the company inspectors had obtained entry to Mrs Lawrie's dairy only on production of their warrant cards which, in truth, gave them no right of entry, the balance of fairness fell in favour of the thieving Mrs Lawrie. Her conviction was quashed.

THE OFFSIDE TRAP, OR THE CASE OF THE INAPPROPRIATE METAPHOR

Case 36: Rodger (Builders) Ltd v. Fawdry
1950 S.C. 483; 1950 S.L.T. 345
(Inner House, Court of Session, Scotland)

*Property—Transfer of ownership—Double sale—Offside goals rule—
Bad faith—Inappropriate metaphor*

(See Forte (Ed.), *Good Faith in Contract and Property Law* (1999): Carey Miller, "Good faith in Scots property law" at p. 103; and Blackie, "Good faith and the Doctrine of Personal Bar" at p. 129.)

Lord Justice-Clerk Thomson liked sporting similes. In *Thomson v. Glasgow Corporation*, 1961 S.L.T. 237 he compared the role of a judge to the role of a referee in a boxing contest. However, for property lawyers he is best remembered for bringing the excitement of the beautiful game to the law on transfer of ownership. After *Rodger (Builders) v. Fawdry* conveyancers have to take care to avoid the offside trap.

Fawdry owned a mansion house and some farms. He contracted to sell the house and farm to Rodger (Builders) Ltd. Part of the price was to be paid on conclusion of the missives, the remainder at the date of settlement. The date of settlement came and went and Rodger (Builders) did not pay. Mr Fawdry did not, like Mariana at the Moated Grange, wait and wait, but rather sought a second suitor and eventually entered a second contract of sale with Adam Bell. Bell knew about the first contract of sale, but was reassured by Fawdry that he had nothing to worry about. In implement of the contract a disposition in favour of Bell's wife, Mrs Marjorie Katharine Montagu Douglas Scott or Hacket Pain or Bell, was delivered. Mrs Bell registered the disposition. On registration of the disposition ownership transferred from Fawdry to Mrs Bell.

Rodger (Builders) went to court. They argued that the disposition in favour of Mrs Bell should be reduced. Fawdry had attempted a double sale. And in the second sale the Bells were in bad faith, for they knew about the existence of the prior contract in favour of Rodger (Builders). As they were in bad faith, their bad faith should be penalised. The disposition should be reduced. This rule was well-established in Scots law: see *Morrison v. Somerville* (1860) 22 D. 1082, *Petrie v. Forsyth* (1874) 2 R. 214, and *Stodart v. Dalzell* (1876) 4 R. 236. The rule even merited its own sub-heading in Morison's *Dictionary*, where cases are gathered under the heading "Private Knowledge of a Prior Right".

The Second Division held that the disposition in favour of Mrs Bell should be reduced and the transference of the real right of ownership avoided. As the Bells knew of the earlier contract, they were in bad faith and they could not rely on the assurance by Fawdry that the first contract had fallen.

Enter Lord Justice-Clerk Thomson, with his sporting metaphor. He said: "The appellants [the Bells] assumed their title would be safe once the goal of the register was reached. But in this branch of law, as in football, offside goals are disallowed. In certain states of knowledge a purchaser is regarded as not being in good faith and goes to the register at his peril."

With these words the rule was rechristened, and centuries of tradition set aside. The leading modern textbook on property law (Professor Reid's *Property* (1996), paras 695 *et seq.*) now refers to "the rule against offside goals".

The case illustrates a broader principle of property law that is crucially important. Generally in property law good faith is irrelevant (see also on that point, **Morrisson v. Robertson, Case 18**). If somebody acquires an item from a non-owner genuinely believing the non-owner is the owner, their good faith does not give them title. Good faith cannot create a property right. However, sometimes—and the offside goals rule is one instance—bad faith can be penalised and as a result a transference of title can be avoided. With the offside goals rule the remedy existed for Rodger (Builders) because the Bells were in bad faith. They knew about the earlier contract, and they did not check to see if the earlier contract had fallen.

At the time of *Rodger (Builders)* it was thought (it would seem incorrectly given *Bouack v. Croll* (1748) Mor. 1695 and 15280) that the rule only applied to competing titles where there had been a double sale, and it was also thought that the appropriate remedy was a decree of reduction. However, since *Rodger (Builders)* the offside goals rule has developed. It now applies where there are competing subordinate real rights (such as a lease and a security), as can be seen in *Trade Development Bank v. Warriner and Mason (Scotland) Ltd*, 1980 S.C. 74, and *Trade Development Bank v. Crittall Windows*, 1983 S.L.T. 510. It has also been held that an appropriate remedy may be an order to make a conveyance as opposed to an order for reduction: *Davidson v. Zani*, 1992 S.C.L.R. 1001.

One final critical observation can be made of Lord Justice-Clerk Thomson. The offside goals rule is an inappropriate metaphor. A party that has been in bad faith in relation to a prior right when acquiring their own real right has a voidable title. The title is capable of being avoided at the instance of the innocent party. But in football an offside goal is never awarded. An offside goal is void, not voidable. And we won't even begin to consider the problems that occur if the defender is level with the pursuer.

WHAT'S IN A NAME?

Case 37: MacCormick v. Lord Advocate
1953 S.C. 396; 1953 S.L.T. 255
(Inner House, Court of Session, Scotland)

Constitutional law—Treaty of Union—Parliamentary sovereignty—Crown

(See Smith, "The Union of 1707 as Fundamental Law" [1957] Pub. L. 99; MacCormick, "Does the United Kingdom Have a Constitution?" (1978) 29 N.I.L.Q. 1; Addo & Smith, "The Relevance of Historical Fact to Certain Arguments Relating to the Legal Significance of the Acts of Union", 1998 J.R. 37.)

When King George VI died in 1952, his elder daughter Elizabeth succeeded to the Throne of the United Kingdom of Great Britain and Northern Ireland, and was crowned Queen in 1953. She took the title of Queen Elizabeth II. Many Scots were offended by this title, and postboxes bearing the royal insignia ER II were attacked (and seldom now appear in Scotland to this day). The point was that while there had been a previous Queen Elizabeth, she had been Queen of England and Wales but most decidedly not of Scotland. John MacCormick, who was rector of Glasgow University at the time and chairman of the Scottish Covenant Association (a nationalist organisation), and Ian Hamilton, then a law student and secretary of the Association, presented a petition to the Court of Session seeking an interdict against the Lord Advocate, as representing the Crown, from publishing a proclamation entitling the new Queen as Elizabeth II. They argued that the title was inconsistent with historical fact and political reality and involved a contravention of article 1 of the Treaty of Union of 1707, and the Acts of Union passed by the English and the Scottish Parliaments to give effect to the Treaty. They also argued that the publication of the proclamation was likely to cause civil disturbance in Scotland, which would be injurious to them as citizens of Scotland.

Their petition was dismissed at first instance, and a reclaiming motion to the Inner House was also dismissed.

The First Division, presided over by Lord President Cooper, dismissed the action on three grounds: (i) the petition was incompetent because the Court had no jurisdiction to decide whether a governmental act such as a proclamation was or was not in conformity with the Treaty of Union; (ii) the petitioners' arguments were irrelevant as article 1 of the Treaty of Union did not prohibit the use of the numeral II; and (iii) MacCormick and Hamilton did not have title to raise the points at issue. To allow them to do so would be to concede a similar right to almost any opponent to almost any political action.

The importance of this case lies not so much in the actual decision but in certain *obiter* remarks made by the Lord President on the doctrine of parliamentary sovereignty and the related question as to whether certain articles of the Treaty of Union are fundamental and unalterable. These issues retain their relevance today in relation to the U.K. Parliament's relationships with other law-making bodies such as the institutions of the European Union, and the devolved Parliament in Scotland and the Northern Ireland Assembly.

Lord President Cooper said that the principle of the unlimited sovereignty of Parliament is a distinctively English principle which had no counterpart in Scottish constitutional law. Since the Parliaments of England and Scotland had been extinguished in 1707, he had difficulty in seeing why it should be supposed that the new Parliament of Great Britain inherited all the peculiar characteristics of the English Parliament but none of the Scottish Parliament. In addition, he was of the opinion that the Treaty and the Acts of Union contain clauses which are declared to be fundamental and unalterable in all time coming and that there is no provision in the Treaty that the Parliament of Great Britain should be absolutely sovereign in the sense that it should be free to alter the Treaty at will. However, he went on to question whether an alleged breach of the Articles of Union would be a justiciable issue in the courts of England or Scotland. The Lord President declined to express an opinion in relation to the Articles which seek to protect the Scottish courts and Scots private law as the issue before the Court was one of public law (but he did go on to say that it is of little avail to ask whether Parliament can do this or that without going on to ask who can stop them if they do).

These views of Lord President Cooper on the peculiarly English nature of the doctrine of Parliamentary sovereignty differ markedly from the views of most English constitutional lawyers who believe that the legislative competence of the U.K. Parliament is unlimited. There have been a few other cases in Scotland where the judges have flirted with the notion that the provisions of the Treaty and the Acts of Union have fundamental status (such as *Gibson v. Lord Advocate*, 1975 S.L.T. 134, the poll tax cases, discussed by Walker and Himsworth, "The Poll Tax and Fundamental Law", 1991 J.R. 45, and the Skye Bridge Toll Cases, such as *Robbie the Pict v. Hingston (No. 2)*, 1998 S.L.T. 1201), but in all of them the courts found some other ground for dismissing the cases in front of them.

So, while Queen Elizabeth can call herself "The Second", the constitutional issue remains unresolved. It should be noted, however, that section 37 of the Scotland Act 1998 expressly provides that the Union legislation "shall have effect subject to this Act" (which sets up the Scottish Parliament). This is intended to ensure that anything done under the Scotland Act which affects or contravenes the terms of the Acts of Union will be given effect to. The existence of this provision implies that the proposition that the earlier Acts are fundamental is, at the very least, arguable.

CONNIE'S CASE

Case 38: Draper v. Thomason, 1954 S.C. 136; 1954 S.L.T. 222 (Inner House, Court of Session, Scotland)

Wills and Succession—Authentication of deeds—Signature—Informal wills

There is nothing like a will to create a family argument. Whenever a person makes a will he or she is effectively saying that the rules on intestacy are not satisfactory. They are, of course, usually entirely satisfactory for the heirs on intestacy. Even more conducive to a family argument is if the will is both ambiguous and informal. If it is ambiguous, surviving relatives can—and do—argue until the cows come home about what the testator really meant; if it is informal it can be argued that it was never intended to be a will in any case.

The Scots as a race are rather reticent when it comes to making formal wills, whether due to a belief in individual immortality or to a disinclination to contemplate one's own demise. But the Scots also are (or at least were, before the explosion of mass and immediate communications) inveterate letter-writers. And in these letters it has been common for writers to indicate what they want to happen to their property after their deaths. Scots law has always been uniquely liberal in recognising the validity of testamentary writings in the most informal manner, and we do not set out the strict requirements of form found in other legal systems, such as English law. The only question in Scots law is whether the provision expresses the concluded testamentary intention of the deceased. The only form that absolutely requires to be followed is that the intention be expressed in writing in a permanent form, and that the writing be signed by the testator.

Mrs Constance Thomason or Tupper (known to her family and friends as "Connie") died in 1952. She had no children, but her husband survived her, as did her sister, Mrs Draper, and a nephew, Mrs Draper's son Billy. She had not made a formal will. However, some 16 years prior to her death she had written to her sister a chatty letter full of news and family gossip, and details of an excursion she was about to undertake the next day to the town of Keswick. About half way through the letter appeared the following passage:

> "By the way, speaking of death! Should anything happen to me (which it will one day) I haven't made a Will, but everything I have is for Billy. Knowing that he will do the right thing".

Nothing did happen to her in Keswick but she did, of course, eventually pass on. Her sister, canny woman, had preserved this letter and Billy, now grown to man's estate, founded upon it to claim all of Connie's property. Connie's widowed husband, and other heirs on intestacy wanted Billy to get nothing.

The first argument was that the letter, being chatty and informal, could not be construed so as to contain formal and important matters like a concluded testamentary intention. That argument failed. "Everything I have is for Billy" was as clear an intention as it was possible to have. The second argument was that the last sentence quoted above limited Billy's absolute right to the property and indicated that he was to take only in trust, the trust purpose being "to do the right thing"—but that purpose was so vague that the trust, and therefore the gift, failed. That argument was rejected as well, on the basis that the words, properly construed, expressed Connie's motives for leaving her property to Billy rather than a condition upon which he took the property.

The third and most vigorously argued challenge was to the signature. Connie had signed herself "Connie" at the end of her letter. The heirs on intestacy tried to argue that for a signature to authenticate a testamentary intention it had to be in formal form, *i.e.* a surname and some indicator of a forename. Again this argument failed. "Connie" was the normal signature of this woman when she wrote to her sister; it would be ludicrous to expect her to sign in any other way. So Billy got his inheritance.

Draper was followed in a better-known case, *Rhodes v. Peterson*, 1972 S.L.T. 98 in which a mother wrote to her daughter Dorothy saying that on her death she wanted Dorothy to have her house, furniture, jewellery and all her little treasures. On her death her sons (doubtless disappointed to discover that they themselves were not their mother's little treasures) challenged the will. The testamentary intention was even clearer than in *Draper*, but the signature was even less formal, for Mrs Peterson signed off her letter "lots of love, Mum". But the Court followed *Draper* and held that since this was the deceased's normal signature in the context in question, the letter amounted to a testamentary document and the wishes contained thereinhad to be given effect to.

The Requirements of Writing (Scotland) Act 1995 puts these cases on a statutory basis. It allows that documents are properly executed (though not probative, or self-evidencing, without a witness) even if printed or typed, which changes the common law rule which required that to be properly executed without a witness the deed had to be handwritten. But the nature of the signature of the granter of the deed (governed by section 7) remains the same. In formal, witnessed, deeds a formal signature (a surname and an indicator of a forename) is required, but in less formal deeds "any name, description, initial or mark" is sufficient if it is established that the name, description, initial or mark was the granter's usual method of signing documents of the type in question. Informal signatures are not presumed to be valid, as formal signatures are, so the onus lies on the party founding on the deed to prove its validity. Neither Billy nor Dorothy had any real difficulty in doing so in their respective cases.

THE OVERDUE DEATH OF JIM CROW

Case 39: Brown v. Board of Education
347 U.S. 483 (1954), 349 U.S. 294 (1955)
(Supreme Court, United States of America)

Race segregation—Civil rights—US constitutional law—Equal protection clause

(See Black, "The Lawfulness of the Segregation Decisions" (1960) 69 Yale L.J. 421; Kurland, *"Brown v. Board of Education* was the Beginning" (1979) Wash. U.L.Q. 309.)

A number of states in the United States of America, predominantly in the South, had since the time of the American Civil War imposed a system of racial segregation on their populations (known in South Africa as apartheid and in the US as "Jim Crow", after a derogatory nineteenth century term for negro which had been popularised in song). The present case was a famous victory against such laws and led to other victories for the Civil Rights movement, which eventually succeeded in expunging directly racial discriminatory laws from the statute books in the United States. It illustrates the power of the US Supreme Court to influence the way in which American society develops.

The nineteenth century Supreme Court had not been inclined to disturb race laws. There are two notorious decisions that have blackened the reputation of the Court since they were handed down and which more recent decisions only partly assuage. In *Scott v. Sandford*, 60 U.S.

393 (1857) the Court held (i) that while a black person could be a citizen of an individual state, he could not be a citizen of the United States and (ii) that state legislation freeing slaves was an unconstitutional interference with citizens' right to property. The decision galvanised both supporters and opponents of slavery to such an extent that many see the decision as one of the major catalysts of the American Civil War. Even after slavery was abolished by constitutional amendment after that war (the 13th and 14th Amendments to the US Constitution), the Supreme Court upheld racial segregation and refused to find that such laws infringed the equal protection clause of the 14th Amendment. In *Plessy v. Ferguson*, 163 U.S. 537 (1896) the Court invented the morally bankrupt doctrine of "separate but equal"—everyone remains equal under the law even when they are separated. So the rules in place in Kansas and 13 other states requiring children to be educated separately depending upon their race seemed to be safe.

The National Association for the Advancement of Colored People (NAACP) had, however, been conducting a strategy of constitutional challenge for some years and by the middle of the twentieth century the Supreme Court was changing its attitudes to race discrimination. The *Plessy* decision was progressively limited within narrower and narrower bounds. The first direct challenge to that decision was, however, in the present case which attacked the policy of separate education for black and white children. While it is clear that the justices had come to accept the utter unsustainability of the "Jim Crow" regime, the consequences of holding school segregation unlawful frightened them. For the practicality of such a decision would be that states would be required *immediately* to open all schools to all races and the economic costs of doing so were enormous. However, the Supreme Court in 1953 acquired a new Chief Justice, Earl Warren, and he came up with the idea of separating the substantive issue of whether segregation was constitutional or not from the issue of what relief to grant if the challenge was successful. So the first case was limited to the issue of constitutionality. Appearing for the plaintiffs was Thurgood Marshall, the legal director of NAACP, who went on to become, in 1967, the first black appointee to the Supreme Court. During the argument he was asked what "equal" meant. He replied that "equal means getting the same thing, at the same time and in the same place". (When later asked why he had appointed Marshall to the Supreme Court, President Johnson said that "it was the right thing to do, the right time to do it, the right man and the right place"). In *Brown* the Court agreed with Marshall. And, to the surprise of many, it did so unanimously. Segregation in state institutions was held to be unlawful as an infringement of every citizen's right to equal protection under the law. *Plessy* was not overruled, but dismissed as irrelevant. The effect of this victory was, symbolically at any rate, profound and heralded a major mind-shift in judicial, political and social thinking in the United States. A year later, the Supreme Court dealt with the remedy to be granted as a result of the first case, but their decision here, though still unanimous, was weak to the point of being meaningless. The plaintiffs and NAACP were required to produce plans for the desegregation of schools across the nation. It took a number of other cases before the Court demanded positive action such as bussing children from one area to schools in other areas: *Green v. County School Board of New Kent County*, 391 U.S. 430 (1968) and *Swann v. Charlotte-Mecklenburg County Board of Education*, 402 U.S. 1 (1971). Anything less would have rendered *Brown* meaningless given the practical segregation in housing that existed long after the decision and to some extent continues today in many US cities.

Brown met with fierce resistance. Ten years after the decision, it was estimated that less than two per cent of previously segregated schools had been desegregated. Other rules, like the rule against mixed-race marriage, remained for another 15 years (*see Loving v. Virginia*, **Case 52**). But, like *Scott* before it, *Brown* galvanised public opinion and breathed life into the civil rights campaign. It was a turning point in American social policy and while today the decision seems inevitable it is as well to remember that a similar anti-black policy survived in South Africa for a further 40 years. The South African constitution then did not permit challenges to apartheid. The power of the law to effect social and political change even when politicians have no stomach to bring about the change themselves is thus starkly revealed, so long as appropriate constitutional mechanisms are in place (as they are, now, in South Africa).

IF YOU FAIL, YOU CAN'T SUCCEED

Case 40: Ross' Judicial Factor v. Martin and Others
1955 S.C. (H.L.) 56; 1955 S.L.T. 117
(House of Lords, Scotland)

Wills and succession— Common calamity—Survivorship clause

The basic aim of testate succession is to identify the intention of the testator and to give effect to it. That intention is found by looking at the terms of the will. Problems arise if the will is ambiguous. The present case is unusual in that the intention of the testatrices was entirely unambiguous but because of the words they had used to express their intent, or their will, the law could not achieve what they clearly wanted.

The Misses Ross, Margery and Hannah, were wealthy spinsters who lived all their lives together in a large house in Edinburgh (rather like *Arsenic and Old Lace* without the arsenic). In June 1938 both Miss

Margery Ross and Miss Hannah Ross made wills, leaving their whole estate to each other, whom failing to various named individuals, including a number of charities. These became the defenders in the case. The wills were in identical terms, other than the fact that Margery left everything to Hannah, while Hannah left everything to Margery. Tragically, in February 1950, there was a gas leak at their home, which poisoned them both, and a day later the two ladies were found dead in their beds. Miss Margery was 79; Miss Hannah was 74.

These facts gave rise to a difficult legal problem in identifying who was to succeed to the valuable estates of these ladies. The problem was that it was impossible to tell which of them had died first, though in fact one of them must have done so. But it is an important principle in the law of succession that a claimant must be alive at the moment of the deceased's death in order to have a valid claim to succeed to any portion of the deceased's estate. This is the rule of "survivorship", and failure to survive (*i.e.* be alive at the date of death) means that the succession claim is lost. Had Hannah died first, then her whole estate would have gone to Margery the survivor, as her will provided; on Margery's subsequent death her will provided that on the failure of Hannah her whole estate (which now included Hannah's share) would go to the defenders. The same result would have followed if Margery had died first—Hannah would succeed, and then because Margery failed Hannah (*i.e.* did not survive Hannah) on Hannah's death the combined estate would go, again, to the defenders. The problem was that this devolution of the estates, which no-one denied was exactly what the sisters intended, could only follow if one survived the other (and, which is the same thing, if one failed the other). But it could not be shown which sister survived and which failed.

In the Outer House, Lord President Cooper (sitting alone) held that it did not matter who died first. Whichever sister died first, they both intended either the other to inherit or the defenders: if the other could not inherit, the defenders took. However, the Crown, who always has an interest in ensuring that estates of persons without relatives fall into intestacy (for then the Crown succeeds: see now the Succession (Scotland) Act 1964, s.7) argued that both sisters died intestate. The Crown reclaimed Lord Cooper's interlocutor, and was successful in both the Inner House and the House of Lords.

The issue revolved around the words used by both sisters in their respective wills. They had both stated that the defenders should succeed only if their sister "predeceased" the testatrix. The Court interpreted these words as effectively creating a conditional legacy in favour of the defenders—the condition being that one sister predecease the other before the defenders could take. The defenders' inability to show how the condition was satisfied was fatal to their claim: the fact that one sister *must have* predeceased the other was nothing to the point. Inability to show that Hannah had predeceased Margery meant that the defenders could not take under Margery's will; and inability to show that Margery had predeceased Hannah meant that the defenders could not take under Hannah's will. So the estate fell into intestacy, notwithstanding the clear intentions of the sisters.

This case was decided under the common law, but that law was altered in 1964. Section 31 of the Succession (Scotland) Act 1964 deals with the situation in which two persons die in circumstances which indicate that they died simultaneously or rendering it uncertain which, if either, survived the other. The general rule in that case is that the elder is deemed to fail the younger. So in the present case Hannah would be deemed to have survived; she would have succeeded to Margery's property; and because she was now dead herself, Margery having "predeceased" her, the whole property of the two sisters would go to the defenders—as they both wanted. But they died too soon for that rule to apply.

The rule in section 31 does not apply if the two persons who die together are husband and wife, and there it is presumed that neither survived the other. This is designed to ensure that the whole property of two spouses does not all go to the blood relatives of one spouse alone, which is all very well except that in facts similar to the present case the same result would be reached and the estate would fall into intestacy contrary to any intention that the parties had. Nor does the rule apply (in cases not involving spouses) where the elder leaves property to the younger, whom failing a third party and the younger dies intestate. For to apply the rule that the younger survives would mean that the younger does not "fail" (even although he or she is dead) and the third party does not succeed, because they can only succeed on the failure of the younger: that is seen as contrary to the elder's intention and so, for the purpose of the "whom failing" clause, the elder is presumed to survive, which means the younger is presumed to fail and the third party is thereby able to succeed.

NURSE RATCHET WOULD HAVE APPROVED

Case 41: Bolam v. Friern Hospital Management Committee [1957] 2 All E.R. 118; [1957] 1 W.L.R. 582 (Queen's Bench Division, High Court, England)

Delict—Medical negligence—Standard of care—Informed consent

(See Teff, "Moving On From *Bolam*" (1998) O.J.L.S. 473; Brazier & Miola, "Bye Bye *Bolam*: A Medical Litigation Revolution" (2000) 8 Med. L.R. 85.)

Mr John Bolam suffered from a mental illness and he was advised by a consultant attached to the Friern Hospital to undergo electro-convulsive therapy, a form of medical treatment which has since rather lost its popularity. It was explained to Mr Bolam that the treatment would involve passing a current of 150 volts through electrodes attached to his head, so that the current would pass through his brain. Convulsions of his body would, he was warned, be a consequence but so, it was hoped, would an amelioration of his mental condition. In that hope, Mr Bolam agreed to the treatment. He was not, however, warned of the risk that the convulsions might lead to bone fracture. The doctor had deliberately failed to warn him that the treatment carried that risk, considering the matter too trivial to concern him with. In doing so, the doctor was following common, though by no means universal, medical practice. The doctor also decided neither to administer the patient with relaxant drugs nor to instruct the attendant nurses to restrain him during the treatment, either of which measures would minimise the risk of fracture. Again, in making this decision, the doctor was following common but not universal medical practice.

During the treatment, the convulsions led to the fracture of Mr Bolam's pelvis on both sides and dislocated both his hips. He sued the hospital, alleging that the doctor had been negligent in three respects: (i) failure to administer relaxant drugs; (ii) failure to provide restraint during the treatment; and (iii) failure to warn him of the risk which he was taking in consenting to the treatment. The defendants pointed out the divergence in medical opinion and claimed that, as a general rule, a doctor is not to be criticised in a court of law for following one school of medical thought rather than another.

The case therefore raises in nice form the question of how medical negligence is to be defined by courts, presided over by judges who are (for the most part) not medically trained. Effectively, the defendants were claiming that the medical profession should be left free to set its own standards. McNair J's charge to the jury goes a long way to accept this and it has since become the *locus classicus* for the definition of professional negligence generally.

McNair J. pointed out that in a situation that involves the use of some special skill and competence, the test whether there has been negligence or not is not the test of the man on the top of the Clapham Omnibus, because he has not got this special skill. Rather the test is the standard of the ordinary skilled man exercising and professing to have that special skill. A defendant is not expected to have the highest degree of expert skill, and it must always be remembered, particularly in medicine, that there may be more than one perfectly proper standard of care. "The true test for establishing negligence in diagnosis and treatment on the part of a doctor", McNair J. quotes the second Lord President Clyde in the Scottish case of *Hunter v. Hanley*, 1955 S.C. 200 as saying, "is whether or not he has been proved to be guilty of such failure as no doctor of ordinary skill would be guilty of if acting with ordinary care". McNair J. accepted this but preferred to put it that a doctor is not guilty of negligence if he has acted in accordance with a practice accepted as proper by a responsible body of medical men. He pointed out, as Lord President Clyde had pointed out, that a doctor is not negligent merely because there is a body of opinion that takes a contrary view. Following this approach, the courts in Scotland and England show much deference to professional practice in cases of professional negligence and have proved themselves unwilling to criticise the exercise of professional judgment. The doctor's judgment may be wrong but it is not necessarily negligence. It may be wrong and it may cause harm, but it is not actionable unless *no* responsible member of the relevant profession would exercise his or her judgment in that manner. The House of Lords has since accepted this test in relation to negligence in treatment in *Whitehouse v. Jordan* [1981] 1 W.L.R. 246 and in relation to negligence in diagnosis in *Maynard v. West Midlands Regional Health Authority* [1984] 1 W.L.R. 634.

The other importance of the case is that it is the first U.K. "informed consent" case, *i.e.* it is the first in which a failure of duty was alleged to be the doctor's failure to inform the patient of the potential risks of the treatment being proposed and for which consent was sought. The two points of note in this aspect of the case are (i) that the same test as that for negligence in treatment and diagnosis was applied (*i.e.* whether no doctor of ordinary skill would have failed to warn of the risk) and (ii) the patient can only win on this basis if he or she can satisfy the court that the result of being informed of the risk of the treatment would have been a refusal to give consent to the treatment. Both these points later received the imprimatur of the House of Lords in *Sidaway v. Bethlem Royal Hospital* [1985] 1 A.C. 871.

Not all courts accept the *Bolam* approach (or the Scottish *Hunter v. Hanley* approach). The High Court of Australia, for example, in *Rogers v. Whittaker* (1992) 175 C.L.R. 479 rejected the proposition that the *Bolam* test applied in informed consent cases. The House of Lords, however, continues to cling to *Bolam*. In *Bolitho v. City and Hackney Health Authority* [1998] A.C. 232 they qualified it to the extent of holding that the body of medical opinion followed by the defendant had to be shown to be logical, defensible and reasonable, but ultimately the authority of *Bolam* was affirmed.

Mr Bolam, incidentally, lost his case; whether he regained his mental health is not recorded by posterity.

SEX WITH AN ALIEN ORGAN

Case 42: MacLennan v. MacLennan
1958 S.C. 105; 1958 S.L.T. 12
(Outer House, Court of Session, Scotland)

Husband and wife—Divorce—Adultery—Artificial insemination

(See Montgomery, 1949 S.L.T. (News) 82; Tallin (1956) 34 Can. Bar Rev. 1 and 166; Middleton, 1956 J.R. 204; and Smith, 1957 S.L.T. (News) 69)

The law always opens itself to ridicule whenever it attempts to regulate sexual activity. This is seen most obviously in the criminal law, but is true also in family law. There are always difficulties in applying with the precision necessary in a just legal system rules which come from propositions untimely ripped from the inspecifics of religious doctrine. The law of adultery is a case in point. Most legal systems in the Christian world, and beyond, originally regarded adultery as an unlawful act, because of the Biblical injunction to chastity. The legal response to an act of adultery varied enormously. In Scotland one response was to permit the putting asunder of the parties to the marriage, this three hundred years before divorce was statutorily introduced into the law of England. Neither the Scottish legislation from the sixteenth, nor the English legislation from the nineteenth, century defined"adultery", for it was considered that everyone knew what that concept entailed. But did they? Do they?

Ronald MacLennan married Margaret Shortland in August 1952, but the marriage was not a success. The couple had separated by May 1954 and Mrs MacLennan shortly thereafter went to the United States of America. In July 1955, in Brooklyn, New York (three months after the magnolia blooms and two months after the cherry blossom), she was safely delivered of a baby girl. Mr MacLennan promptly sued her for divorce. Defending the action, Mrs MacLennan claimed that she had conceived the child with semen obtained not through a licentious connexion but through artificial insemination from an anonymous donor. So the Court of Session was faced for the first time with the question of defining adultery: more specifically the question was whether artificial insemination of a woman without the consent of her husband amounted to adultery. Concerning this petty little question a surprising amount of judicial and academic ink has been spilt, illustrating once again that lawyers can find room for more angels on the head of a pin than nearly anyone else.

Mr MacLennan's argument was two-fold. First, his wife's act was such a grave breach of the marriage contract that it was the equivalent to, and should have the same effect as, adultery. Given the terms of the statutory law, which limited divorce to specific grounds which could not be extended by judicial development, this argument was bound to fail. The second argument was that the insertion into a wife's body of semen from a man not her husband was such as to adulterate the stock, which was the definition of adultery. Mrs MacLennan argued that adultery was committed only when the physical act of intercourse occurred and that her husband had the onus of proving that.

Lord Wheatley considered that such authority as existed in Scots law (the Book of Deuteronomy, the writings of St Paul and the works of the Canonists) indicated that adultery required "*conjuncto corporum*". The purpose of adultery as a ground for divorce could be gleaned from the preamble to the Divorce Act 1563, c. 10, which denounces those who have no regard to the commandments of God but only to their own sensualities, filthy lusts and pleasure. The Institutional writers talk variously (and coyly) of "fidelity to the marital bed", "having knowledge of another" or, rather more opaquely, "the sin of incontinence" (this last from Bell's *Dictionary* (7th ed.) at p. 25). However expressed, Lord Wheatley saw all the references as pointing to the need for sexual intercourse. If so, can AID amount to sexual intercourse? The Institutional writers do not, for obvious reasons, address that question, but Lord Wheatley took the view that since procreation is not a necessary concomitant of sexual intercourse, it cannot define it. This leaves the physical act, the absence of which with AID means that there is no adultery: adultery is, in Lord Wheatley's memorable phrase, "physical contact with an alien and unlawful organ".

There were some awkward precedents that Lord Wheatley had to deal with. Some English decisions had suggested that actual penetration was not required for adultery. In *Russell v. Russell*, 1924 A.C. 687 Lord Dunedin had stated (*obiter*) that "fecundation *ab extra* is, I doubt not, adultery". And in *Sapsford v. Sapsford*, 1954 P. 394 the judge held "manual satisfaction" (a rather recondite reference to onanism) to be sufficient for adultery. The facts in both these cases involved sexual intimacy which AID lacks; and in any case the Court of Appeal decision in *Dennis v. Dennis* (1955) P. 153 has been taken to settle the point for English law that adultery requires some degree of penile penetration of the vagina.

The issue is relevant only in those countries that retain adultery as an automatic ground for divorce. There is little justification for doing so today, when people by and large are sexually more imaginative and when the opportunities for destroying a marriage by a variety of means are so much greater than before. Apart from anything else, it is a gross waste of public money to give court time to individuals arguing about whether the nature of their sexual experiences is such as to be a concern of the law. A worse example even than AID is the case of *Baxter v. Baxter* [1947] 2 All E.R. 886, in which the House of Lords were asked to address the question whether penetrative sexual intercourse between a man and his wife was truly "sexual intercourse" when the man wore a condom. Within what scale of values is it important that the highest court in the land gives an opinion on this matter?

And did Mr MacLennan get his divorce? In fact he did. Lord Wheatley's opinion was limited to the relevancy of the defence, and once it was held relevant Mrs MacLennan was required to provide further and better particulars of the AID procedure. This she failed to do, and therefore her adultery was conclusively established by her bearing a child more than 14 months after the last episode of sexual intercourse between the parties to the marriage.

DELIVERING US FROM EVIL

Case 43: Attorney-General of the Government of Israel v. Eichmann, 36 I.L.R. (1961) 5 and 277 (District Court and Supreme Court, Israel)

War Crimes—Crimes against humanity—Jurisdiction—Superior Orders

(See http://www.pbs.org/eichmann/study.htm)

Eichmann, an Austrian like Hitler, took an active role in supervising the Final Solution programme, and was linked with the notorious death camp of Auschwitz where he observed "progress". After the Nazi defeat in 1945, Eichmann escaped to South America and was found living in Argentina in 1960. Now, no extradition treaty was in place between Argentina and Israel. So Eichmann was kidnapped, brought to Israel and put on trial under the Nazi and Nazi Collaborators (Punishment) Law 1950 which concerned war crimes, crimes against the Jewish people and crimes against humanity. This prosecution raised a number of important legal issues.

First and foremost, did the Israeli court have jurisdiction to try a man for crimes committed in another country? In public international law, there are five bases of criminal jurisdiction: territorial (*i.e.* that the crime was committed in the territory of the trying state), nationality (*i.e.* that the accused is a national of the trying state), universal, protective and passive personality. The first two were clearly inapplicable and the last (where a state has jurisdiction when one of its nationals is the victim) was politically controversial. But jurisdiction was founded on the other two grounds. Universal jurisdiction entitles all States to prosecute regardless of the place where the crime was committed and jurisdiction can be based solely on the presence of the individual within the nation's boundaries. It applies only to a very small category of crimes adjudged to be offensive to the international community as a whole, *e.g.* piracy, war crimes, crimes against humanity and genocide. It was held to apply here. Protective jurisdiction rests on a notion of harm against the security, territorial integrity or political independence of the State. This too was held to justify jurisdiction over Eichmann because of the special connection which the State of Israel had with the crimes charged. The court said that "[t]o argue that there is no connection [between the Final Solution and the State of Israel] is like cutting away a tree root and branch and saying to its trunk: I have not hurt you."

The second legal issue was that since the Israeli Nazi Collaborators (Punishment) Law 1950 punished acts committed outside Israel and before its establishment as a State against people who could not be Israeli citizens the Act could be claimed to conflict with international law and so to exceed the powers of the Israeli legislature. The Supreme Court rejected this argument on the basis that the prohibition against *ex post facto* legislation had not yet become a rule of customary international law. An academic point has been made that while Israel did not exist before 1948, it was an enemy of Nazi Germany as the successor to the British mandate of Palestine. Consequently, it was entitled to the rights Britain would have enjoyed had the mandate continued. Israel could thus be characterised as a belligerent by proxy.

The third issue was the "Superior Orders" defence, which had of course figured prominently in the *Nuremberg Trial* (**Case 32**). It failed here, and indeed was unlikely to have worked even if it had been held applicable. For there was little evidence to suggest that any duress forced Eichmann to behave in the way he had done. He maintained that he had not known what was going on at Auschwitz and upon discovery had been devastated by what he saw, and had tried to halt the progress of the Final Solution. He also claimed only to have been involved in the evacuation of Jews to concentration camps, not their subsequent extermination. But his subordinates spoke of repeated visits made by him to Auschwitz. Their averments implicated Eichmann as a key mechanic of the Holocaust enacting Himmler's orders, "efficiently". His dedication was displayed by "all kind of tricks and trickery, [he] managed to get priority for his death trains, knowing that by doing so he was actually harming Germany's war effort. He told his friends; 'I know the war is lost, but I am still going to win *my* war'".

The fourth issue was the validity of the witness evidence against him. In the context of genocide, choosing which witnesses are to give evidence is always a delicate task. Ultimately one witness was to give extremely poignant evidence which embraced in calm and clinical terms the horror of the Holocaust. A man who had arrived in Auschwitz with his family testified as to what happened when families were split up according to gender and usefulness for labour. This man was moved to one side, his wife and infant daughter to the other. They were then removed to their fate: certain death. The witness indicated that his young daughter was wearing a red coat which he and his wife had bought her in happier days. He said: "You ask 'What does the Holocaust mean to me?' It means a red dot getting smaller and smaller."

Eichmann was convicted and sentenced to death and this was upheld on appeal to the Israeli Supreme Court. He was executed on June 1, 1962. He remains the only person to have been sentenced to death and executed in Israel. His ashes were "scattered over the Mediterranean waters lest they defile Jewish soil".

On a political level, it has been suggested that the trial served primarily to advance Israel's claim to represent *all* Jewish people. Perhaps the trial provided "closure" for Holocaust survivors and it is commonly accepted that this is a real and important function of enforcing justice, removing impunity and beginning the rebuilding process for victims. The Israeli Prime Minister David Ben-Gurion indicated that the trial would have an important purpose in educating Israeli youth about the Holocaust. Auschwitz camp commander Hoess stated: "Eichmann explained to me that it was especially the children who have to be killed first, because where is the logic in killing a generation of older people and leaving alive a generation of young people [who could wreak revenge]".

Little did Eichmann know how prophetic those words were

THE POUND OF FLESH

Case 44: White and Carter (Councils) Ltd v. McGregor
1962 S.C. (H.L.) 1; 1962 S.L.T. 9
(House of Lords, Scotland)

Contract—Repudiation—Breach

(See Scott, "Contract—Repudiation—Performance by Innocent Party", 1962 C.L.J. 12; Furmiston, "The Case of the Insistent Performer" 1962 Mod. L.R. 314; Goodhart, "Measure of Damages When a Contract is Repudiated", 1962 L.Q.R. 263.)

The law of contract can be harsh. The law will accept that harshness on the basis that if people want to be harsh with themselves, then so be it. For contracts are *voluntarily undertaken* obligations, and for that reason the law tolerates a higher level of inequity than it would with imposed obligations. A person may escape from a contract if forced or tricked into it, but not otherwise. And certainly not just because a contract is less beneficial than was expected, or was unexpectedly detrimental.

White and Carter (Councils) was a company that supplied litter bins to local authorities, making profit from the advertisements carried thereon. William McGregor was the owner of a garage in Clydebank, which he advertised in this way from 1954 to 1957. At the end of that period, his general manager, Mr Ward, signed a contract for a further three years of advertising, not knowing that Mr McGregor had decided to terminate this method of advertising since he did not find it particularly cost-effective. However, Mr Ward was acting within his apparent or ostensible authority as Mr McGregor's agent and it was not disputed that he had created a valid contract between the garage owner and the advertisers.

One of the terms of the contract was that if the garage proprietor failed to pay any of the monthly payments for the adverts and the amount remained unpaid for a period of four weeks, then the whole amount due for the remainder of the three years would immediately become payable. Mr McGregor, on the day the contract was signed by his manager, wrote to the advertisers asking them to cancel the contract. Their response was modelled on that of the deaf adder of Scripture, and five months later they commenced advertising Mr McGregor's garage. Then they sent him the first bill. When he refused to pay and that refusal had lasted four weeks, they sued him for the whole amount, as provided for in the contract. Mr McGregor argued that there was no contract, since he had repudiated it, and that his repudiation of a valid contract rendered him not liable under the contract, though he accepted liability in damages for the advertiser's loss (which was far less than the contractual stipulation).

Mr McGregor accepted that a valid contract had been entered into, but he argued that the advertisers were not entitled to seek to enforce it if he repudiated it before they had taken any action under the contract. In other words, after his letter of repudiation, White and Carter (Councils) had no right subsequently to commence performing their side of the contract. He was effectively arguing that it was unfair to hold him liable under a contract that he had attempted to escape from and under which the pursuers could choose, with little loss, not to do anything. Seeking the full amount under a term of the contract was little more than seeking a pound of flesh—his flesh. Following their earlier decision in *Langford & Co v. Dutch*, 1952 S.C. 15, the Court of Session accepted his argument, but the House of Lords (by a slim majority) did not.

A contract is a voluntarily undertaken obligation whereby both parties agree to do something. Once it is completed then the law will give effect to it, unless one of the parties can have it reduced on grounds such as fraud, illegality (see *Morgan Guaranty*, **Case 89**), or facility and circumvention (see *Anderson v. The Beacon Fellowship*, **Case 79**); or it can be avoided on a statutory ground such as being within the Unfair Contract Terms Act 1977. Accordingly Scots law, in common with other systems whose rules derive from the traditions of Roman law, generally requires that parties should perform their contractual obligations. It is not the role of the court, said Lord Hodson, to rewrite the terms of an improvident contract, and there is no escape merely because the terms turn out to be less favourable than anticipated. Of course, if one party wants to escape, the other has the choice to allow them to do so (effectively making a new contract to cancel the old) but there is no legal obligation on the other to do so. The whole point of contracts is that they are legally enforceable, whether or not it is fair to do so. So even although White and Carter (Councils) could have, without any real loss to themselves, accepted Mr McGregor's repudiation, they were not obliged to do so and they were within their contractual rights to perform their side of the bargain and extract the full payment from him. Lord Reid speculated that this might not be so if the person seeking to enforce the contract has no legitimate interest, financial or otherwise, in doing so, but that was not the situation here where the pursuers would receive great financial benefit in enforcing the contract. They had an interest to enforce the contract and had no obligation to be nice to Mr McGregor. English law, which is not derived from Roman law, has resisted this House of Lords decision. Indeed, Lord Denning once said that he would follow it only on virtually identical facts (*Attica v. Ferrostahl* [1976] Lloyd's Rep. 250). In Scotland, though, the courts have found the decision less objectionable: see, for example, *Salaried Staff of London Loan Co Ltd v. Swaers and Wells*, 1985 S.L.T. 326.

ODE TO JOY

Case 45: Van Gend en Loos [1963] E.C.R. 1 (European Court of Justice)

European Law—Free movement of goods—Direct effect of Treaty of Rome

In 1958, a Dutch firm, Van Gend en Loos, was importing adhesive from Germany, paying customs duty of three per cent. Although the

Netherlands had ratified the Treaty of Rome, establishing the European Community in 1957, in 1959 it ratified a Benelux customs protocol, which raised the duty payable to eight per cent. The firm protested that this breached Article 12 [now 25] of the EC Treaty (prohibiting new tariffs), and took the case to the Amsterdam Customs Court (Tariefcommissie). Unsure of the effect of the Treaty, the Amsterdam Court referred the case (under Article 177 [now 234]) to the European Court of Justice (ECJ) for a ruling on: (i) whether articles of the Treaty had a direct effect on the legal position of individuals and firms, and (ii) whether the eight per cent duty constituted an "unlawful increase" forbidden by Article 12.

Van Gend en Loos is an important case because it showed the clash, in the Community's infancy, between two widely differing views of what the EC Treaty meant. The Dutch Government, backed up by Belgium and the Court's own Advocate-General, saw the Treaty through the prism of classical international law: that is to say, that any treaty's effect on domestic law was a matter not of international law but of national constitutional law, interpreted by the national constitutional court. The Dutch and Belgians saw the Treaty as taking effect between the Member States, but not between them and their citizens.

However, the European Court of Justice disagreed with this view, holding instead that the European Community formed "a new legal order of international law", which had as its subjects not only the contracting Member States, but also their citizens. Therefore the EC Treaty produced "direct effects" and created individual rights which national courts were under a duty to protect. The new eight per cent duty was struck down.

With the benefit of hindsight, we can see that the Court had no choice. Had they accepted the arguments of the Dutch Government that the ECJ had no jurisdiction over what was essentially a Dutch constitutional matter, then Article 12, designed to cover the whole Community, would only have covered those countries whose constitutional law accepted the primacy of international treaties. Therefore, Van Gend en Loos might have won their case in the Netherlands Constitutional Court, but companies in the U.K., whose law did not recognise the primacy of international treaties, would not have had the same protection. In terms of classic international law, this is not incorrect; but the uniformity of application which is at the heart of Community legislation demanded direct effect.

So *Van Gend en Loos* gave citizens rights under the Treaty against both their own and other countries. At the same time, it imposed on national courts the duty to protect these rights, making these courts the main appliers of Community law. A new legal order indeed, marking out the EC Treaty as something apart from other international treaties, something altogether *sui generis*. Community law is now a direct source of legal rules applicable in the domestic legal systems of the member states.

HEDLEY BYRNE LIABILITY

Case 46: Hedley Byrne & Co v. Heller & Partners
[1964] A.C. 465; [1963] 2 All E.R. 575; [1963] 3 W.L.R. 101
(House of Lords, England)

Delict—Economic loss—Negligent misstatements—Proximity

(See Wilkinson & Forte, "Pure Economic Loss—A Scottish Perspective", 1985 J.R. 1; McBride & Hughes, "*Hedley Byrne* in the House of Lords: An Interpretation" (1995) 15 Leg. Stud. 376).

Hedley Byrne & Co, the plaintiffs in this most fundamental of cases, were advertising agents. In 1957 they were commissioned by a firm known as Easipower Ltd to produce for the latter a large advertising campaign. The costs would be about £100,000 and it would involve Hedley Byrne in substantial outlays. So, in order to ensure that Easipower would be able to pay their bills, Hedley Byrne contacted their own bankers, who in turn contacted the bankers of Easipower, a firm of merchant bankers known as Heller and Partners. Heller and Partners, the defendants, gave (gratuitously) a report suggesting that Easipower were a sound financial partner. As a result of this report, Hedley Byrne accepted the commission. Easipower promptly went into liquidation, and Hedley Byrne suffered losses in the outlays they had made to the tune of over £17,500. They sued the defendants for giving the favourable report, which led, they argued, directly to their losses.

The judge at first instance, McNair J., found that the defendants had indeed been negligent in drawing up the financial report on Easipower, but he also held that the losses sued for were irrecoverable on the basis that there was no duty of care not to cause pure economic loss. The Court of Appeal upheld his decision, following their own earlier decision to that effect in *Candler v. Crane Christmas & Co* [1951] 2 K.B. 164. However, the House of Lords overturned the Court of Appeal, overruled *Candler v. Crane Christmas* and held that there could indeed be a duty of care to avoid causing pure economic loss. Unfortunately, though interestingly, the ground upon which their Lordships made their decision seems to have changed as the years have gone by.

One thing that is clear is that the test for recovery of economic loss is different from and stricter than the foreseeability test for recovery of physical loss (which was laid down in *Donoghue v. Stevenson*, **Case**

27). The reason why the law imposes a stricter test on claims for economic losses is that while physical losses have their own inherent limitations (and so the existence of a duty of care can be determined simply by whether the loss suffered is foreseeable), economic losses can foreseeably multiply consequentially with no obvious cut-off point to liability. In addition, there is far less moral imperative to avoid causing another economic losses in a capitalist system than to cause physical harm. But what is the stricter test to be applied? Today, the law talks (unhelpfully) about "proximity" as the extra element in the test over and above foreseeability, and while the word did not appear in *Hedley Byrne* that concept is traced to this case.

Hedley Byrne lays down the general principle that pure economic loss will be recoverable if it had been caused by the negligent misstatement of a person acting in the exercise of a certain skill, having held himself out as possessing the requisite skill to make the statement and having knowingly permitted the receiver of the statement to rely upon it. The problem for future cases was working out which aspect of that holding rendered the relationship between plaintiff and defendant so "proximate" that the latter owed the former a duty of care? Was it the fact that the defendant was exercising special skill (as was assumed in *Mutual Life & Citizens Assurance Co v. Evatt* [1971] A.C. 793), or the fact that the negligence lay in the giving of financial advice (such as in *Caparo Industries v. Dickman* [1990] 2 A.C. 605), or the fact that the negligence lay in the making of statements (the "law of negligent misstatements", as it was taught in the 1970s and early 1980s)? And did the case completely overturn the previously understood rule that there was no liability for pure economic loss, or did it merely establish an exception to that rule? And if the latter, what was the basis of the exception? In *Anns v. London Borough of Merton* the House of Lords seemed to have accepted that *Hedley Byrne* was not simply an exception to the rule, but had reversed the rule; *Anns* was, however, overturned in *Murphy v. Brentwood Council*. *Hedley Byrne* seems today to be regarded as an exception, but one so flexible that "*Hedley Byrne* liability" can arise in a whole variety of circumstances. In **Junior Books v. The Veitchi (Case 69)** the House of Lords accepted liability in a case in which the defenders had been negligent in laying a floor in a factory owned by the pursuers, putting the pursuers to the cost of replacing it; in *Spring v. Guardian Assurance* [1994] 3 All E.R. 129 the House of Lords accepted that negligently given unfavourable reports were as actionable as negligently given favourable reports; in *White v. Jones* [1995] 2 A.C. 207 *Hedley Byrne* was used to establish liability when a solicitor who had been instructed by a testator to draw up a will in favour of the plaintiff negligently delayed until after the testator's death, so depriving the plaintiff of the inheritance; and finally in **McFarlane v. Tayside Health Board (Case 99)** (a case as far removed from the giving of financial advice as it is possible to imagine) "*Hedley Byrne* liability" was not established when parents of a child born after a failed sterilisation operation sued to recover the costs of bringing up that child. In all these cases, the important issue was the assumption of responsibility. In other words, if the pursuer can show that the defender has assumed responsibility for the former's economic wellbeing then this will be sufficient to establish the element of proximity which is the added extra over and above foreseeability in the *Donoghue v. Stevenson* sense. The element of proximity (which sounds like a matter of fact) is now dependent, in new types of claim, on whether the claim is "fair, just and reasonable" (a matter of judicial policy).

NB: The whole reasoning of the House of Lords in *Hedley Byrne* was *obiter*, for in the facts of the case there was no liability since the defendants had given their negligent financial advice on a "no-liability" basis and it had been accepted as such by the plaintiffs. So the advertising agents had to suffer the loss of their £17,500.

THE ST NINIAN'S ISLE TREASURE CASE

Case 47: Lord Advocate v. Aberdeen University and Budge
1963 S.C. 533; 1963 S.L.T. 361
(Inner House, Court of Session, Scotland)

Property—Abandoned property—Feudal law and Udal law—Crown property prerogative—Classification of property

(See Smith, Editorial Excursus, *Stair Memorial Encyclopaedia of the Laws of Scotland*, 15, 317–329).

Students from the University of Aberdeen were on a field trip, excavating a site on St Ninian's Isle in Shetland. They came across a fabulous horde of treasure, hidden away underground; this turned out to be eighth or ninth century, probably having belonged (then) to the Celtic Church which was predominant in the area at that period of time. Since the treasure dated to a time of great Viking aggression, it is likely that it had been buried during one of the frequent Viking incursions. The University removed the treasure to Aberdeen, where it intended to display the goods at its museum in Marischal College. The Lord Advocate, representing the Crown, sued the University for delivery of the treasure, founding upon the Crown's property prerogative *quod nullius est fit domini regis*, or that which is owned by no-one falls into the ownership of the Crown. The University resisted the claim with the difficult argument that Scots law, at least in this regard, did not apply to the Islands of Shetland. An historical excursus was necessary to back up this claim.

Shetland originally came under the jurisdiction of the Norwegian Crown. James III of Scotland married the daughter of the King of Denmark and Norway and with her received a valuable dowry. But the King of Norway had fallen on hard times and could not raise the money to pay this dowry. So instead in 1468 he "impignorated" his lands in Orkney and Shetland to the Scottish Crown. (Impignorating is to kings what pawning is to paupers). Needless to say, the pledge has never been redeemed and the Northern Isles remain part of Scotland today. But the point is that the law applicable in these islands was and remained for some time after the impignoration Norse law. In 1274 good King Magnus Hakonsson, Magnus the Law-Mender, had promulgated a code of law instituting a form of land-holding known as Udal Law. Scotland was at around the same time becoming progressively normandised and the form of land-holding known as Feudal tenure, with the Crown as ultimate feudal overlord in a pyramid of greater barons, lesser barons, and still lesser local land-holders, took hold over nearly all of the mainland. Both systems had a rule for ownership of buried treasure, but the rules were different. Feudal law said that since the Crown was the ultimate feudal superior buried treasure which had no longer any owner fell to the Crown; the Code of King Magnus decreed that buried treasure should be split three ways, between the Crown, the finder and the land-owner. The land-owner had a claim not because the treasure became part of his land by being buried, but on the theory that since land passes down the generations of successors, the land-owner is likely to be the heir of the person who buried the treasure in the first place. The question in the case was, which law applied?

The Crown argued that an Act of the Scottish Privy Council, dated 1611, had stated that Scots law was to apply in Orkney and Shetland rather than the "foreyne law" which the inhabitants of the Islands had been applying for their own personal gain; the University argued that the Act was irrelevant to the nature of the land holding, which remained Udal, as recognised by the Court of Session in the cases of *Smith v. Lerwick Harbour Trustees* (1903) 5 F. 680 and *Lord Advocate v. Balfour*, 1907 S.C. 1360. The Second Division held that the onus of proving that Scots law did not apply rested with the University, and that since they had failed to discharge this onus, Scots law rather than the Norse law of good King Magnus applied to the case, with the result that the Crown owned the treasure.

They also pointed out, however, that even if Udal law had applied that would have had no effect on ownership of the treasure. Udal law was land law (*i.e.* the law of heritable property). But treasure does not become heritable merely because it is buried in land. It does not "accede" to the land: it remained moveable. So the rule of law to be applied was that governing moveables, and there was no doubt that the

1611 Act required Scots law to apply to determine ownership of the moveable treasure. So, as so often happens, the Crown won.

PARLIAMENT ALWAYS WINS

Case 48: Burmah Oil Co v. Lord Advocate
[1965] A.C. 75; [1964] 2 All E.R. 348
(House of Lords, Scotland)

Royal prerogative—Damages—Parliamentary sovereignty

(See Goodhart, "The Burmah Oil Case and the War Damage Act 1965" (1966) 82 L.Q.R. 97.)

And so, too, does Parliament. This case arose from events during World War II. In January 1942 the Japanese armies invaded Burma and in February the General Officer Commanding the British Forces in Burma issued instructions that the oil installations belonging to the Burmah Oil Company near Rangoon should be destroyed as and when necessary to prevent them being of use to the enemy. These orders were carried out on March 7, 1942 and on the following day the Japanese entered Rangoon. It was not disputed that the destruction was lawful; it was assumed that it was carried out under the Royal Prerogative and it was accepted that the military situation at the time rendered the destruction expedient for the defence of His Majesty's other territories. But after the war, Burmah Oil claimed that they were entitled to compensation, amounting to many millions of pounds, out of public funds. They raised the action in Scotland because it was time-barred in England. But it was one of those cases where both parties were "deep-pocket litigants" and the amount of money involved was so great that whoever lost in the lower courts would inevitably appeal as far as they could go. So the case was always going to end up in the House of Lords, whichever jurisdiction it started in.

The judges reviewed the use of the royal prerogative in times of war over many centuries, examined the views of the institutional writers on the issue and considered the writings of other learned authorities, such as Grotius. Any student who wishes to know about the historical development of the royal prerogative in time of war will find the speeches fascinating reading.

Their Lordships decided, by a majority of three to two, that there was at common law a legal right to compensation, though not necessarily to the full cost of reinstatement. Their reasoning was that if, in the exercise of the Royal Prerogative of war, a subject was deprived of property for the benefit of the state he was entitled to compensation unless the case fell within an exception to the general rule. The relevant exception in this case was for what is called "battle damage", that is to say accidental or deliberate damage done in battle or for the necessities of battle, such as the destruction of property caused in the retaking of a town from the enemy. The exception did not extend to destruction which was part of a deliberate strategy to deny to the enemy industrial resources and facilities, which is really a form of economic warfare. The destruction of Burmah Oil Company's installations fell into the latter category and did not fall into the exception of battle damage.

So the decision went in favour of the Burmah Oil Company. But they did not get their compensation.

The Government of the day was unwilling to accept the Court's decision and pay the compensation. So the following year they introduced, and Parliament passed, the War Damage Act 1965 which abolished rights at common law to compensation in respect of damage to or destruction of property effected by or on the authority of the Crown during or in contemplation of war. Most unusually, the Act was given retrospective effect and so it denied the company, in 1965, compensation for damage sustained in 1942, despite a decision in 1964 of the House of Lords that they were entitled to it. The case illustrates graphically the sovereignty of the U.K. Parliament. Subject to the United Kingdom's obligations under EC law (see *Factortame*, **Case 80**) if the U.K. Parliament does not like a decision of the courts, it can pass an Act which nullifies the decision, even retrospectively, and there is nothing that anyone can do about it.

IT'S A LONG WAY TO BELLAHOUSTON

Case 49: Williams v. A. & W. Hemphill Ltd
1966 S.C. (H.L.) 31; 1966 S.L.T. 259
(House of Lords, Scotland)

Delict—Vicarious Liability—Scope of Employment

Fewer cases were reported in the law reports in Scotland in 1966 than in any other year before or since. But amongst them are some brilliant ones. This is the best. It is about a journey made by some boys through Scotland on a summer's day in the back of a lorry. It ended in tragedy. The lorry had an accident. Its driver was negligent. People were killed. The pursuer was one of the boys. He survived, but was left paraplegic. He sued for compensation. He sued the driver's employer. Everyone knows that employers are automatically liable for the negligence of their employees at work. Employers insure against these things. The properly advised claimant goes after them, and not after the employee. But this time there seemed to be a legal difficulty: Was the driver still at work at the moment of the accident? For an employer is only vicariously liable for the delict of an employee if the negligence was committed by the employee while acting "within the scope of his employment", or as it is sometimes put, "in the course of his employment".

The journey was from a bit of the country north of Oban to Glasgow. Even the sketchiest knowledge of the lay out of Scotland shows that the driver was at the moment of the accident wildly off the route. Oban is on the western edge of Scotland, and a long way north of Glasgow. So, naturally, he should have driven south and eventually taken the high road down the banks of Loch Lomond. But at the moment of the accident he was in fact getting further and further away from the end of what should have been that delightful journey. He was nearly as far south as Glasgow. But he was about 35 miles further east, and had been following a route that, if he had persisted in it, would have taken him to Denmark. In fact, at the moment of the collision he had for a short time even left that route, and was travelling on a route that would have led in the end to the North Pole. But he was not totally lost. He was where he was, because he had been persuaded by some of his cargo of boys to go on to Dollar, a town near the north side of the Firth of Forth. Only then did he plan to turn round and travel west to Glasgow. It is 97 miles from where they started north of Oban to Glasgow by the normal, sensible route. It is 148 miles by this wandering route.

However, there was reason for it. The prospect of Dollar was bonnier to the boys than that of the banks of Loch Lomond. What gave Dollar the edge in their eyes were not bonnie banks but (as Burns said of Ayr) the bonnie lassies. How did they know that Dollar was the place for that? The boys had been camping. They were members of the Boys Brigade (103 Company from Bellahouston). The girls were members of the equivalent female organisation, the Girls Guildry. The judges in the House of Lords got all that right. But the judge at first instance got his youth organisations in a twist, and referred to the girls repeatedly, and quite wrongly, as "girl guides", members of a rival organisation. (Today, he might have been less confused. The Girls Guildry, founded in Glasgow by one Dr Somerville, who later gave it up to become, instead, the President of the Society for the Conversion of the Jews, is now the Girls Brigade). These GGs were camping next to the BBs. The adult in charge of the BBs gave permission for his BBs to go to the station near Oban where the GGs were to catch a train to their homes, at Dollar. The BBs, young gentlemen all, did that to assist the GGs with their luggage. Thus enthused, the BBs persuaded the lorry driver to drive them to Stirling Station. Stirling is way to the east out of the route to Glasgow. But the GGs were to change trains there and would need more help with their luggage. Sure and stedfast, the BBs provided that help. Really fired up in Stirling, it made sense to persuade the driver to go those extra miles to meet the GGs of Dollar, at their own home station for a fond farewell. Tragically only a few miles short of that anticipated moving event, the accident occurred.

This case raises the wider question that arises in all situations where the employee was both in some sense doing the employer's work and simultaneously doing something else. The general rule confirmed is that where the employee can be seen as doing the employer's work and something else at the same time the employer will still be vicariously liable unless, looked at in a common sense way, the employer's work has no real connection with the context.

The rule formulated for journey deviation cases, and how to apply it, is that the journey, despite a deviation, is still part of the context of the employer's work unless the deviation has become an "independent" journey undertaken not for the employer but for somebody else. In applying that rule to the facts it is necessary to consider the relative dominance of the employer's and of any other person's purposes as they have a bearing on the journey at the moment of the accident. The geography of the route, the relative lengths of the different bits of it, are all relevant but are not to be weighed in mathematical sum to determine this question. As Lord Pearce, giving the judgment for all the House of Lords judges, famously said: "The more dominant are the current obligations of the master's [*i.e.* employer's] business in connection with [this journey] the less weight is to be attached to the navigational extravagances of the servant [*i.e.* employee]". Looked at in this way the journey at the moment of the accident was not an "independent" journey for the boys to say farewell to the girls of Dollar: it was still, looked at from a common sense point of view, part of a journey the employee driver was employed to make, a journey from north of Oban to Glasgow. So the employer (or his insurers) were liable and the injured boys got their compensation.

Much more recently the House of Lords has developed the concept of vicarious liability so that it exists whenever there is a sufficiently close connection between the act complained of and the employment (see *Lister v. Hesley Hall*, May 3, 2001, following decisions of the Supreme Court of Canada in *Bazley v. Curry* (1999) 174 D.L.R. (4th) 45 and *Jacobi v. Griffiths* (1999) 174 D.L.R. (4th) 71). On that test the result in *Williams* is less surprising and so it may be seen as an early precursor to the modern approach.

A CASE OF WHISKY AND ELECTRICAL GOODS

Case 50: Consten and Grundig v. Commission
[1966] E.C.R. 299; [1966] C.M.L.R. 418
(European Court of Justice)

European Law—Competition law—Anti-competitive agreement

(See Fulda, "The First Anti-Trust Decisions" (1965) 65 Colum. L.R. 625.)

Have you ever wondered why only some brands of Johnny Walker whisky are available in this country? The application of European Community competition law lies behind this mystery and the legal outcome in the present case helps to explain why. *Consten and Grundig* was a landmark European Court of Justice decision on competition law and, although it is to a certain extent outdated, the principal points raised remain important.

The factual background is fairly straightforward, involving an agreement between Grundig, a major manufacturer in West Germany of electrical and electronic equipment, and Consten, a French distributor of its products. The agreement provided for an exclusive distributorship for the territory of France and it included three main features: (i) it imposed an obligation on Consten, similar to that imposed on Grundig's distributors in other Member States, not to export the contract goods from France; (ii) Grundig undertook not to sell directly to anyone in France; and (iii) Grundig assigned the trade mark attached to each piece of equipment for its sale in France.

There are clear commercial reasons why such exclusive distributorships are entered into between producers and distributors of goods. A producer may have difficulty in competing effectively with competing brands of goods unless a distributor, aware of national or regional tastes and consumer preferences, markets and promotes the product effectively, particularly with novel or luxury goods. In order to ensure the loyalty and marketing expertise of the distributor, the producer will require to offer some form of commercial protection to the distributor by allocating it an exclusive sales territory, otherwise other distributors and retailers would attempt to free-ride on the back of their promotional expenditure.

However, the effect of European Community competition law means the position is not so simple. When the Treaty of Rome was ratified, the principal aim was to create a Common Market (subsequently the internal market) by integrating the national markets across Europe. Partly in order to achieve this aim, and the aim of improving the economic well-being of European people as a whole, the Treaty contains competition rules aimed at controlling monopoly power (Article 82 [previously 86]- "abuse of a dominant position") and cartels (Article 81 [previously 85] - "anti-competitive agreements"). Accordingly these rules are aimed at market power but also more fundamentally at market integration within the Community.

In this case, a French company obtained Grundig's products in another Member State, and sought to import them into France. Consten brought an action to stop the resale of the goods. A complaint was made by the French company to the Commission, which ruled that the contracts restricted competition within Article 81(1) and were not entitled to an exemption as the absolute territorial protection created was not indispensable to the agreement. On appeal to the European Court of Justice it was argued that vertical agreements (between parties at different levels of the market, *e.g.* producer and distributor) were not affected by Article 81 as it should only apply to restrictions of inter-brand competition, *i.e.* between producers of competing brands including the most heinous breach of any system of competition law—a price-fixing producers' cartel. The Court rejected this argument and held that Article 81 could also apply to vertical agreements containing restrictions on intra-brand competition. However, they stressed that the Commission should not have prohibited the whole agreement but merely the clauses which created the absolute territorial protection ("ATP"), namely those assigning the trade-mark.

This was a crucial case and the Court sought to achieve a balance by prohibiting the ATP, whilst providing that some territorial exclusivity was not necessarily prohibited. Nonetheless, the line between legal territorial restrictions and illegal ATP was never particularly clear. This reached crisis point in the 1970s in the Distillers case. Distillers claimed they would never penetrate the French market effectively with its Johnny Walker Red Label brand unless it gave its French distributor absolute protection from "free-riders" seeking to cash in on the distributor's promotional and marketing expertise, notably the company's U.K. distributors. They imposed an export ban on their U.K. distributors but as this ban was prohibited under the competition rules laid down in *Consten & Grundig*, Distillers decided the only effective action was to cease to provide that brand at all to its U.K. distributors. So no more Red Label here.

In the face of criticism of the strict approach adopted by the Commission to vertical agreements there have been some important developments. The European Court, in a series of judgments, has adopted a more lenient approach towards certain vertical restraints, for example stating that the restrictions were necessary for the agreement to proceed in the first place ("ancillary restraints": see *Remia v.*

Commission [1985] E.C.R. 2545), or that some degree of exclusivity is required where it is necessary to develop the product ("open exclusivity": see *Nungesser v. Commission* [1982] E.C.R. 2015). In addition, the Commission introduced a series of block exemption Regulations, including Regulation 1983/83 on exclusive distribution, which exempt agreements from the prohibition in so far as agreements follow their requirements and do not create ATP by isolating national markets totally.

However, the Community authorities have continued to be criticised for their strict approach, and have been urged to look at vertical agreements only where the producer has market power and can therefore act in a way that is detrimental to consumers. The change in approach finally adopted in the Block Exemption Regulation 2790/1999 might incidentally increase consumer choice among whisky brands in Scotland.

THE SCOTTISH MIRANDA

Case 51: Miln v. Cullen, 1967 J.C. 21
(High Court of Justiciary, Scotland)

Evidence — Criminal law — Corroboration — Self-incrimination — Fairness

Clearly, the way that police deal with suspects is important for the liberty of us all. As always, fundamental legal principles can be extracted from factually unimportant cases. Such is the case of *Miln v. Cullen*.

Early one evening in April 1965, a lorry was involved in a collision with a motor car. Some minutes later a police car happened upon the scene. The lorry driver spoke to the police and pointed out Cullen, who was standing by the road, as being the driver of the car, and accused him of being the cause of the accident, and drunk. The police approached Cullen and asked him if he had been the driver. After a couple of hiccoughs, Cullen admitted that he was the driver and, subsequently, he admitted that he was drunk. He was charged with driving while unfit to drive through drink or drugs.

At his trial, the only direct evidence led that he had been driving the car was that of the lorry driver. But corroboration of that fact is required to establish guilt (see *Moorov*, **Case 26**). The prosecutor sought to rely on his admission given in response to the policeman's question. But he had not been warned that he was under suspicion, nor that any answer he gave to the question would be taken down and might be used in evidence. The sheriff-substitute held that the admission had been unfairly obtained and dismissed the charge. On appeal, the High Court of Justiciary pointed out that the line between fairly obtained (and therefore admissible) evidence and unfairly obtained (and therefore inadmissible) evidence was a fine one, but that it must not be drawn in such a way as unduly hampers the search for the truth. The rule against self-incrimination was not absolute, otherwise all confessions would be worthless. Rather, an accused's self-incrimination may be used as evidence so long as it is made voluntarily and without pressure. That was the test of fairness. In the circumstances of the present case there was no unfairness and therefore Cullen's reply to the policeman's question was admissible evidence which could act as corroboration of the lorry driver's evidence that Cullen was driving the car.

The importance of this case really lies in its backing away from an apparently much stricter test in an earlier, and better-known, decision, *Chalmers v. H.M. Advocate*, 1954 J.C. 66. Here, a youth suspected of murder was being interrogated by the police. He led them to a field and pointed out a spot where the wallet of the murdered man was found. The High Court of Justiciary held that these actings could not be used in evidence since they were unfair. The case had been interpreted as disallowing any evidence of incriminating statements once a person falls under suspicion, but that test was found to be unduly hampering of the police's investigations of crime. Since *Miln v. Cullen* it is clear that "fairness" is a much more fluid concept, in the determination of which all the circumstances of the case are to be taken into account. Answers to questions are normally unfair if the suspect is not informed that his answers may be used in evidence (*Tonge v. H.M. Advocate*, 1982 J.C. 130) or if he is not informed that he is not obliged to answer the questions (*H.M. Advocate v. Docherty*, 1981 J.C. 6) but these are not absolute rules. Unfairness is assessed as an overall impression and no one fact is determining in all cases. This is as it should be for otherwise the police could avoid all challenges by simply "reading the rights" without checking that the suspect actually understood what was being said. But, of course, that would never happen in real life. Would it?

VIRGINIA IS FOR LOVERS

Case 52: Loving v. Virginia, 388 U.S. 1 (1967)
(Supreme Court, United States of America)

Marriage—Ban on interracial marriage—US constitutional law— Equal protection

(See Wadlington, "The Loving case: Virginia's Anti-Miscegenation Statute in Historical Perspective", 52 Va L. Rev. 1189, (1966). See also the motion picture, *Mr and Mrs Loving* (TVM) (1996).)

Mildred Jeter and Richard Loving were brought up in Central Point, Caroline County in the State of Virginia. Situated in the north of the state midway between the birthplace of George Washington and the shrine to Stonewall Jackson it is just over an hour's drive to the national capital, Washington. Although the state of Virginia had reacted negatively to the call for educational integration in *Brown v. Board of Education* **(Case 39)**, Central Point itself was a town where there was integrated education, and racial mixing was common. Mildred and Richard had attended the same school.

In June 1958 they got married in Washington, then immediately returned to the Dogwood State. Within four months they were charged on a Grand Jury felony indictment. The punishment for their offence, if they were convicted, was confinement in the penitentiary for not less than one nor more than five years. In January 1959 they pled guilty to the charge and were sentenced to the minimum period of one year in jail. The trial judge, however, suspended the sentence for a period of 25 years on the condition that the Lovings left the State and did not return to Virginia together.

Clearly the Lovings were really nasty people, guilty of some dreadful crime from which the citizens of Virginia had to be protected. Drug pushing perhaps? Assaulting aged citizens? Transporting minors across the state line? Actually, it was none of these. Their crime was getting married. But it was not a horrid marriage. Richard had not ravished an underage Mildred; Mildred had not lured Richard into a bigamous trap. Nevertheless, in getting married to each other they had broken a Statute enacted in 1924 to preserve racial integrity in Virginia. This made it an offence for any white person to intermarry with a coloured person, either in Virginia (where it was directly prohibited) or anywhere else in the world (so as to stop residents avoiding the prohibition simply by going out of state). The terms "white person" applied only to a person who had no trace whatever of any blood other than Caucasian. Persons with one-sixteenth or less of the blood of American Indians were also deemed to be white persons. This was, apparently, due to the desire to recognise as an integral and honoured part of the white race the descendants of John Rolfe (the child abuser) and Pocahontas (the child he abused). Coloured persons were defined to include every person in whom there was ascertainable any negro blood. Mr and Mrs Loving were of different races. The trial judge was shocked: "Almighty God", he declared, "created the races white, black, yellow, malay and red, and he placed them on separate continents. And but for the interference with his arrangement there would be no cause for such marriages. The fact that he separated the races shows that he did not intend for the races to mix".

Statutes like the Virginian one were a common feature of life in most post-war American states. They had flourished in the 1920s when the Klu Klux Klan was at the height of its membership during what the Supreme Court delicately referred to as the "period of extreme nativism". In 1952 some 31 of the 48 states had laws prohibiting interracial marriage. Between 1952 and 1967 14 states repealed their laws outlawing interracial marriages—Arizona, California, Colorado, Idaho, Indiana, Montana, Nebraska, Nevada, North Dakota, Oregon, South Dakota, Utah and Wyoming. Maryland repealed its law on the subject after the start of the *Loving* litigation. In addition to Virginia at the time of the *Loving* decision prohibitions against interracial marriage existed in 15 other states—Alabama, Arkansas, Delaware, Florida, Georgia, Kentucky, Louisiana, Mississippi, Missouri, North Carolina, Oklahoma, South Carolina, Tennessee, Texas and West Virginia.

The Lovings challenged the constitutionality of the statute under which they were charged. The Supreme Court of Virginia threw out their challenge, relying on their earlier decision in *Naim v. Naim*, 87 S.E. 2d 749 (1955) which had concluded that the state had a legitimate purpose to "preserve the racial integrity of its citizens" and to prevent "the corruption of the blood", the emergence of "a mongrel breed of citizens" and "the obliteration of racial pride".

The case finally reached the Supreme Court in April 1967. The decision delivered during the summer of love, in June 1967, upheld the Lovings' claim. Their challenge was based on the Fourteenth Amendment to the US Constitution which provides, *inter alia*, that "[no] State shall ...deny to any person within its jurisdiction the equal protection of the laws". The state argued that because both the participants in an interracial marriage were punished equally the statute did not involve invidious discrimination based upon race. This argument had worked in *Pace v. Alabama* (1883) in which the Supreme Court had upheld a law that punished interracial fornication more severely than same-race fornication, but in the present case the Supreme Court rejected the equal application argument. They noted that Virginia's statute rested solely upon distinctions drawn according to race. Over the years the Court had consistently repudiated distinctions between citizens solely because of their ancestry as being "odious to free people whose institutions are founded upon the doctrine of equality. Where there were racial classifications they were to be subject to the "most rigid scrutiny". If they were to be upheld they must be shown to be necessary to the accomplishment of some permissible state objective independent of the racial discrimination which it was the object of the Fourteenth Amendment to eliminate. The Court could see no legitimate overriding purpose. The fact that Virginia prohibited only interracial marriages involving white persons demonstrated that racial classifications must stand on their own justification as measures designed to maintain White Supremacy. The Court had no doubt that restricting freedom to marry solely because of racial classifications violated the central meaning of the Equal Protection Clause.

The statute, like the practice of sterilisation of the mentally weak, accepted in *Buck v. Bell* (Case 24), had been adapted by the Nazis in Germany in the notorious Nuremberg laws prohibiting marriage with Jews. More recently the case has taken on a new significance as a symbol for those in the gay and lesbian community who are seeking freedom to marry for same-sex couples. Anti-gay marriages bills were produced in at least 20 states in the mid 1990s as a reaction to the possibility (never, in fact, realised) that the state of Hawaii would recognise same-sex marriage. South Dakota's bill read: "Any marriage between persons of the same gender is null and void from the beginning" (SD House Bill 1184). This bore a striking resemblance to the Virginia law which *Loving* had put an end to: "All marriages between a white person and a colored person shall be absolutely void without any decree of divorce or other legal process" (VA Code Ann 20.57).

HONEYSUCKLE COTTAGE

Case 53: Sweet v. Parsley [1970] A.C. 132
(House of Lords, England)

Criminal law—Legal process—Statutory interpretation—Crime of absolute liability

Living in the country can be dangerous. Remember Constable Oates, the village bobby from *The Code of the Woosters*, who suffered agonies at the hands of a local resident, Stephanie Byng, aggrieved at him for letting himself be bitten by her Aberdeen terrier, the dog Bartholemew?

Another Stephanie, though altogether more innocent, was at the heart of the present case.

Stephanie Lavinia Sweet, a school teacher, lived in a farm house called Fries Farm, in the parish of Gosford, near to Woodstock in Oxfordshire. There was honeysuckle growing around the lintel of the front door, roses in the borders, badgers at the bottom of the garden, probably fairies too, and a babbling stream in the distance. Butterflies. Country things. Niceness.

The farmhouse was large and Miss Sweet let out some rooms, to young people. One evening, Sergeant Parsley, the local policeman, called, but he was not on a social visit. He had a search warrant, for he suspected drugs. Unhappily, he had reason to be suspicious. Miss Sweet's tenants were, totally unknown to her, pot smokers. Sergeant Parsley found all the equipment, together with some cannabis and even remnants of LSD. What he did not find were the tenants, who had run away. No matter, he arrested Miss Sweet.

Miss Sweet was charged with, and convicted of, an offence under the Dangerous Drugs Act 1965, s.5 of which made it an offence for any person who occupied premises which were used for the purposes of smoking cannabis either (i) "to permit those premises to be used" for that purpose or (ii) "to be concerned in the management of any premises used" for that purpose. Being entirely unaware of what the tenants were doing, she could not be said to have "permitted" her house to be used for the purpose of smoking cannabis. But on a literal interpretation of the statute, she was clearly "concerned in the management of" the premises (the farmhouse) in which cannabis was smoked. The Court of Appeal upheld her conviction, and she appealed further to the House of Lords.

Their Lordships quashed the conviction. The literal meaning of the words in the statute could not be applied, for the court had to take account of the principle that crimes as a general rule require *mens rea* with the result that to obtain a conviction a guilty mind must be shown by the prosecutor to exist. This Miss Sweet clearly did not have. Parliament can, of course, create crimes of absolute liability but it must be presumed that it does not do so. This presumption is rebuttable but only when it is shown in the clearest possible language and with no room for doubt that Parliament meant to criminalise particular actions without any intent on the part of the accused. In the present case, the question was whether Miss Sweet was concerned in the management of premises used for the purposes of smoking pot and that question could easily be interpreted to mean that, for a conviction, she had to be shown to be concerned in the management of premises she knew would be so used. Lord Morris went further and held that Fries Farm was not "used for the purposes of smoking cannabis" just because it was a place where cannabis was smoked: if one of the tenants had taken sugar in his tea, Lord Morris pointed out, it would be factually accurate and at the same time ludicrous to say that the farm was "used for the purposes of eating sugar".

This decision of the domestic law is consistent with the presumption of innocence that courts must apply in criminal cases and now contained in Article 6(2) of the European Convention on Human Rights. This Convention was used by a sheriff to avoid High Court precedents where the High Court had not followed *Sweet v. Parsley*. In *Kiely v. Lunn*, 1983 S.L.T. 207 and *MacIntyre v. Annan*, 1991 S.C.C.R. 465 the statute at issue was the Education (Scotland) Act 1980 which made it an offence for a parent whose child failed to attend school regularly without reasonable excuse. The High Court of Justiciary had interpreted this provision as creating a crime of strict liability—the parent was guilty whenever the child had no reasonable excuse, and any reasonable excuse of the parent (the one being charged) was irrelevant. But in *O'Hagan v. Rea*, 2001 S.L.T. (Sh. Ct) 30 the sheriff held that this was inconsistent with Article 6(2) of the ECHR and that the statute should be interpreted to permit the parent a defence of having a reasonable excuse (such as, for example, being unable to control the movements of the child). This is interpreting the law consistently also with *Sweet*.

MALTESE CROSS-ROADS

Case 54: Chaplin v. Boys
[1971] A.C. 356; [1969] 2 All E.R. 1085
(House of Lords, England)

Delict—Negligence—Assessment of damages—International private law

(See Rodger, "*Boygues* and the Scottish Choice of Law Rules in Delict: Reconsidering *McElroy v. McAllister*", 1995 S.P.L.Q. 58, and "*The Halley*: Holed and Now Sunk", 1996 S.P.L.Q. 397; Rogerson, "Choice of Law in Tort: A Missed Opportunity" (1995) 45 I.C.L.Q. 650).

Being a member of H.M. Armed Forces is a dangerous occupation. However, on signing up for the Royal Air Force, David Boys would be unaware that the source of his danger was the Royal Navy and be constituted not by sophisticated anti-aircraft weaponry but by a small car. He probably assumed that being stationed in Malta would involve little more than sun, sea and sand and that there would be greater perils in his military life than riding pillion on a motorbike on the dusty roads of Malta. Unfortunately, Boys' military career ended as a result of an accident in which Richard Chaplin, also stationed in Malta though with the Royal Navy, collided into the motorbike upon which Boys had been travelling. Boys suffered a fractured skull in the accident, remained unconscious for three days thereafter and as a result was permanently deaf in his right ear. He was subsequently discharged from the RAF where he had ranked as a junior technician.

Boys raised an action against Chaplin claiming damages for his injuries arising out of the accident. Chaplin admitted that he had been driving negligently and that he was liable to Boys. However the major issue in this case concerned the extent of damages to which Boys was entitled. The incident took place in Malta, and under Maltese law Boys would only have received his expenses and his direct financial loss, amounting to some £53. Under English law he would have been entitled to £2,250 covering his out of pocket expenses, prospective loss of earnings due to his incapacity and for the pain and suffering caused by his injuries in addition to the £53 financial loss. The question was, which legal system governed the assessment of damages? Existing authority in both English law and Scots law provided a test for liability known as the "double actionability" rule (*Phillips v. Eyre* (1870) L.R. 6 QB 1; *McElroy v. McAllister*, 1949 S.C. 110). Although the rule was slightly different in the two jurisdictions, this basically meant that in order to succeed with a claim in delict one had to be able to make a claim both under the law of the forum (the court hearing the case— known as the "*lex fori*") and under the law of the place where the delict was committed (know as the "*lex loci delicti*"). The question for the court to decide was whether (and how) to avoid the application of the double actionability rule which would limit Boys' claim to the overlapping £53, and provide him with the damages recognised by English law. All nine judges involved in the case from Mimo J. in the Queen's Bench Division through the Court of Appeal to the House of Lords agreed that the plaintiff should be granted the English and not the Maltese award of damages, *i.e.* the higher sum. Unfortunately this was about the only issue the judges agreed upon and it is difficult to ascertain any clear *ratio decidendi* (the reason on which the decision is based). In the House of Lords, three judges (Lords Guest, Donavon and Pearson) considered that the *lex fori* (*i.e.* English law) applied as this was a question of quantification of damages rather than liability. They said that the double actionability rule applied only to the latter and that the former, being a question of remedy, had to be dealt with by the law of the forum (for a court can only give the remedies it has in its domestic law and not those recognised elsewhere). However, the judgment which has been adopted subsequently as the most important and authoritative pronouncement is by Lord Wilberforce (Lord Hodson's judgment is a variation on a similar theme) and this created what has become known as the flexible exception to the double actionability rule. Lord Wilberforce considered that it may be appropriate to consider whether the foreign rule ought to be applied as a matter of policy and this would depend on the circumstances of the case. In this case it would be inappropriate to apply Maltese law given the identity of the parties and the circumstances involving two British subjects temporarily resident in Malta for the purpose of serving in the British armed forces. The event, in other words, was far more British than Maltese. This suggested that the Maltese rule should not be applied and that the plaintiff should be able to claim the damages which would be awarded under English law.

The flexible exception created by Lords Wilberforce and Hodson has been followed and applied in various English cases subsequently. (See e.g. *Coupland v. Arabian Gulf Petroleum Co* [1983] 1 W.L.R. 1136; *Johnson v. Coventry Churchill International Ltd* [1992] 3 All E.R. 14). Although various questions remained unanswered, the scope of the exception to the general rule was confirmed and extended by the Privy Council in *Red Sea Insurance Co Ltd v. Boygues SA and Others* [1994] 3 All E.R. 749. This confirmed that the flexible exception may apply to the whole case, and not merely to one sub-issue as Lord Wilberforce had suggested (the type of damages at issue in *Chaplin v. Boys*). More importantly, *Red Sea* provided that the flexible exception could apply to both parts of the double actionability rule, and lead to application of the *lex loci delicti* alone, ignoring the *lex fori*, a development which surprised some commentators. However, *Red Sea* was only part of the reform process which culminated in the Private International Law (Miscellaneous Provisions) Act 1995. Part III of this Act abolished the double actionability rule and provides a new general rule that the applicable law shall be the "*lex loci delicti*" and this law alone will be applied to determine delictual disputes. However, *Chaplin v. Boys* has not been totally killed off. The double actionability rule continues to apply to defamation actions. Furthermore, the 1995 Act adopts Lord Wilberforce's flexible exception and allows for displacement of the general rule where it is substantially more appropriate for another applicable law to decide a dispute, taking into account all the circumstances and the interests of justice. Stay tuned for more classic Chaplin repeats.

READER, I MARRIED HIM

Case 55: Corbett v. Corbett
[1971] P. 110; [1970] 2 W.L.R. 1306; [1970] 2 All E.R. 33
(Queen's Bench Division, High Court, England)

Marriage—Nullity of marriage—Transsexual—Definition of "woman"

(See Kennedy, "Transsexualism and the Single-Sex Marriage", in *Treat Me Right* (Clarendon, 1988); Campbell, "Successful Sex in Succession", 1998 J.R. 257 and 325)

George Jamieson (now Lady Rowallan) was a working class lad. He had always been a feminine child, deeply desirous of being a girl. He joined the Merchant Marine at the age of 16, encountered there extensive on-board sexual activity, but found the whole experience deeply unsatisfying. He left after 18 months. Sometime thereafter he commenced taking oestrogen and in 1960, in Casablanca, he underwent an operation to remove his testicles and the internal tissue of his penis, and to fashion with the remaining skin of his penis an artificial vagina. This she used (apparently successfully) in her later sexual encounters with men. She joined a troupe of male and female impersonators in a Paris nightclub. She changed her name to April Ashley by what the English call "deed poll", and the British Ministry of National Insurance issued her with a woman's national insurance card. She became a stunningly beautiful and highly successful fashion model, being photographed by all the greats in the early 1960s.

Arthur Corbett came from a vastly different background. A scion of a wealthy aristocratic family, he was married with children, though he was deeply unhappy with his life. One of his few pleasures (other than the anticipation of succeeding to a title) was dressing up in women's clothes. Even this, however, left him dissatisfied since the effect was never quite right. Arthur met April in 1961 and was immediately bowled over by her appearance and, one hopes, her personality. They started their own nightclub in Spain, at Marbella, and Arthur purchased a villa for them there. Arthur's wife divorced him. Arthur became obsessed with the thought of marrying April and giving her the title he would later inherit. After much persuasion, April agreed to marry Arthur, and the deed was done in Gibraltar in 1963. There were attempts at sexual intercourse thereafter, which ended with Arthur in tears, wailing "I can't, I can't". Poor Arthur.

The couple separated soon afterwards. April then sought maintenance from Arthur, including a claim to the villa in Spain. At that point Arthur petitioned the court for a decree of nullity of marriage, the ground being that he had married a man. The case was heard before Mr Justice Ormrod who, unusually, was medically as well as legally qualified. Ormrod J. gave a judgment which has since come to dominate English law in relation to the treatment of transsexuals.

The judge pointed out that legal relations can be classified into those in which sex is entirely irrelevant (such as contract, tort and much of criminal law), those in which sex is relevant (such as insurance and pensions law) and those in which sex is an essential determinant. Into this last category he placed marriage because (and circularly) marriage by definition is the union of one man and one woman. He claimed that, in marriage, the capacity for "*natural* hetero-sexual intercourse" is an essential element, and that a "woman" for the purposes of marriage is a person who is "*naturally* capable of performing the essential role of a woman in marriage". As well as being entirely self-referential ('a woman is a person who can be a woman in marriage') this is assertion without authority that sex for legal purposes cannot be altered by artificial intervention. He pointed out that there are at least four ways in which gender can be defined: chromosomal, gonadal, genital and psychological; and some would add hormonal. If the first three of these are (before surgical intervention) congruent, he said, then that is the sex of the individual for the purposes of the law. So April Ashley, who used to be George Jamieson, and is now Lady Rowallan, is, was and always shall be a man. Poor April.

This result has been followed in English law in the fields of criminal law (*R. v. Tan* [1983] Q.B. 1053) and employment law (*White v. British Sugar Corporation* [1977] 1 R.L.R. 121) and though it has been held not to breach the European Convention on Human Rights (*Rees v. United Kingdom* (1987) 8 E.H.R.R. 56, *Cossey v. United Kingdom* (1991) 13 E.H.R.R. 622, *Sheffield & Horsham v. United Kingdom* [1998] 2 F.L.R. 928), the European Court of Justice has held that to discriminate in employment against a person because of their transsexualism is unlawful (*P. v. S. and Cornwall County Council* [1996] I.R.L.R. 347). Other countries take a different approach from *Corbett* and adopt what is sometimes called a "cluster analysis", whereby all the different factors that make up a person's sex are weighed in order to determine where the preponderance lies—and, crucially, there is no requirement that the factors be determined only in their pre-surgical state (*M.T. v. J.T.* (1976) 334 A2d 204 (New Jersey), *R. v. Harris & McGuinness* (1988) 35 A. Crim. R. 146 (Australia), *M. v. M.* [1991] N.Z.F.L.R. 337, *Attorney General v. Otahuhu Family Court* (1995) 1 N.Z.L.R. 603 (New Zealand)). There is no direct authority in Scotland, but *Forbes Sempill, Petitioners* (unreported, 1967) raises similar issues. In that case a person naturally "inter-sex", who had been brought up a female but who in adult life decided to live as a male, sought to inherit a title of honour which passed down the male line. Lord Hunter in the Outer House of the Court of Session identified the four criteria for sex determination later listed by Ormrod J., but the Scottish judge accepted that no single criterion could determine the issue. Rather, what was called for was an examination of the balance of all the relevant criteria. Though he does not directly address the issue of deliberate and artificial changes to one or more of the criteria, his holding that the petitioner was male suggests that he took account of such changes, for the petitioner had undergone many years of hormonal treatment to emphasise his male appearance. One matter upon which both judges were agreed was the importance of the sexual functionality of the genitals being examined. Ormrod J. had made much of April's inability to provide a "natural cavity" for the purposes of sexual intercourse; Lord Hunter in *Forbes Sempill* questioned the petitioner's wife about the extent to which he provided her with "satisfaction". She declared herself satisfied, and the petitioner was declared male.

BRÛNNHILDE STIRS

Case 56: McKendrick & Ors v. Sinclair, 1972 S.L.T. 110 (House of Lords, Scotland)

Delict—Assythment—Wrongful death—Legal process—Desuetude of remedies

(See Smith, "Designation of Delictual Actions: Damn Injuria Damn", 1972 S.L.T. (News) 125; Hunter, "The End of Assythment", 1973 S.L.T. (News) 1).

Arthur Craig lived with his elder sister and his two younger brothers. He was the sole breadwinner in the family, their parents having died some time previously. He worked as a labourer at Hamilton Brickworks Limited. On March 3, 1967, one of his duties was to help load bricks from an electric conveyor belt leading from the brick kiln to a loading lorry. Due to negligent maintenance, the conveyor belt was conducting live electricity. Arthur Craig's body came into contact with the conveyor belt. He received an electric shock from which he died. He was 19 years old.

Not only was this a personal tragedy for his orphaned siblings, but it was an economic disaster in that they lost their sole source of support. They were rendered destitute, as a direct result of the defender's negligence. Now, one of the tensions in the law of delict is the extent to which wrongdoers should be made to pay. If claims for damages can be made too widely, business defenders would go out of business; but if claims are too strictly limited, it is the taxpayer, through the social security and welfare system, that often has to pick up the bill. The present case illustrates this point precisely: who was to pay for the upkeep of these children? Should it be the person who negligently killed the sole breadwinner in the family, or was it to be the state? (If the latter, the amount paid would be far less in real terms). But there is another consideration. The law likes certain family relationships and is indifferent to others. And it recognises and protects the favoured relationships while ignoring the others. Had Arthur been the children's father or had he been the husband of one of the survivors, then a claim for compensation for what some systems (though not, usually, Scots law) call "wrongful death" could have been made by the surviving siblings, reflecting the favoured status of "parent" and "spouse". Unfortunately, as a result of earlier cases (*Greenhorn v. Addie* (1855) 17 D. 860 and *Eisten v. North British Railway Co* (1870) 8 M. 980) there was a rule in the law of negligence which limited wrongful death claims to children and spouses of persons negligently killed and so the claim was not available to surviving siblings, even when they had been dependent on the economic support of the deceased. The pursuers in the present case therefore turned to the ancient remedy of *assythment*. This was the old Scots remedy whereby money was payable to the relatives of a person criminally killed by another, in order to buy off the wrath of vengeful relatives. There never had been doubt that siblings could claim for assythment, and the issue in the present case was whether the action still existed in modern law, or whether it had been superseded by the development of the law of negligence (with its exclusion of claims by siblings).

The Lord Ordinary allowed a proof before answer, having repelled the defender's plea-in-law that the action for assythment was no longer competent. That decision was overturned by the Second Division, though on the ground that the pursuers had no title to sue and that their averments were lacking in specification. Only Lord Wheatley held that assythment was now obsolete, while Lord Justice-Clerk Grant reserved his opinion. In the House of Lords the Second Division's decision was affirmed, on the basis that in the absence of a criminal charge the current claim for assythment was irrelevantly pleaded. On whether it remained part of Scots law, Lord Kilbrandon reserved his opinion, though Lord Reid expressed the view that a remedy of the common law did not disappear from the law merely because it had not been sought by anyone for some centuries. Lord Simon of Glaisdale was doubtful whether the reawakening of the action would serve any useful purpose, given the changes in law and social circumstances since the last case of assythment over 200 years previously. "This Brûnnhilde would awake in our uncongenial modern Niebelheim", he said, before being carried away into further flights of fancy: "Even if this Sleeping Beauty were so attractive as to tempt your Lordships to favour her with your kisses, she could not possibly live happily ever after". Neither, of course, could the unfortunate siblings of Arthur Craig.

Lord Reid and Lord Kilbrandon called upon the Scottish Law Commission to amend the law of wrongful death to allow claims by siblings where they are the deceased's next of kin and dependent upon him for support. The Scottish Law Commission so recommended, but when Parliament acted, with the Damages (Scotland) Act 1976, the class of survivors entitled to sue for damages on the wrongful death of a relative was not extended to siblings. So even today anyone in the position of the Craig children would recover nothing from the person who had negligently killed their sole source of support, and their upkeep would be thrown on to the public purse. Oh, and assythment was expressly abolished by the 1976 Act.

The terminology of the law is of little concern to pursuers, but it is of concern both to legal practitioners and to legal scholars. The Roman law of damages was, by and large, to be found in either the *lex aquilia*, which provided reparation for physical injury, or the *actio injuriarum*, which provided damages for affront. Perhaps because the loss to survivors in an action for wrongful death was not a direct physical injury to the survivors personally, the habit had grown sometime in the nineteenth century of describing survivors' claims as an *actio injuriarum*. The culprit seems to have been that never before known to have nodded Homer, Lord President Inglis in *Eisten* (further information about Lord Inglis is found in Case 13). The House of Lords in *McKendrick*, however, (or at least the Scottish representatives on the Judicial Committee) took the opportunity to restore the correct terminology: actions for delict involving either death or personal injury are traced from the *lex aquilia* and this includes survivors' claims. Affront based delicts like defamation come from the *actio injuriarum*. The importance of making the distinction is that the *lex aquilia* requires fault to be shown by the pursuer, which can be established by negligence, or failure to take due care, while the *actio injuriarum* requires intent to injure, which is a more culpable form of fault.

THE RUG TRADE, OR HOW TO WIND UP YOUR FRIENDS

Case 57: Re Westbourne Galleries Ltd
(Ebrahimi v. Westbourne Galleries Ltd)
[1973] A.C. 360
(House of Lords, England)

Company law—Minority shareholder rights—"Just and equitable" winding up

(See Chesterman, "The 'Just and Equitable' Winding up of Small Private Companies" (1973) 36 M.L.R. 129; Prentice, "Winding up on the Just and Equitable Ground: the Partnership Analogy" [1973] 89 L.Q.R. 107; Clark, "Just and Equitable Winding Up: Wound Up?" 2001 S.L.T. (News) 108.)

Asher Nazar Achoury was an entrepreneur who ran various small businesses including a store selling carpets, called the "Oriental Carpet Co". In 1945 Shokrollah Ebrahimi joined Nazar as a partner in this business. Now, it is of the nature of a partnership that the partners co-operate in running a business. However, the relationship between Ebrahimi and Nazar was odd. While there was no doubt that Ebrahimi was assumed as a partner Nazar, throughout their time in business together, appeared to view—and certainly treated—Ebrahimi as an employee. The business traded successfully for some years and in 1953 the Oriental Carpet Co moved to Westbourne Grove, London. In 1958 the firm incorporated as Westbourne Galleries Ltd. One thousand shares were issued in the new company, Nazar and Ebrahimi each holding 400 shares, and Nazar's son George holding 200 shares; and all three were appointed directors. Each of them expected to be involved in running the company as directors—and therefore, while the company made substantial profits, the profits were not distributed as dividends to the three as shareholders, but instead were paid to them as directors' salaries.

As time went on Ebrahimi started to express concerns at Nazar's external interests. Nazar purchased carpets during his business trips and sold them on to the company. Ebrahimi believed that Nazar was taking too much profit to the detriment of the company and made certain accusations about Nazar's behaviour. Though never substantiated, these allegations caused ill feeling between the parties and their working relationship broke down. Nazar and his son put a motion to the company general meeting seeking the removal of Ebrahimi as a director. In company law a director can be removed by the votes of a majority of shares at a general meeting (see Companies Act 1948, s.184, now Companies Act 1985, s.303). Nazar and his son with 600 votes outvoted Ebrahimi who was thus removed as a director. And when he was removed as director he no longer obtained a salary. And, of course, Nazar and son continued to pay directors' salaries rather than dividends to shareholders. The end result was that Ebrahimi had a substantial investment in Westbourne Galleries Ltd, but no way to make any money from it. He therefore tried to get out of the company and sell his shares, but Nazar and son did not wish to purchase them.

The principle of majority rule in company law causes difficulties for those shareholders in the minority. The law has, therefore, ameliorated their position, both at common law (see *Foss v. Harbottle* (1840) 2 Hare 461, which created some exceptions to the majority rule) and by statute (see, at the time of this case, the Companies Act 1948, s.222(f) and now the Insolvency Act 1986, s.122(1)(g) which allows a company to be wound up on just and equitable grounds at the behest of any individual shareholder).

Failing a sale of the shares, Ebrahimi sought to have the company wound up. He argued that given the nature of his relationship with Nazar, having been in partnership for some years before incorporating, and the previous administration of the company, he had certain legitimate expectations to be involved in running the company, and to share in the profits. He had no strictly defined legal right to do so. However, the remedy he sought was based on justice and equity.

The House of Lords agreed. It was stressed that the remedy was based on equitable considerations, and that these varied depending upon the nature of the case. However, it was also noted that the equitable considerations could arise in relation to small companies where three factors were present: (i) the company was based on a relationship of mutual confidence, *e.g.* a partnership incorporating; (ii) there was an understanding that certain shareholders would participate in the management of the company; and (iii) there is difficulty in the minority shareholder selling their shares and leaving the company.

So the court ordered the company to be wound up. Nazar's refusal to purchase Ebrahimi's shares meant that the only way Ebrahimi could escape from the company was to destroy it. The result was, as Lord Cross noted, that a minority shareholder in a small company now had an effective threat. If the relationship with their other shareholders failed and they wanted out of a company, and wished a proper price for their shareholding, they could now threaten to have the company wound up. But the enduring moral of the tale is, pick your partners properly.

ABORTIVE RIGHTS

Case 58: Roe v. Wade, 410 U.S. 113 (1973)
(Supreme Court, United States of America)

Abortion— US   *Constitutional*   *Law— Privacy— Lawyer-client*
relationship

(See Dellinger & Sperling, "Abortion and the Supreme Court: The Retreat from *Roe v. Wade* (1989) Univ. Penn. L.R. 83; Bell, "Analysis of the US Judgments on Validity of Abortion Legislation" (1993) 1 Fem. Leg. Stud. 91).

Along with its companion ruling *Doe v. Bolton*, 410 U.S. 179 (1973), this case can lay claim to be the most famous decision of the US Supreme Court. It was the focus of a class action, an overtly political move and a vehicle for the twentieth century's most active women's movement in their efforts to establish a right of a woman to terminate her pregnancy.

Norma McCorvey (the real name of the pseudonymous Jane Roe) faced an unwanted pregnancy, but she lived in Texas where, in common with the other 50 states in the US, abortion was a criminal offence, unless carried out for the purpose of saving the life of the mother. Rather than subjecting herself to the dangers of a back-street abortion, McCorvey sought assistance from an abortion referral service, who put her in touch with Sarah Weddington, a lawyer. She told the lawyer that she had been raped. This allowed an easy route to challenge the ban on abortions, arguing that in circumstances of rape prohibiting abortion was an infringement of the victim's constitutional rights. But the lawyer rejected this route, preferring the much more difficult, and more high-profile, route of challenging the abortion prohibition in all circumstances. The lawyer was using the case to further the political campaign to secure abortion rights. She was blunt about this, describing McCorvey's role as "ancillary to the primary focus of all women". (McCorvey eventually gave birth and dropped out of the litigation, but the case went ahead—she was irrelevant). The high risk tactic paid off, for the Supreme Court delivered a judgment which overturned a century of restrictive legislation and ignited a moral and at times violent debate which still rages on and continues to dominate the political landscape in God's Own Country.

By a 7–2 majority the Supreme Court declared that the constitutional right of privacy (developed by the Court from the Due Process Clause of the 14th Amendment (see *Griswold v. Connecticut*, 381 U.S. 479 (1965); *Eisenstadt v. Baird*, 405 U.S. 438 (1972)) encompassed a woman's decision to abort. But the right to abort was not unqualified. The Court set out a framework for the regulation of abortion, dividing the pregnancy into trimesters and holding constitutional increasing regulation depending on how far the pregnancy had advanced. During the first trimester a woman's choice must be unfettered by State interference (except for rules such as who may carry out abortions). During the second trimester the State can apply restrictions so long as there are compelling reasons to do so concerning women's health. During the third and final trimester the State may constitutionally prohibit abortion, except where the life or health of the woman is threatened by the continuance of the pregnancy. *Roe*, therefore, does not give a woman an unfettered right to abortion. After the first trimester other interests than hers can be seen to colonise women's reproductive freedom.

Many people do not like even the limited freedom conferred by this decision. National campaigns by the far right and the Catholic church have sought to promote the rights of the unborn child and putative father, but their efforts to convert such campaigns into legislative provision have so far been unsuccessful. A more fruitful approach for abortion opponents has been to encourage state legislatures to impose restrictions on the practical rather than the legal availability of abortion. In *Webster v. Reproductive Services*, 492 U.S. 490 (1989) a Missouri state law prohibiting abortions in public facilities or by public employees was upheld, alongside a requirement that women undergo foetal viability tests. Both were viewed not as obstacles to a woman's "right to choose" but as permissible means to further the state's interest in protecting human life. *Planned Parenthood Southeastern Pennsylvania v. Casey*, 505 U.S. 833 (1992) came close to overruling *Roe*, but did not quite do so. It did, however, increase states' latitude during the second trimester by modifying the test to be applied in judging the constitutionality of restrictions to women's access to abortion. Prior to then the state had to show a "compelling interest" in imposing the limitation, but after *Planned Parenthood* the state had to show merely that the limitation did not impose an "undue burden" or "substantial obstacle" on the woman seeking abortion. States have satisfied this lesser test by imposing waiting periods, informed consent clauses, statistical reporting, licensing clinics and other regulatory requirements.

More directly the private health care system that dominates the US exposes funding of abortions to political attack (see *Maher v. Roe*, 432 U.S. 464 (1977) and *Harris v. McCrae*, 488 U.S. 297 (1980)). This has been possible because of the inherent weakness in *Roe's* founding on privacy rather than on a woman-centred notion of bodily integrity: that approach casts the right as a negative one to be left alone rather than as a positive one of access. This does nothing to assist the campaign for safe and accessible medical procedures but rather legitimates the authorities' opting out of financial assistance. The effect of the financial restrictions is predictable—the poorer the woman is the less likely she is to be able to access abortion services, causing serious health risks to those who most need financial assistance and state support to secure a safe abortion.

MARX IS RIGHT AS USUAL, OR THE ART OF CLUBMANSHIP

Case 59: Charter v. Race Relations Board [1973] A.C. 868 (House of Lords, England)

Discrimination—Racial discrimination—Public or private club

(See Jackson, "Can Clubs Discriminate?" (1973) 36 Mod. L.R. 529; Plender, "A Question of Public Concern" (1975) 38 Mod. L.R. 93.)

Amarjit Singh Shah worked as a postal and telegraph officer in London. He was a Conservative. He applied for, and obtained, membership of the East Ham Conservative Association. He then sought membership of the East Ham Conservative Club which provided entertainment and recreation facilities at their premises in East Ham. His application to join the Club was turned down, on the casting vote of the chairman, allegedly on the basis of Mr Shah's Indian origin. Mr Shah sought a remedy, with the help of the Race Relations Board, under the Race Relations Act 1968. He was unsuccessful in Westminster County Court and he appealed to the Court of Appeal who upheld Mr Shah's complaint and determined that the Club had acted unlawfully. The East Ham Conservative Club appealed to the House of Lords.

Prior to 1965 there had never been anything unlawful in any body adopting and applying racist policies and both formal and informal colour bars were by no means uncommon in the United Kingdom. The Race Relations Act 1965 provided a limited range of remedies for those refused entry to public places like cinemas and dance halls. The 1968 Act extended these to cover jobs and housing and prohibited discrimination on racial grounds in the provision of goods, facilities or services to the public. But it was not and is not unlawful to discriminate in private life. So, for example, you can refuse to associate in private with another person just because of the colour of his or her skin. To do so means that you are a bad person, but it does not mean that you are acting unlawfully. Further, you are allowed to associate with others who think like you do and to prohibit others from joining you—you can establish "members-only" clubs. So the issue for the House of Lords was whether the East Ham Conservative Club was a private group of like-minded individuals or was a public body providing services to members of the public. The Conservative Association was unquestionably the latter and membership of that had in the past always allowed membership of the Conservative Club.

The majority in the House of Lords held that the club was not providing a service to the "public at large" or to a "section of the public". They were prepared to recognise that there was a real distinction between joining the East Ham Conservative Association (open to any member of the public) and joining the East Ham Conservative Club (open only to members of the Association). The technical step from one to the other had never been invoked in the past, but their Lordships accepted that it was not a mere convenient fiction. But this means that the formal mark was deemed to be the criterion for determination of the public/private divide rather than the objective reality. It is a shame that this lack of attention to what actually happens as opposed to the formal steps gone through should have been so influential in the early days of this legislation.

Lord Morris of Borth-y-Gest dissented. He noted that the legislation restricted people's freedom to act in the public sphere. It was restricted, however, only where the motivation is the colour of a person's skin. Thus it was perfectly acceptable for bodies like colleges to exclude people on the grounds that they failed to measure up to the challenge of scholarship. Similarly clubs may be restricted to those skilled in a particular sport or owing allegiance to a particular political party. Nor would there be any problem with clubs restricted to those who share the same religious faith or who have "deep pockets". If groups want exclusivity that is quite acceptable. There must, however, be public policy limitations, identified by the legislation, which people's right to choose their companions must not cross. For this is the message of the race and ethnicity legislation, and subsequently in gender and disability discrimination legislation.

So, the complaint did not in the end succeed and the case remains the cornerstone of the notion of the private club exception, as well as a graphic illustration of the perspicacity of Marx's remark (the other Marx, that is) that he would not want to join any club that would accept him as member.

Similar issues were raised in the US Supreme Court decision of *Dale v. Boy Scouts of America*, 530 U.S. 640 (2000), where the defendants sought to exclude from its organisation gay people, on the basis that to allow them membership would compromise the principles of decency and clean-living for which it thought it stood. The Supreme Court did not challenge the Boy Scouts' assertion that gayness was inconsistent with decency and clean-living and upheld the organisation's right to exclude gay people on the basis of its freedom of association. The withdrawal of economic support that followed the decision has rendered their victory entirely Pyrrhic.

NOT SO SLIM PICKINS FOR THE RAILWAYS

Case 60: British Railways Board v. Pickin [1974] A.C. 765 (House of Lords, England)

Constitutional law—Judicial review—Parliamentary sovereignty

George Pickin was a railway enthusiast interested, as we all should be, in the preservation of railways. When the Clevedon-Yatton branch line in Somerset closed, he purchased from the owner of lands adjoining the railway, for a mere 10 shillings (half a pound), a piece of land and that brought with it the rail track, including the metal rails and the sleepers. He was able to do so because the Bristol and Exeter Railway Act 1836 provided that when a railway was abandoned, the ownership of the land passed to the owners of the adjoining land. There were apparently about one hundred early nineteenth century Acts of this nature, relating to railway lines in various parts of the country—probably as a *quid pro quo* for the compulsory purchase of the land to build the railways in the first place.

In the middle of the twentieth century numerous stretches of railway line were becoming redundant and would be closed down. British

Railways Board realised that if these old provisions took effect it would deny them of valuable land rights. They therefore promoted a private bill in Parliament which became the British Railways Act 1969. Section 18 of that Act repealed the earlier Acts which vested the ownership of abandoned railways in the adjoining landowners. British Railways Board was then free to sell the land, for profit.

Mr Pickin wanted to challenge this Act, which deprived him of his rights, but it is of course a well-established principle that Parliament is supreme and the courts have to give effect to Acts of Parliament, however unfair—a supreme legislature, like a dictatorship, is allowed to be unfair if it wants to be. So instead of attacking the doctrine of Parliamentary sovereignty by challenging the Act itself, Mr Pickin attacked the way the Act had been passed. He argued that British Railways Board had fraudulently concealed certain matters from Parliament and its officers and thus misled Parliament into granting rights to them. He argued that the court should either disregard s.18 or, if it was proved that Parliament had been misled, nullify the benefit to the Board and require them to hold it in trust for him. While accepting that none of these arguments would work in relation to a public general Act, he contended that there was a difference between public Acts and private Acts. He founded on the House of Lords decision in the Scottish case of *Mackenzie v. Stewart* (1754) Mor. 7443 and 15459. There, a private Act of Parliament had been obtained fraudulently and deprived Mackenzie of his estate; and its provisions appear to have been disregarded by the Court. However, in the present case, Lord Reid explained away the earlier decision as being based on a proper construction of the Act rather than a disregarding of its provisions. In Lord Reid's opinion, the law was correctly stated by Lord Campbell in *Edinburgh and Dalkeith Railway Co. v. Wauchope* (1842) 8 Cl. & F. 710 (another case involving a railway enthusiast—a very early one—and a private Act of Parliament). Lord Campbell said: "All that a court of justice can look to is the parliamentary roll; they see that an Act has passed both Houses of Parliament, and that it has received the Royal Assent, and no court of justice can inquire into the manner in which it was introduced into Parliament, what was done previously to its being introduced, or what passed in Parliament during the various stages of its process through both Houses of Parliament. I therefore trust that no such inquiry will hereafter be entered into ... and that due effect will be given to every Act of Parliament, both private as well as public, upon the just construction which appears to arise upon it".

Lord Reid pointed out that for more than a century both Parliament and the courts had been careful not to act so as to cause conflict between them and that the whole trend of authority was clearly against permitting any investigation into the matter in which an Act reached the statute book. So Mr Pickin lost his case.

It should be noted that, in relation to the Scottish Parliament, the principle upon which this case was decided has been put into statutory form. Section 28(5) of the Scotland Act 1998 provides that the validity of an Act of the Scottish Parliament is not affected by any invalidity in the proceedings of the Parliament leading to its enactment, thus making the position of Acts of the Scottish Parliament, in this respect, similar to Acts of the U.K. Parliament, and different from subordinate legislation which may be challenged on the ground of procedural impropriety. The courts do, however, have the power to decide that an Act of the Scottish Parliament is not law because it is beyond the Parliament's legislative competence (*e.g.* by being inconsistent with either European Community law or the European Convention on Human Rights). So Acts of the Scottish Parliament, unlike Acts of the U.K. Parliament, can be challenged in the courts, but Acts of neither Parliament can be challenged on grounds similar to those raised by Mr Pickin. One can only hope that he found solace in his railways.

RACHMAN LIVES, BUT LOSES

Case 61: Dyson Holdings Ltd v. Fox
[1975] 3 All E.R. 1030; [1975] 3 W.L.R. 744
(Court of Appeal, England)

Landlord and tenant—Husband, wife and unmarried couples—
"Family"—Legal process—Escape from precedent

Jack Wright was a bachelor and Olive Agnes Fox was a spinster, who met in 1920, fell in love, and lived happily ever after (which in their case lasted for over 40 years until Mr Wright's death in 1961). They had lived modestly, in rented accommodation, which had been taken in the name of Mr Wright. Olive was known as Mrs Wright. But in fact they never married. In 1940, their house having been bombed, they moved to 3 Old Road, Lewisham, where they lived together for the rest of Jack's life. After his death, Olive continued to live there. She was never late with the rent. She gave no trouble to her neighbours. However, 12 years after Jack's death, when Olive was 73, the landlords discovered that she was not, in fact, Jack's widow, but "merely" the woman who had lived with him for all these years as if she were his wife. The landlords sought to evict this old woman from her home on the ground that she had no right to the tenancy. They could then rent the property out to someone else at a higher rent.

Had Olive and Jack been married, Olive would have a legal entitlement to remain in her home, because statute provided that on the death of a tenant the tenant's widow could take over the tenancy. But Olive was not (at least not in strict legal terms) a widow. However, the same statute also provided that on the death of a tenant who had no widow, the tenancy could be taken over by a "member of the tenant's family". Olive claimed to be a member of Jack's family.

When Parliament first introduced the Rent Acts, "family" was a relationship of husband, wife, and their children. Unmarried couples lived "in sin" and not "in family". The Court of Appeal in 1950 had been faced with a similar claim to Olive's, in *Gammans v. Ekins* [1950] 2 All E.R. 140, and had held that the words "member of the tenant's family" could not be interpreted to include the man who had lived with a deceased tenant as if he were married to her, when in fact he was not. Olive's major problem was that decisions of the Court of Appeal are precedents which bind all courts in England short of the House of Lords, including the Court of Appeal itself. How, then, could she avoid *Gammans*?

The Court held that all that *Gammans* decided was that the word "family" was to be given a non-technical meaning which reflected its popular usage. In 1950 its popular usage did not include cohabitants in a conjugal but unmarried relationship. *Gammans* was neither overruled nor distinguished, but simply given a very narrow *ratio*. In 1975, the Court of Appeal could follow *Gammans* by giving the word "family" its popular non-technical meaning, even while accepting that that meaning had altered due to changes in social perceptions. Society accepted unmarried cohabiting couples and the word "family" could be used to include relationships such as that between Olive and Jack. So Olive was able to stay in the home she had lived in for over 30 years.

There are numerous cases raising the same issue under the same Rent Acts, with varying fact scenarios. The most important recent decision is that of the House of Lords in *Fitzpatrick v. Sterling Housing Association* [1999] 4 All E.R. 707 in which the cohabitants were a gay couple. The same issue arose on the death of the tenant. Could his partner be regarded as a member of his "family"? Had society developed in its views of domestic relations that the popular non-technical meaning of the word could now be held to include a same-sex couple? By a slim majority the House of Lords held yes, on the basis that "family" had to be looked at in a functional rather than a formal sense—in other words the court should look at how the relationship operated rather than what it looked like. This was another case in which the landlords were trying to evict a survivor of a couple, this time founding on the sexual orientation of the couple, for had Mr Fitzpatrick been a straight woman rather than a gay man the landlords would have had to accept, on the basis of *Dyson Holdings*, that the survivor had a legal right to remain in his or her home. *Dyson* had been doubted in a few cases after its decision, but the House of Lords gave it unequivocal support in *Fitzpatrick* and it is now unchallengeable as a precedent. *Dyson* was the catalyst for *Fitzpatrick* and the result in the latter case was possible only because the majority refused to discriminate between a gay couple and a non-gay couple.

The Housing (Scotland) Act 2001 grants express statutory protection to tenants in the position of both Olive Fox and Martin Fitzpatrick.

SEXISM IN THE SKIES

Case 62: Defrenne (No.2) [1976] E.C.R. 455
(European Court of Justice)

European Law—Equal treatment—Discrimination—Direct effect of Treaty of Rome

Gabrielle Defrenne, an air hostess working for Sabena, sued the airline for paying her less than male cabin stewards doing the same job, claiming that this was sex discrimination in breach of Article 119 of the EC Treaty, which requires "equal pay for equal work". The Belgian Labour Court asked the European Court of Justice (ECJ) to decide whether or not Article 119 [now 141 after amendments by the Treaty of Amsterdam] had direct effect.

According to the European Judges, Article 119 has two aims. First, the Court held that Article 119 was designed to prevent countries which discriminated against women from enjoying a competitive advantage over countries which had implemented equal-pay provisions. Secondly, it also served to advance social progress, an objective of the Community laid out in the Preamble to the Treaty.

The Court then drew a distinction between "direct and overt discrimination" and "indirect and disguised discrimination". In cases falling under the former category, Article 119 was directly applicable, giving rights to individuals which national courts had a duty to uphold. In cases falling under the latter category, Community or national legislation would have to be passed before the article could be judicially implemented.

The U.K. Government and the European Commission argued that Article 119 could not be invoked between individuals, but only between individuals and the State. (Ms Defrenne was not employed by the Belgian State; Sabena, though state-owned, is a separate legal entity). The ECJ, however, held that Article 119 applied to all agreements intended to regulate paid labour. In other words, employees in both the private and public sectors could challenge their employers in national courts on the basis of the EC Treaty. The article has "horizontal" as well as "vertical" effect (*i.e.* it applied between citizens as well as between citizen and state).

Objections were raised by the U.K. and Irish Governments that this ruling could impose massive retroactive costs on small businesses. Article 119 provided that equal pay should be ensured during the first stage of the transitional period, which ended in December 1961. If it had direct effect, that effect should have commenced at that point. However, at the time, neither the Commission nor the Member-States considered that it did. *Defrenne* posed the danger that private individuals would face massive claims for back-pay, based not on national law but on provisions of an international Treaty which neither they, nor their governments, nor the Commission itself, thought could directly affect them. Therefore, the Court overruled its own Advocate-General and decreed that the direct effect of Article 119 could not be relied on to support claims which predated the Court's judgment, unless legal proceedings had already been brought.

That part of the judgment, while defensible in terms of practicality, is perhaps hardest to defend in terms of legal reasoning; direct effect should really have taken place from 1962 onwards. Notwithstanding that, *Defrenne* is a landmark case, allowing the EC Treaty to be relied upon by all workers to claim equal pay for equal work, and to do so in their own national courts.

THE CASE OF THE DUTCH SOLDIER BOYS

Case 63: Engel and Others v. The Netherlands
(1976) 1 E.H.R.R. 647
(European Court of Human Rights)

Human Rights—Right to liberty—Right to a fair trial—Freedom from discrimination—Arts. 5, 6 and 14, ECHR

Some people are just not meant to be soldiers. Conscription might seem a good idea to states that want to maintain a strong army, but in countries like the Netherlands, where the torch of personal liberty has burned brightly for many centuries, there are some people who find it very difficult to fit into the disciplines of army life, with its requirements for unquestioning and unthinking obedience. One such was Mr Engel. So too were his chums, Mr Dona and Mr Schul. All three were active in a voluntary organisation, the Conscript Servicemen's Association, a body set up to look after the interests of conscripts. The Dutch Army itself viewed this body with suspicion, but, being law-abiding, tolerated it and recognised that it had some legitimacy to speak for the conscripted soldiers. Mr Engel stood for election as vice-president of the Conscript Servicemen's Association; Mr Dona and Mr Schul were involved in the writing and publication of the association's newsletter. They were intelligent young men. Mr Engel was a doctoral candidate at Utrecht University, having recently submitted his thesis. A date was set for the *viva*. He really wasn't meant for the army.

In March 1971 Mr Engel wanted to attend a meeting of the Conscript Servicemen's Association, at which he was standing for election as Vice-President but instead of asking for time off, he told his commanding officer that he was sick that day and would have to stay at home (he was not sick and he did not stay at home). This, inevitably, was discovered. Mr Engel was punished with four days of what was called "light arrest", which effectively confined him to barracks. But his doctoral examination was five days away and he needed to go home to prepare. So he did. This led to a penalty of three days of "aggravated arrest", which again he ignored, and so he was subjected to two days of "strict arrest", which involved locking him in a cell.

Meantime, Mr Dona and Mr Schul published in their newsletter an article critical of one of the great generals, who had been negotiating with the Association, but (it was alleged in the article) went back on his word. They were charged with undermining military discipline and were subjected to four months retraining in a disciplinary unit. Both they and Mr Engel complained to the European Court that their treatment amounted to various infringements of the European Convention on Human Rights.

They first argued that the impairments of their freedom of movement inherent in military service was an infringement of their right to liberty as protected by Article 5. This argument was rejected on the basis that Article 5 is concerned with deprivations of physical liberty rather than simply limitations on movement. It prohibited (except in specified circumstances) locking people up but did not prohibit the state requiring people to be in particular places at particular times. So while Mr Engel had a relevant claim in respect of his "strict arrest", the other two did not. And due to procedural flaws in the way that Mr Engel had been subjected to arrest, it could not be said to have been carried out in accordance with the law and it was, therefore, an infringement of Article 5.

The major issue under Article 6 was whether the application of military discipline was a criminal or a civil matter. This was important since if it were the former it would be subject to the higher protections contained in Article 6(2) and (3) in addition to the general right to a fair trial contained in Article 6(1). The Court held that the concept of "criminal" proceedings has an autonomous meaning but that this autonomy only works one way. In other words, if the domestic system regards the process as criminal then, for ECHR purposes, it is indeed criminal; but if the domestic system regards the process as civil, it may nevertheless be regarded as criminal for ECHR purposes. For otherwise a state could escape Article 6(2) and (3) simply by designating all its processes as "civil". In determining whether a process is "criminal" or not account is to be taken of the nature of the offence and the severity of the punishment. (For a recent Scottish application of this rule, explicitly founding on *Engel*, see *S. v. Miller*, 2001 S.L.T. 531). In the present case, taking account especially of the punishment, the Court held that Mr Engel had been subjected to only disciplinary (*i.e.* civil) proceedings, while Mr Dona and Mr Schul had been subjected to criminal proceedings. In both cases, however, there was an infringement of Article 6(1) since the hearings had not been held in public.

Perhaps the most interesting claim was that the soldier boys had been discriminated against and that therefore Article 14 had been infringed. The Dutch system of military justice differed depending upon the rank of the soldier involved. With the so-called "light arrest", while lower ranks had to serve their time in their barracks, officers would be confined to their own homes. That, remember, is what Mr Engel had wanted so that he could prepare for his exam and he would have been allowed this had he been of officer rank. The Court, however, dismissed this argument. They pointed out that armies of their nature and of necessity are hierarchical institutions, each rank having different duties and responsibilities. The differentiation in military justice according to rank had, therefore, some rational basis and because it was not arbitrary the different treatment was not discriminatory. This illustrates the important point that different treatment is not unlawful discrimination if it has some rational and justifiable basis.

So, Engel and his chums won on Articles 5 and 6 and lost on Article 14. But none of them should have been in the army.

SOCRATES SURVIVES (BUT IS FINED)

Case 64: Handyside v. United Kingdom
(1976) 1 E.H.R.R. 737
(European Court of Human Rights)

Human Rights—Freedom of expression—Art. 10, ECHR—"Necessary in a democratic society"—Proportionality—Margin of appreciation

(See Hutchinson, "The Margin of Appreciation Doctrine in the European Court of Human Rights" (1999) 48 I.C.L.Q. 638.)

One of the primary purposes of the criminal law is to control behaviour, or to stop people from doing certain things. But that necessarily limits individual freedoms, and the criminal law therefore has to have good reason for doing so, otherwise it is arbitrary and pernicious, which is intolerable to the European Convention on Human Rights. Sometimes the reason behind the law is obviously good, such as the law against murder. Sometimes, however, the reason for a criminal prohibition is good or bad depending only upon one's own moral outlook. The ban on gay sex was justifiable or not depending upon how one regarded homosexuality (see *Norris v. Ireland*, **Case 77**). Laws prohibiting actions that will corrupt or deprave others are good or bad depending on what is understood by corruption or depravity. Is, for example, consensual sado-masochism so corrupt and depraved that it is justified to punish those who consensually indulge? (The answer is yes: *Laskey v. United Kingdom*, **Case 87**). Is consensual gay group sex equally corrupt and depraved? (The answer is no: *A.D.T. v. United Kingdom* [2000] 2 F.L.R. 697).

Mr Richard Handyside (a modern Socrates) was accused of corrupting the youth—but whether he did so depended entirely on one's view of "corruption". He was the publisher of a book written for children above the age of 12. It was called *The Little Red School Book* and was deliberately radical, provocative and, for those who want children to remain obedient and respectful little souls, dangerous. It made declarations such as "all grown-ups are paper tigers". It told children not to feel guilty about things just because adults disapproved of them, like masturbation, having sex, or smoking pot. It had sections explaining abortion, pornography, homosexuality, and orgasm. It asked (rhetorically) whether teachers deserved unquestioned respect. The book was published widely throughout Europe, and Mr Handyside thought that it was about time that there was a British edition. So he published in the United Kingdom. The British Government took an instant dislike to the book (or, at any rate, decided to take a dislike after the *Daily Mirror* and the *Sunday Times* carried reports of editorial outrage). The Metropolitan Police, after being asked to investigate by the Home Secretary, charged Mr Handyside under the (English) Obscene Publications Act 1959, which prohibits the publications of works which "tend to deprave and corrupt" those who would read them. He was convicted, and fined £50. Interestingly, attempts to prosecute the distributors in Scotland failed.

Mr Handyside complained to the European Court of Human Rights that his right to freedom of expression, protected by Article 10 of the European Convention on Human Rights, had been infringed by the English law under which he was charged and convicted. The U.K. Government accepted that his rights had been limited, but pleaded the defence in Article 10(2), that the restrictions to his freedom of expression were "necessary in a democratic society ... for the protection of morals". It should have been hard for them to establish this defence: *The Little Red Schoolbook* was freely circulating in many European countries without the destruction of their democracy, so in what sense could it be said that the English law was "necessary" for democracy? The first significance of the European Court's ruling in *Handyside* is that the test of "necessity" was held to be far less strict than its literal meaning might suggest. Necessity, said the Court, does not mean "indispensable" for democracy. Rather, to justify an infringement, the state must identify the purpose that its law seeks to achieve and show that that purpose is legitimate within a democracy. Then the state must show that the limitation on the freedom is proportionate to the identified legitimate aim, in the sense that it goes no further than is necessary to achieve the aim. The English Act clearly, the Court held, had a legitimate aim, being the protection of morals. But did it go too far? Was it disproportionate to that aim?

These were the real questions of import and, rather oddly, it is the Court's refusal to answer them that constitutes the most important element of the case. The Court held that different states in Europe might give a different answer to the questions, depending upon their perception of morality and depravity, with the result that the domestic courts in each member state are in a better position than the European Court to make the necessary judgment. As such, it would be illegitimate for the European Court to substitute its own judgment for that already reached by a domestic court. In short, domestic legal systems have what the Court called a "margin of appreciation" and the role of the European Court was limited to ensuring that rules of domestic law did not stray so far beyond that margin that they were clearly more draconian than was necessary to achieve their aim. Mr Handyside's conviction came within the margin of appreciation and did not, therefore, amount to an infringement of his rights under the European Convention.

The doctrine of the margin of appreciation means that the European Court has no role in setting down common standards and it is, therefore, an inherently conservative human rights forum. However, because the justification for the margin of appreciation is that "different countries do things differently", it can have no role to play in determining a human rights claim in the wholly domestic sphere, where the issue is the standard in a single country. This fact, together with the fact that the European Convention lays down minimum and not maximum rights, means that domestic courts are free to be, and ought to be, more radical in their protections of human rights than the European Court is. Mr Handyside might not be convicted today.

RUNNING RINGS ROUND THE TAXMAN

Case 65: Lord Advocate v. Royal Bank of Scotland
1977 S.C. 155; 1978 S.L.T. 38
(Inner House, Court of Session, Scotland)

Debt—Diligence and enforcement of debt—Companies—Floating charge—Arrestment

(See Wilson "Effectively Executed Diligence", 1978 J.R. 253; Campbell, "Receivers' Powers" (1978) 23 J.L.S.S. 275; Gretton, "Diligence, Trusts, and Floating Charges" (1981) 26 J.L.S.S. 57; Sim, "The Receiver and Effectually Executed Diligence", 1984 S.L.T. (News) 25; Wortley, "Squaring the Circle: Revisiting the Receiver and Effectually Executed Diligence", 2000 J.R. 325.)

There are some perils in having a legal system where judicial decisions form a primary source of law. The full implications of a decision may not be apparent from the facts before the judges. Accordingly a decision may be reached which, in a different context, has absurd effects. The present case illustrates this danger. It is a decision which is almost universally condemned by academic commentators (which is what such individuals are for). It involves the complicated area of debt enforcement.

Every legal system that permits one person to borrow money from another must have a means of enforcing repaying if the borrower defaults (*i.e.* cannot or will not repay the debt when due)—otherwise no-one would be willing to lend money to anyone else and commercial advancement would be stifled. Scotland, like all developed legal systems, has a variety of enforcement mechanisms. One common method of debt enforcement is the right in security, where the debtor agrees that if he defaults the creditor can sell a specified item to satisfy the debt—the most common example is the home loan mortgage where a person borrows money to buy a house and uses the house as security so that if he or she fails to repay on time the lender can sell the house. Another method of debt enforcement is arrestment whereby, with the court's authority, the creditor can seize or attach the debtor's bank account—if the debtor then continues to fail to pay an action of "furthcoming" can transfer the frozen bank account to the creditor. Yet another method, but available only in relation to company debtors, is the floating charge, which is a form of security without specifying which item of the debtor's property is secured. Companies prefer this to a fixed security since that would inhibit the company's dealing with the secured item during the term of the debt. A floating charge "floats" until the company goes into receivership, at which point the charge "attaches" to the company assets and the holder of the floating charge has to be paid by the receiver out of the assets before other (unsecured) creditors.

This myriad of enforcement mechanisms is all very well, except that different creditors might choose different methods of enforcing different debts, but enforce them against the same item of property. In that case, the law must provide a means of ranking the claims. Arrestment, for example, seizes or attaches a bank account without (yet) transferring ownership; but a floating charge attaches to all the company's assets including its bank account. If one creditor arrests a company's bank account and another creditor has a floating charge which attaches to all the company's assets (including the bank account), who gets paid?

Imperial Hotels (Aberdeen) Ltd borrowed a sizeable sum and granted a floating charge to the lender. It then got in to financial difficulties and was unable to pay its tax bill. The Inland Revenue, which were owed £4,850.49, arrested Imperial Hotels' bank account on May 23, 1974. As Imperial Hotels' financial position worsened the lender became increasingly concerned about its loan and, on July 17, 1974, appointed Frank Mycroft (a regular character in case reports of the late 1970s and early 1980s) as receiver. The floating charge therefore attached all of Imperial Hotels' assets, including the bank account. The question was: who had priority to the bank account? Was it the Inland Revenue, which had arrested the account two months before the floating charge attached? Or was it Mr Mycroft, the receiver? Did the floating charge trump the arrestment?

To decide which party ranked first the Court had to interpret the Companies (Floating Charges and Receivers) (Scotland) Act 1972. This provided that the receiver prevailed over creditors unless they had "effectually executed diligence". Arrestment is a form of diligence (which simply means debt-enforcement) but was it "effectually executed"? The First Division held that the diligence would be "effectually executed" only if the arrestment had been followed by furthcoming (*i.e.* the transfer of the account to the Revenue) before the floating charge attached. This had not happened in this case and so the receiver prevailed.

Now, this decision is problematic in its own terms because the effect of furthcoming is to transfer the bank account to the arresting creditor, and would mean that the bank account would never be caught by the floating charge. But the real problems come when the unforeseen consequences involving third parties are considered.

If there is a bank account the customer may transfer that account to a third party. This is done using an assignation. It is only effective to transfer the account when the bank receives intimation of the transfer. If an arrestment is made before intimation has taken place then the arrestment prevails over the assignation, and the arresting creditor takes priority over the third party.

If the customer intimates an assignation of the bank account before a receiver is appointed (*i.e.* before the floating charge attaches) then the customer no longer owns the bank account and it is removed from the scope of the floating charge. So if the receiver is appointed after intimation the third party will prevail over the receiver.

While the three competitions—between arrester and third party; between receiver and third party; and between arrester and receiver—are simply resolved in themselves, their interaction with each other causes a problem.

Consider the following sequence of events: (i) A company's bank account is arrested. (ii) The assignation of the company's bank account to a third party is intimated to the bank. (iii) A receiver is called in, and the floating charge granted by the company attaches. (iv) The arresting creditor seeks furthcoming.

The order of ranking in this case is irresolvable. The arrester takes priority over the third party. The third party takes priority over the receiver. As a result of *Lord Advocate v. Royal Bank* the receiver takes priority over the arrester. And, of course, the arrester takes priority over the third party who takes priority over the receiver. And so on. And so on. Forever.

This conundrum is referred to as a circle of priorities, and the problem can only be resolved by legislation or by a later court overruling *Lord Advocate v. Royal Bank*. For that reason, among many others, academics tend to regard *Lord Advocate v. Royal Bank* as wrongly decided, but it is still the law. For the moment.

L'AFFAIRE COHN-BENDIT, OR THE CASE OF DANNY THE RED

Case 66: Minister of the Interior v. Cohn-Bendit
[1980] 1 C.M.L.R. 543
(Conseil d'Etat, France)

European law—Supremacy—Free movement of persons—Directives

(See Tatham, "Effect of EC Directives in France: The Development of the *Cohn-Bendit* Jurisprudence" (1991) 40 I.C.L.Q. 907.)

History grabs some people at birth and then never lets go. This is the case for Daniel Cohn-Bendit. He was born on April 4, 1945 in France from German Jewish parents who had run away from Nazi Germany. Orphaned at the age of 16, he chose the German nationality in order to avoid French military service. He spent his childhood in France and his teenage years in Germany. However, it was in France, in the University of Nanterre (Paris) that he decided to study sociology. Cohn-Bendit actively participated in the student revolt, which aimed at "breaking up the encrusted structures in the university, in politics and in society". In the rage of the May '68 French turmoil, he stood out in the crowd with his good looks, his charisma, his high spirit and his anti-authoritarian views. He became a symbol. As a result, the Minister of the Interior made an expulsion order against him on May 24, 1968. He was forced to move back to Frankfurt where he continued to be an active political radical. Among many things, he founded a revolutionary political group (the "Revolutionary Struggle") and launched the city magazine "*Pflasterstrand*". Simultaneously, he worked as a teacher in an anti-authoritarian Kindergarten and as a salesperson in the Karl-Marx bookstore next to the University. In the light of these activities, the French Minister of the Interior refused to cancel the exclusion order in February 1976.

Cohn-Bendit relied on Community rules governing free movement of persons to challenge the exclusion order before the *Tribunal Administratif* (the lowest administrative court in France). The *Tribunal Administratif* suspended the proceedings and referred two questions for a preliminary ruling by the European Court of Justice with respect to the interpretation of Directive 64/221 on the free movement of persons. The Minister of the Interior sought the annulment of that judgment before the *Conseil d'Etat* (the highest court in France dealing with administrative law). It held that "directives cannot be invoked by persons within the jurisdiction of those Member States in order to support a legal action undertaken against an administrative act taken with regard to an individual". Therefore, the case had to be referred back to the *Tribunal Administratif* and not to the European Court of Justice.

The *Conseil d'Etat*'s decision was in flagrant contradiction with the ECJ's decisions in *Van Duyn* [1974] E.C.R. 1337 and *Rutilli* [1975] E.C.R. 1219. It was not the first time, however, that a national court showed resistance towards the ECJ's ambition to become a federal constitutional court. Indeed, the relationship between the national and the European jurisdiction has not always been an easy one. National courts have been protective of their judicial sovereignty as shown by the German Federal Tax Court in *Bundesfinanzhof* [1982] 1 C.M.L.R. 527 or in the British House of Lords' decision in *Finnegan* [1990] 2 All E.R. 546. Nevertheless, the greatest resistance can be found in the *Cohn-Bendit* decision. It has become the most well-known rebellion against the supremacy of EC law. Although, in recent years the national courts have settled down, the spirit of *l'Affaire Cohn-Bendit* has served to give warning to the ECJ that its ambitions have not gone unnoticed.

What really makes this 21-year-old French case still so grabbing to us today? Is it the scent of freedom and madness carried along by the

1968 students' revolt? Could it be the character of Cohn-Bendit himself? Could it possibly be the resistance of one man against the system, or the resistance of one system against a higher order? Whatever it is, *l'Affaire Cohn-Bendit* symbolises a certain idea of resistance against conformity and marching orders. The individual and the particular will not be melted in the collective without a fight.

As far as Daniel Cohn-Bendit is concerned, when his exclusion order was finally lifted in 1978, he did not want to leave Germany any more. He joined the German Green Party, and in 1994 became a member of the European Parliament for the Greens. In 1998, he stood in the election of the European Parliament in France, the only election open to non-nationals. When he was elected, *"Les frontières on s'en fout!"* (We don't care about borders!), the 1968 student slogan, takes all his meaning.

CASSIS DE DIJON

Case 67: Rewe Zentral AG v. Bundesmonopolverwaltung für Branntwein [1979] E.C.R. 649
(European Court of Justice)

European law—Free movement of goods—public health exception

(See Alter and Meunier-Aitsahalia, "Judicial Politics in the European Community: European Integration and the Pathbreaking *Cassis de Dijon* Decision", (1994) 26 Comparative Political Studies 535)

A German company, Rewe Zentral AG, wanted to import a French liqueur called "Cassis de Dijon". Under German law, only liqueurs with an alcohol content of 25 per cent or more could be marketed as "Cassis". The French product had an alcohol content of 15–20 per cent. The German authorities decided that "Cassis de Dijon" could thus be imported, but not sold in Germany. The firm claimed that this was a breach of Article 30 [now 28] of the EC Treaty, which forbids quantitative restrictions on imports or measures having equivalent effect.

The German Government argued that their rules were not discriminatory; they had imposed no quota, for the obstacle to trade resulted merely from France and Germany requiring different levels of alcohol content. They also invoked the public policy defences of Article 36 [now 30]. They claimed to be protecting consumers, saying that if the 25 per cent requirement were overruled, then the weaker French law would cover drink sold in Germany, which would lead to German producers demanding a similar relaxation in German law. Any relaxation of the French law would automatically apply in Germany too, and eventually the law with the lowest standards would apply everywhere. Germany also claimed that lowering the alcohol content would lead to a greater tolerance of alcohol, increased proliferation of alcoholic beverages and thus indirectly to more widespread alcoholism.

The Court, in its judgment, made no reference at all to discrimination. Instead, it took the view that the infringement of Article 30 arose from the fact that "Cassis de Dijon" could not lawfully be placed on the German market, and then began analysing the justifications offered for the exclusion.

The public health argument was the first to be demolished, since a wide range of weak, moderate and strong alcoholic products were already available, and in any case the stronger forms of Cassis were usually taken in diluted form.

Neither did the Court feel that consumer protection required mandatory alcohol fixing of alcohol content. Enough information could be conveyed to the consumer simply by labelling origin and alcohol content.

The Court held that the true purpose of the 25 per cent requirement was to exclude the products of other countries, which did not meet that requirement. It was therefore an obstacle to trade incompatible with Article 30.

Cassis de Dijon is a landmark case because of the doctrine it gave birth to, that products exported from one Member-State must be admitted to the importing Member-State if it has been lawfully produced, *i.e.* according to the rules and processes of manufacture which are customary in the exporting country. Any measure which obstructs this, even if not intended to be discriminatory, will be struck down.

This uncompromising attitude against quotas and measures having equivalent effect is important because quotas, even more than tariffs, are capable of distorting international free trade; the volume of imports cannot expand to meet increased demand, nor can the increased efficiency of exporters gain them access to the protected markets.

WRONGFUL LIFE

Case 68: McKay v. Essex Health Authority
[1982] 1 Q.B. 1166; [1982] 2 All E.R. 771
(Court of Appeal, England)

Delict—Damages for being born alive—Disabled child—Abortion

(See Teff, "The Action for 'Wrongful Life' in England and the United States" (1985) 34 I.C.L.Q. 423; Norrie, "Wrongful Life in Scots Law: No Right, No Remedy", 1990 J.R. 205)

Mrs Jacinta McKay fell pregnant in February 1975. Shortly thereafter she came in contact with a person who was suffering from rubella (German measles). Knowing that this disease carries a high risk of severe and irreversible damage to unborn children, by inhibiting the proper development of the child in the womb, Mrs McKay attended hospital for a blood check. After the blood test she was informed that she and the unborn child were free from rubella. The pregnancy continued, and in August 1975, prematurely, a little girl was born. She was named Mary. Unfortunately, she was severely disabled. Her disabilities had been caused by the rubella which her mother had indeed contracted. Had Mrs McKay been informed that she had contracted rubella, she would have terminated the pregnancy, which would have been lawful under the Abortion Act 1967. The hospital's negligence in carrying out the blood test deprived her of this opportunity. But when an action was raised against the hospital, it was not Mrs McKay who sued—it was Mary, the child.

This was an action for what is known as "wrongful life", which is not to be confused with actions for "wrongful birth". Both arise from the failure of someone to prevent a pregnancy or to terminate it, but their legal bases are very different. The latter are raised by parents and are competent, at least for some of the losses suffered (see *McFarlane v. Tayside Health Board*, **Case 99**); the former would be raised by the child him- or herself. *McKay* is the first (and last) time that such a claim had ever been made in England but they are more common (though seldom successful) in the United States of America. The early American cases involved children born with social disadvantages. In *Zepeda v. Zepeda*, 41 Ill. App. (2d) 240 (1963) an illegitimate child sued his father for negligently conferring an injury—life as an illegitimate child—on him. In *Williams v. New York*, 223 NE (2d) 849 (1963) a similar claim was made against the state of New York which ran a mental institution, the alleged negligence being the failure to prevent one resident (the father of the subsequent child) from raping another (the mother). Both claims failed on the ground that social disadvantage was not a cognisable loss in law. Later claims were made when children were born with physical or mental disadvantages rather than social ones and, occasionally, damages have been awarded. In *Park v. Chessin*, 400 N.Y.S. (2d) 110 (1977), for example, the court held that since abortion was (by then) legal, a breach of duty which deprived the parent of the right to choose an abortion was tortious not only to the parent but to the child. The court held that the child had a "right to be born whole or not at all". And in *Turpin v. Sortini*, 31 Cal. (3d) 220 (1982) a child was awarded damages to cover the extra expenses it would face in life as a result of its injuries caused by disease which could only have been prevented by aborting the child.

In *McKay*, the Court of Appeal was not impressed by these American decisions, and Mary's claim was rejected, on three related grounds. First, the court held that the doctor owed no duty of care to the child, at least not to the extent that the duty could only be fulfilled by terminating her existence. Once rubella had been contracted, Mary's health was doomed, and no-one could be blamed for that (remembering that the law of delict only gives damages if the injured party can find someone to "blame"). So if the doctors did owe her a duty, the only way they could prevent her suffering was to abort her and the court was not willing to recognise a duty to abort. Secondly, the court held that there were public policy reasons against allowing the claim: it would mean regarding the life of a handicapped child as not only less valuable than the life of a normal child but so much less valuable that it was not worth preserving. That, considered the court, was bad social policy and demeaning to the disabled. Thirdly, it would be entirely impossible to assess the extent of the loss suffered, because the law of damages operates by comparing the position of the pursuer with and without the negligence: in the present case that would involve putting a monetary value on the difference between Mary's disabled life and her non-existence. But non-existence (as opposed to death) cannot have a monetary value. So no damages can be awarded.

The case was based on the English common law but the matter is now governed by statute, for section 4(5) of the Congenital Disabilities (Civil Liability) Act 1976 provides (in terms not easy to understand) that actions for wrongful life are not competent.

However, the 1976 Act does not apply to Scotland, and the matter remains to be dealt with by the common law here. But the same result as in *McKay* would be reached. A claim effectively the same was raised in rather different circumstances in *P's Curator Bonis v. Criminal Injuries Compensation Board*, 1997 S.L.T. 1180. A child sought compensation from the Criminal Injuries Compensation Board, claiming to be a person who suffered personal injury directly attributable to a crime of violence. What had happened was that her mother had been raped by her (the mother's) own father and the child had been conceived, to be later born with congenital abnormalities. The claim was rejected and on appeal to the Court of Session the reasoning in *McKay* was followed to uphold that rejection. So in Scotland too there is no remedy for the so-called delict of "wrongful life". Life may be nasty, brutish and short, but it is never wrongful.

NOT BED-TIME READING

Case 69: Junior Books Ltd v. Veitchi Ltd
1982 S.C. (H.L.) 244; 1982 S.L.T. 492
(House of Lords, Scotland)

Delict—Negligence—Economic loss—Proximity

(See Markesinis, "An Expanding Tort Law—The Price of a Rigid Contract Law" (1987) 103 L.Q.R. 354; Stephenson, "Goodbye *Junior Books*" (1988) 138 New L.J. 483; Logie, "The Final Demise of *Junior Books*?" 1989 J.R. 5.)

A book distribution company called Junior Books entered into a contract for the construction of a factory for their business. The contractors subcontracted the floor-laying in the factory to the Veitchi Co. It was alleged by Junior Books that the workmanship by the Veitchi Co was so defective that the floor surface required to be removed immediately and replaced in order to avoid expensive long-term maintenance. Junior Books sued for the cost of replacement and the losses they would suffer while the work was being carried out. The problem for the pursuers was that this was a claim for what is called "pure economic loss", which is not usually recoverable. However, the House of Lords held by a majority, Lord Brandon dissenting, in favour of Junior Books and allowed recovery of the pure economic losses allegedly suffered. Lord Roskill identified eight factors as helping to determine that there was a sufficient degree of proximity between the parties, such that there was a close and special relationship between them. Indeed their relationship was akin to contract: the key aspects were that the Veitchi Co was a nominated sub-contractor and they knew that Junior Books were relying on them and the quality of their work.

This is the most famous Scottish case on the question of recovery of economic losses in negligence. The law of delict in both Scotland and England has long grappled with the complex question of whether one can sue for one's economic losses arising from another's negligence, never quite liking the straightforward answer: yes, why not? The first difficulty is to ascertain what is meant by economic loss. At first glance, one could say that all losses are economic in that they have some financial basis, *e.g.* a car damaged as a result of negligence may cost £x to repair and this is obviously a financial loss. However, the law classifies certain types of losses as being either physical injury or property damage, and these are recoverable under the normal principles of recovery laid down in ***Donoghue v. Stevenson*** **Case 27**, while economic losses following a physical injury, for example medical costs and loss of earnings, are recoverable as consequential economic losses, provided a duty of care is owed in respect of the physical injury. At the other end of the spectrum, there are secondary economic losses, where a loss is derived from injury to someone else or damage to another's property, and it has been held that these economic losses are never recoverable. (See, *e.g. **Reavis v. Clan Line Steamers***, **Case 23**). What about those situations where someone merely suffers economic loss as a result of another's actions where there is no physical injury or property damage, for instance if negligent investment advice is given and a range of people rely on the advice and lose their hard earned savings as a result? Should there be limits on the recovery of such losses? On the one hand the principle of corrective justice would suggest that the negligent party is liable for all losses, whereas the principle of distributive justice would seek to consider liability from the perspective of a fair distribution of risks and losses in society.

The first occasion in which the higher courts in either jurisdiction confirmed that pure, or primary, economic loss was potentially recoverable was in ***Hedley Byrne & Co Ltd v. Heller & Partners Ltd***, **Case 46**. There, the House of Lords held that pure economic loss could be recovered if it had resulted from negligent misstatements which the defendants knew the plaintiffs would rely on. The importance of *Junior Books* is that it applied the principle in *Hedley Byrne*, though rather more widely than the factual circumstances of negligent misstatements: the principle was that of proximity, as established by the pursuers' reliance.

It needs to be remembered that this case took place in 1982 during an expansive phase of delictual liability in the House of Lords following *Anns v. Merton London Borough Council* [1978] A.C. 728. According to that case, there is a two stage test of liability to be applied, the second stage of which is to consider whether there were any public policy reasons to deny liability, and the floodgates argument (*i.e.* that this would open up the floodgates to litigation) being disregarded. However, since *Junior Books*, *Anns* has been overruled by the House of Lords, and *Murphy v. Brentwood District Council* [1990] 2 All E.R. 908 and *Caparo v. Dickman* [1990] 1 All E.R. 568 signalled a change in direction by their Lordships to a more restrictive approach to delictual liability, involving an incremental approach and a three stage test of liability. Accordingly, the *Junior Books* authority may be doubtful, and it also sits uneasily with the rules against recovery for secondary economic loss and in respect of defective property.

It has been suggested that *Junior Books* should now be viewed as an unlawful interference with contract case, and it has also been considered as limited to its facts or cases involving a contractual chain (see *Strathford E.K. Ltd v. HML Design Ltd*, 1999 S.L.T. 121, discussed by

Rodger at (2001) 6 S.L.P.Q. 35). However, a better approach is to consider it as a clear application of *Hedley Byrne* principles requiring the establishment of a special relationship or proximity. The moral of the story though for children is that it is better to grow up to be a "cowboy" builder than a "cowboy" floor-layer.

I CAN'T BELIEVE IT'S NOT A MONOPOLY!

Case 70: Garden Cottage Foods Ltd v. Milk Marketing Board
[1984] 1 A.C. 130; [1983] 2 A.C. 770
(House of Lords, England)

European law—Competition law—Abuse of a dominant position

(See Hoskins, "*Garden Cottage* revisited: the availability of damages in the national courts for breaches of EEC competition rules" [1992] 6 E.C.L.R. 257.)

In the early 1980s the Milk Marketing Board, ("MMB"), a statutory authority, produced 75 per cent of the butter produced in England and Wales and was the largest producer of bulk butter exported from the U.K. Garden Cottage Foods Ltd ("GCF") was an altogether smaller concern. It operated from the home of Mr and Mrs Bunch in Crowborough, East Sussex, who were its only employees. The purchase and sale of bulk butter accounted for 80 per cent of the company's turnover, 90 per cent of its purchases were from the MMB and 95 per cent of its resales were exported to a single purchaser in the Netherlands. The MMB in 1982 decided to alter its distribution strategy and it appointed four independent distributors to handle the sales of bulk butter for export. Mr Bunch was informed that he should discuss the availability of supplies with those distributors.

In the business equivalent of David and Goliath, GCF applied for an interlocutory injunction restraining the defendants from withholding supplies of butter from them and from refusing to maintain normal business relations. They claimed that the MMB's actions breached Article 86 of the EEC Treaty, which prohibits the abuse of a dominant market position—competition law jargon for a monopoly. The House of Lords overturned the Court of Appeal and held that the claimant was not entitled to injunctive relief. However, the majority suggested that it would be possible to bring a claim alleging infringement of the Community competition rules as a "breach of a statutory duty". This remains the most important case concerning Community competition law in the U.K. courts (see also the Scottish case of *Argyll v. Distillers*,

1987 S.L.T. 514), and although there has been no final award of damages by a U.K. court on the basis of Community competition rules, it is clear that this remedy would be available despite the *obiter* nature of the House of Lords' pronouncements. There has also been pressure from the European Court in recent years to ensure that appropriate remedies are available in national courts. (See, for example, *Francovich v. The Italian Republic*, Cases C-6 & 9/90 [1996] E.C.R. I–5357, [1993] 2 C.M.L.R. 66.) However, the difficulties in obtaining interim relief have been criticised as jeopardising the continuing viability of companies which are subjected to anti-competitive conduct, and the courts still have to clarify a number of issues as to the limits of liability under Community competition rules.

This case is interesting as there has subsequently been considerable jurisprudence in European courts on the legality of the refusal to supply goods or services under Community competition law by a company in a dominant market position. Further, the MMB's operation formed part of the Community market for milk products under the Common Agricultural Policy, heavily criticised at the time for the creation of the European "butter mountain". Some final points should be noted. As a result of the recent Amsterdam Treaty the principal Community competition rules are now contained in Articles 81 and 82 of the EC Treaty [previously Articles 85 and 86]. Further, during 1999 the successor to the Milk Marketing Board, Milk Marque, was the subject of a competition law inquiry in the U.K. by the Monopolies and Mergers Commission (now the Competition Commission). Finally, the Competition Act 1998 has recently taken effect in the U.K. and this models U.K. competition law on Articles 81 and 82.

A TALE OF TWO CAUSES

Case 71: Khaliq v. H.M. Advocate
1984 J.C. 23; 1984 S.L.T. 137
(High Court of Justiciary, Scotland)

Criminal law—Endangering lives—Supplying lawful but harmful substances—Causation

(See www.lawscot.org.uk/whatis/famous_cases.html)

Mr Raja Khaliq and Mr Raja Ahmed ran a small corner shop in the Saltmarket in Glasgow. They sold all sorts of household provisions, tinned food, milk, sweeties, clothes pegs, glue. Evostik glue. Between 1981 and 1983 they sold lots and lots of glue, to lots and lots of children.

With the glue, they sold empty crisp packets, tins and tubes. An innocent observer might well have thought that the children were building some model, or Useful Gift For Mother's Day, as instructed by *Blue Peter*. But the reality was far less benign. The children were abusing the solvents contained in the glue, by placing it in the crisp packets, putting the packets to their noses and mouths, and inhaling. They were, in the jargon, "glue sniffing". The shopkeepers knew, it was alleged, the purpose to which these kits were being put when they sold them to the children, and they were charged with supplying glue and empty crisp packets to children, knowing that the children intended to inhale the vapours of the glue, so putting themselves at risk of serious injury or death. The shopkeepers pleaded that this was no crime known to the law of Scotland, and that in any case it was the children who were placing themselves at risk, rather than them.

They argued that many things sold in shops, like kitchen knives for example, are dangerous if misused but that does not mean that the shopkeepers who sell them are criminals. It might be different if statute prohibited the sale, but statute does not prohibit the sale of kitchen knives, or of glue. Glue is not a "dangerous drug" for the purposes of the control of drugs legislation. They argued that if this charge did constitute a crime, it could do so only as a result of the High Court declaring a new crime (see *H.M. Advocate v. Greenhuff*, **Case 6**) which, they claimed, it no longer had the power to do.

The trial judge held that, if there is a power to declare new crimes, it inhered in a quorum of the High Court and certainly not in him. But he also held that since Parliament had expressed its disapproval of glue-sniffing, by passing the Solvent Abuse (Scotland) Act 1983, which made that activity a ground of referral to the children's hearing, he was entitled to find that the supply of goods designed to be used in this harmful activity was the known crime of intending to cause harm to another. On appeal, he was upheld. Criminal conduct, the High Court held, includes conduct which causes real injury to the person. So the only question was whether the acts of the shopkeepers in selling their glue-sniffing kits "caused" injury to the children. The prosecutor was held entitled to attempt to prove this and the trial judge was held correct to hold the indictment competent. The Court emphasised that to hold the shopkeepers criminally responsible is not to create a new crime but simply to recognise a new way of committing an old crime.

Apart from the potential use of the so-called "declaratory power", the major issue in the present case was the extent to which an accused can be held criminally liable for an act which only causes harm because another person has independently done something—in other words, was the fact that the children themselves sniffed the glue a *novus actus interveniens*? The Court held that it was not, so that the supplier of harmful substances can be found guilty of endangering the health or life of the person supplied. This has obvious implications for the fight against drug dealers and suppliers. In *Ulhaq v. H.M. Advocate*, 1990 S.C.C.R. 593 a shopkeeper was held properly convicted of culpably and recklessly endangering lives and health when he sold lighter fuel, knowing that the purchasers would use this to inhale the vapours.*Khaliq* was taken to its logical conclusion in *Lord Advocate's Reference (No. 1 of 1994)*, 1995 S.C.C.R. 177 where a trial judge was held to have been wrong in acquitting a person accused of culpable homicide by supplying the deceased with amphetamines from which she died. The High Court explicitly held that the causal link between the supply of the drug and the death was not broken by the deceased's voluntary act of taking the drug. The law of England seems to be somewhat different: see *R. v. Dalby* [1982] 1 All E.R. 916.

THE GCHQ CASE

Case 72: Council of Civil Service Unions and Others v. Minister for the Civil Service
[1985] A.C. 374; [1984] 3 All E.R. 935
(House of Lords, England)

Administrative law—Judicial review—Royal prerogative—National security

(See Wade, "Procedure and Prerogative in Public Law" (1985) 101 L.Q.R. 180).

Not long after Mrs Thatcher became Prime Minister in 1979, there arose a great deal of industrial unrest between the civil service trade unions and the government about civil service conditions of employment. The trade unions organised a campaign of industrial action designed to do as much damage as possible to government agencies. Government Communications Headquarters (GCHQ) in Cheltenham was (and is) a surveillance centre whose functions were (and are) to ensure the security of U.K. military communications and to provide signals intelligence for the government. Strike action at GCHQ virtually shut down parts of their operations. Mrs Thatcher who, as Prime Minister, was also the Minister for the Civil Service lost patience and she issued an oral instruction that the staff of GCHQ would no longer be allowed to be members of trade unions. The power to issue such instructions came from an Order in Council which had been made under the royal prerogative. There had been a long-standing practice of consultation with the trade unions over proposed changes in the staff's conditions of service. On this occasion there was none.

The trade unions applied for judicial review of the (Prime) Minister's instruction, seeking a declaration that it was invalid on the ground that she had acted unfairly in removing the fundamental right to belong to a trade union without consultation. The Minister argued that instructions issued under a power which emanated from the royal prerogative and not from a statute were not open to review by the courts and that the requirements of national security overrode any duty to consult the staff. At first instance the judge granted the application, but the Court of Appeal allowed the Minister's appeal on the ground of national security. The unions appealed to the House of Lords. There, the judges held that the Minister had indeed acted unfairly in failing to consult prior to making her decision, but dismissed the appeal on the ground of national security.

The case is important both for what the judges had to say about judicial review of prerogative powers and also for a new classification of the grounds for judicial review.

Lord Scarman said that judicial review had reached the stage where it could be said with confidence that if the subject matter in respect of which the prerogative power is exercised is a matter on which a court can adjudicate, the exercise of the power is subject to judicial review. The controlling factor is not the *source* of the power. Lord Roskill added that he could see no logical reason why the fact that the source of the power is the prerogative and not statute should deprive the citizen of the right to challenge the manner of its exercise. However, prerogative powers relating to the making of treaties, the defence of the realm, the prerogative of mercy, the granting of honours, the dissolution of Parliament and the appointment of ministers would not be susceptible to judicial review because their nature and subject matter is such as not to be amenable to the judicial process. All the judges agreed that Mrs Thatcher's instructions were not immune to judicial review just because the instructions were issued under a power derived from the prerogative. They also agreed that the staff at GCHQ had a legitimate expectation of consultation before important changes were made to their conditions of service. However, the Minister had provided evidence that she feared that consultation would have given rise to industrial action which would have endangered national security. The question of whether the instruction was necessitated by the requirements of national security was a matter for the executive, not the judges, since only the executive had access to the information to enable a judgment to be made. Thus the judges had to dismiss the appeal.

Lord Diplock took the opportunity to devise a new nomenclature for the classification of the grounds of judicial review which has since become widely accepted. The grounds on which administrative action is subject to control by judicial review can be classified under three heads: illegality, irrationality and procedural impropriety. By "illegality", Lord Diplock meant that the decision-maker must understand correctly the law that regulates his or her decision-making power and give effect to it. By "irrationality", he meant what is referred to as "*Wednesbury* unreasonableness" (see **Case 33**). This applies to a decision which is so outrageous in its defiance of logic or of accepted moral standards that no sensible person who has applied his mind to the question to be decided could have arrived at it. According to Lord Diplock, this is a question which judges by their training and experience should be well-equipped to answer. By "procedural irregularity", Lord Diplock had in mind something wider than a failure to observe the basic rules of natural justice. It covers failure to observe procedural rules expressly laid down in the legislation which confers the power to make decisions, even when such failure does not involve a denial of natural justice.

Lord Diplock added that developments in administrative law might in time add further grounds for judicial review, such as proportionality, a principle well-recognised in European Human Rights law (see Case 64).

HITTING THE FAN

Case 73: RHM Bakeries v. Strathclyde Regional Council
1985 S.C. (H.L.) 17; 1985 S.L.T. 214
(House of Lords, Scotland)

Delict—Nuisance—Fault-based, or strict liability?

(See Reid, "The Basis of Liability in Nuisance", 1997 J.R. 162; McManus, "Culpa and the Law of Nuisance", 1997 J.R. 259).

Scottish people have a renowned sweet tooth, a penchant for sugary food like tablet and an unenviable tooth decay record: we eat cream buns, fudge doughnuts and Danish pastries that would make the people of Copenhagen wince. Bakeries play a prominent part in the culinary aspirations of the Scottish people and therefore a tale of our pies, bridies and iced buns floating in sewage is apt to bring a tear to the eye and bile to the gullet.

Strathclyde Regional Council was claimed to be the largest local authority territory in West Europe. In this case the might of the Regional Council, renowned for its non-readiness to admit liability in any situation, was sued by a local bakery company. In September 1978 a main brick sewer in the Paton Street/Duke Street area of Glasgow burst and collapsed. The Regional Council was the authority responsible for the sewerage system. Repair work was being executed by contractors on behalf of the local authority when flooding occurred during a period of heavy rainfall. As a result, the pursuer's bakery premises were flooded and they sued the Regional Council for damages to their premises. They claimed that they were entitled to damages for the wrong of nuisance.

Entitlement to sue and claim damages under the law of nuisance is based on the principle that a proprietor of land is entitled to enjoyment of their property without interference. Accordingly, there is a duty not to use one's land in an unreasonable way and thereby prejudice a neighbour's enjoyment of their own land (see Lord President Cooper in *Watt v. Jamieson*, 1954 S.C. 56 at 58.) This was all accepted. The issue for decision was the appropriate test in order to succeed in a nuisance claim. Was it necessary for the pursuer to show that the "author" of the nuisance, in this case the Regional Council as the authority in control of the sewerage system, was at fault, for instance by failing to take reasonable precautions in maintaining their property? Or was nuisance a delict of strict liability where the occurrence of the event was all that needed to be shown?

This issue was made more difficult by two factors. First, there was considerable doubt about existing Scottish authority in *Kerr v. The Earl of Orkney* (1857) 20 D. 298. In that case a dam had been built across a stream on which the pursuer had a mill about half a mile downstream. After heavy rains the dam burst, the waters swept away the pursuer's mills and the defender who had built the dam was held liable in damages, though it has always been unclear whether liability there was based on fault or on the mere happening of the event. In the present case Lord Fraser of Tullybelton concluded that the true basis of *Kerr* was culpa, or fault, of the defender. Accordingly, the House of Lords in this case confirmed (some would suggest they decided for the first time) that, under Scots law, in order to succeed in a claim for damages for nuisance one requires to show fault on the defender's part. Another potential obstacle to this outcome was the rule in the English case of *Rylands v. Fletcher* (1868) L.R. 3 H.L. 330, which imposes strict liability. However, Lord Fraser pointed out the historical differences in the approaches to liability of the two legal systems with Scots law's traditional approach to delictual liability based on *culpa* reflected in its law on nuisance. These two difficulties having been disposed of, the way was open to affirm that for an action for nuisance in Scots law, fault had to be averred by the pursuer. This meant that the pursuer was required, in the pleadings, to state the nature of the defender's fault, although an exact account would not be required, as it would often be impossible to know. For example, it could be sufficient to state that normally maintained sewers do not collapse and it is then for the defender to show that the harm was not his fault, for example because it is caused by a third party outwith the defender's responsibility.

This case is interesting because it reaffirms the distinctive approach of Scots law and the treatment of English authority as non-binding. The case also demonstrates the frequent practice in modern times of English Law Lords concurring with the single speech by a Scottish Law Lord in an appeal on Scots law. And it also illustrates the full appeal process in Scots civil law from the Sheriff Court, via Sheriff Principal and Inner House to the House of Lords. Interestingly, in a dispute which proceeded all the way to the House of Lords on the issue of the basis of liability, Lord Fraser concluded that there was not much difference in the practical result! A clear demonstration of the argumentative nature of lawyers and undoubtedly considerable fees would have been earned in the appeal process—enough to pay for a few cream buns in the Court common room.

MAMMA MIA

Case 74: Gillick v. West Norfolk & Wisbech
Area Health Authority
[1986] A.C. 112; [1985] 3 W.L.R. 830; [1985] 3 All E.R. 402
(House of Lords, England)

Medical treatment—Parent and child—Capacity of child to consent to treatment—Contraception and abortion advice and treatment

(See Williams, "The Gillick Saga" (1985) 135 New L.J. 117; Norrie, "Gillick Again: The House of Lords Decides", 1986 S.L.T. (News) 69; Bridgeman, "Old Enough to Know Best?" (1993) 13 Leg. Stud. 69).

Mrs Gillick was the mother of ten children. She sought assurances from her local health authority that they would not give contraceptive advice or treatment to any of her daughters without her knowledge and consent before they reached the age of 16. These the authority refused to give, referring to recently issued Department of Health guidance to the effect that with children under 16 attempts should always be made to involve their parents but that in exceptional cases doctors may prescribe contraceptives without parental consent. The plaintiff raised an action seeking to have this guidance declared unlawful. Though she won her case in the Court of Appeal, the House of Lords, by a majority of three to two, held that it was lawful for a doctor to provide contraceptive or abortion advice or treatment to girls under the age of 16 without parental knowledge or consent. The speeches are, however, ambiguous as to when it is lawful to do so, though the case is the genesis of the concept of the "Gillick-competent" child, that is one who has the mental maturity to understand the nature and consequences of medical treatment and thus is *prima facie* capable of consenting thereto. In English law Gillick-competency is merely the starting point for the determination of legal capacity, and issues of parents' rights and children's welfare are also relevant to that determination. Lord Fraser suggested that as well as competency to understand, the medical treatment or procedure must be in the child's best interests before it is lawful. Lord Templeman suggested that unlawful treatment could become lawful if the child's parents consented to it (an approach followed—though not explicitly—in *Re J. (Circumcision)* [2000] 1 F.L.R. 571 in which it was held that genital mutilation was not in a boy child's best interests but could lawfully be carried out if both parents consented). Only Lord Scarman took the view that a mature understanding of the nature and possible consequences of proposed medical treatment was sufficient in itself both to give the child capacity to consent and to rob the parents of the right of veto. Legislation in Scotland (the Age of Legal Capacity (Scotland) Act 1991, s.2(4)) follows the Scarman approach. Another issue which remained unresolved by the House of Lords is whether capacity to consent carries with it capacity to refuse. In subsequent cases (*Re R. (A Minor) (Medical Treatment)* [1991] 4 All E.R. 177, *Re W. (A Minor) (Medical Treatment)* [1992] 4 All E.R. 627) the Court of Appeal has held that the court can override a child's refusal or indeed can veto treatment the child wishes to consent to, all on the basis of the child's interests. Scots law would appear to take the more logical view that since the point of consent is to give the opportunity to refuse, capacity to consent includes capacity to refuse treatment: see the sheriff's decision in *Houston, Applicant*, 1996 S.C.L.R. 943.

The House of Lords in *Gillick* also held (this time by a majority of four to one) that while it was a criminal act for a male person to have sexual intercourse with a girl under the age of 16, a doctor who prescribes contraception to such a girl is not committing the offence of aiding and abetting a criminal act, so long as he or she honestly believes that his or her prescribing of contraception is necessary for the physical, emotional and mental health of the patient.

The case is of wider import than in relation to contraceptive, or other medical, treatment. Their Lordships took the opportunity to explore the very nature of the parent and child relationship, in particular the concept of "parental rights". Parental right was held to derive from parental responsibility, and to be a dwindling concept which existed only insofar as was necessary to provide the child with appropriate guidance and protection. This way of looking at the parent and child relationship was given statutory recognition in England in the Children Act 1989 and in Scotland in the Children (Scotland) Act 1995.

GRASPING THE NETTLE

Case 75: Marshall v. Southampton and South West Hampshire Area Health Authority [1986] E.C.R. 723 (European Court of Justice)

European law—Equal pay—Sex discrimination—Direct effect of directives

(See Arnull, "The Direct Effect of Directives: Grasping the Nettle" (1986) 35 I.C.L.Q. 939; Martin, "Furthering the Effectiveness of EC Directives" (1994) 43 I.C.L.Q. 26; Craig, "Directives: Direct Effect, Indirect Effect and the Construction of National Legislation" (1997) 2 Edin. L.R. 519.)

Miss Marshall worked for a Health Authority in the United Kingdom. At the age of 62 she was dismissed, since she had passed the mandatory retirement age, which was 60 for women and 65 for men. In fact, an exception had already been made for her to stay on until the age of 62. She raised an action against the Authority, claiming that the lower age for women was sex discrimination contrary to Directive 76/207. This Directive ensures equal treatment for women and men "including the conditions governing dismissal". Obviously that worked in favour of Miss Marshall, but it was balanced by Article 1(2) of the Directive which took pains to exclude social security from the Directive's ambit. The Court of Appeal referred the matter to the European Court of Justice, on the question of whether the retirement provisions were contrary to the Directive and, if so, whether Miss Marshall could rely on the directive in her claim for wrongful dismissal.

The European Court held that the retirement provisions concerned conditions of employment rather than social security and so did indeed breach the Directive. But the reason the case is important is on the question of whether it could be relied on to give direct effect. You see, Directives, according to Article 189 [now 249] of the EC Treaty, tell Member-States what aims are to be achieved, but leave the means to be decided by the Member-State. In other words, they impose obligations on Member-States, not on individuals. In this case, the time-limit had long since expired, but the U.K. Government had taken no action to equalise retirement ages—they had, in other words, failed in their obligations. The question was whether the Directive would therefore have direct effect, giving rights to individuals like Miss Marshall, which the British courts could enforce.

However, giving direct effect to this Directive could cause serious problems. Giving rights to an employee means imposing duties on the employer. In *Marshall,* this was not a problem, since the employer, the Health Authority, was an organ of the State, the same State to which the Directive had been addressed and which had failed to implement it properly. But to impose such a heavy burden on private employers because of a Directive which their own country has not implemented, and which will almost always take effect retroactively, was not acceptable.

So, the Court held that because, under Article 189, Directives bound only those Member-States to whom they were addressed, they could not impose duties on individuals, but only on their addressee, the State. At the same time individuals could rely on rights given by Directives against the State (though not against other individuals). This is the theory of the so-called "Horizontal" application of directives. (For "vertical" application of the EC Treaty itself, see *Defrenne*, **Case 62**).

This compromise is unsatisfactory in several ways. In particular, as the U.K. argued, it discriminates between the rights of State employees and those of private-sector employees. The Court's answer was that this could be avoided by correct implementation of Directives into national law.

Touché. But in *Defrenne* **(Case 62)**, Article 119 of the EC Treaty was held to bind private parties as well as the State. Given that the obligation to comply with Directives is as much a Treaty obligation as the Treaty itself, and Directives have been held to have as much binding effect as any other piece of Community legislation, can it not can be argued that the same should be true of Directives?

There is a good case against giving Directives "horizontal effect" (*i.e.* between individuals); it could create doubt about discrepancies between directives and the national legislation needed to implement them, leaving individuals unsure about their obligations. In many cases, such uncertainty will have been resolved in earlier proceedings against the national authorities, yet even with them, *Marshall* rules out the possibility of horizontal effect. The inevitable result is an uneven application of Directives.

GEORGE AND LINDA

Case 76: Grant v. Edwards
[1986] Ch. 638; [1986] 3 W.L.R. 114; [1986] 2 All E.R. 426
(Court of Appeal, England)

Property— Constructive trusts— Cohabitation

(See Sufrin, "Intention and Detriment" (1987) 50 Mod.L.R. 94; Ferguson, "Constructive Trusts: A Note of Caution" (1993) 109 L.Q.R. 114.)

It is a truth universally acknowledged that marriage is a bribe to make a housekeeper think she's a householder. Can she get her bribe without the cost?

Linda Grant's husband deserted her in 1967, leaving her with two young sons, aged two and four, to bring up alone. At about the same time, George Edwards' wife left him, taking their children (and most of their furniture) with her. So when Linda and George met they had much in common. And they got on well. Their friendship developed into a close personal relationship, and in 1968 Linda became pregnant by George. In the latter stages of her pregnancy, Linda moved, with her two sons, to a flat owned by George's brother, and on the birth of the new baby, George and Linda started looking for a house to live in together. In December 1969 such a house was purchased. Title was taken in the name of George and his brother, George explaining to Linda that it was better to leave her name off the title deeds since this would avoid complicating her divorce from her deserting husband. Linda accepted this but, particularly after returning to work in 1972 (about a year after the birth of another child and shortly after her divorce came through), she made substantial contributions to the general household expenses, in particular for the feeding and bringing up of the children. These contributions allowed George to make the mortgage payments. George and Linda's relationship broke down in 1980 and the parties separated.

Now, the greatest practical benefit that the law gives to married couples is access to the divorce court, with its almost unique power to order one party to give some of their property to the other. But, being not married to George, Linda could not divorce him and could not, therefore, seek an order for financial provision. She turned, therefore, to the common law doctrine of the common intention constructive trust. This had been developed by the House of Lords as a means of providing an equitable distribution of property between spouses in situations not covered by financial provision on divorce: see *Pettitt v. Pettitt* [1970] A.C. 777 and *Gissing v. Gissing* [1971] A.C. 886. Linda would be able to claim a share of the home in which she had lived with George and their children, if she could show a common intention between her and George, acted upon by her, that she should have a beneficial interest in the property. If she could show such an intention, equity would not allow George to deny it but would rather construct a trust to give effect to it (*i.e.* George would own the property not outright but only subject to a trust for them both, the trust obliging him to make over a share of the property to Linda).

The Court of Appeal accepted that Linda's indirect contributions to the mortgage payments evidenced both a common intention, and that she had acted upon it, and they held that she was entitled to a half interest in the house.

Cases such as this are brave attempts by the courts to use existing doctrine to achieve purposes which Parliament has not yet seen fit to achieve such as, in the present case, protection of the financial position of cohabitants. That it is more flexible than legislation is shown in the case of *Tinsley v. Milligan* [1994] 1 A.C. 340 where a constructive trust was found to arise over property lived in by a lesbian couple, even although same-sex relationships are almost entirely ignored by statute even when unmarried cohabitants are recognised. But common law remedies are clumsy and awkward to apply, as is evidenced by the high number of these cases which reach the House of Lords. The most important House of Lords case after *Grant v. Edwards* is that of *Lloyd's Bank plc v. Rosset* [1991] 1 A.C. 107, which attempted to limit the application of the constructive trust by requiring evidence of a direct financial contribution by the claimant to the purchase price of the property. *Grant* was not overruled, but it is difficult to see how the same result could have been reached after *Rosset*.

Other legal systems attempt to achieve the same end by various different means. In Canada, for example, the courts have extended the doctrine of unjustified enrichment to the economic loser in a cohabitation (see *Pettkus v. Becker* (1980) 117 D.L.R. (3rd) 257 and *Peter v. Beblow* (1993) 101 D.L.R. (4th) 621). In Australia, cohabitation is seen as a sort of joint venture, so that "profits" have to be shared (see *Muschinski v. Dodds* (1985) 160 C.L.R. 583 and *Baumgartner v. Baumgartner* (1987) 164 C.L.R. 137). And New Zealand adopts a "reasonable expectations" approach (see *Gillies v. Keogh* [1989] 2 N.Z.L.R. 327 and *Lankow v. Rose* [1995] 1 N.Z.L.R. 277). Some jurisdictions now deal with the question of financial settlement on the break up of an unmarried relationship by statute. This is the case in most Canadian provinces and Australian states, amongst others. None of the above approaches has been attempted in Scotland to give benefit to cohabitants, though the case of *Shilliday v. Smith*, 1998 S.L.T. 976

suggests that a claim for unjustified enrichment might, at least in some circumstances, work.

Case 77: Norris v. Ireland (1991) 13 E.H.R.R. 186 (European Court of Human Rights)

Human Rights—Right to private life—Homosexuality—Arts. 8 and 25, ECHR— "Victim"

(See Johnson, "A Comparison of Sexual Privacy Rights in the United States and the United Kingdom", 1992 Colum. J. Transnational L. 697)

David Norris, an academic at Trinity College, whose alumni included Oscar Wilde, was an activist for gay law reform, a renowned expert on that other great Irish dissident James Joyce, and a member of the Second Chamber of the Irish Parliament, the *Seanad Eireann*. He challenged the laws applicable in Ireland which prohibited homosexual acts in private between consenting males. He was represented in the Irish Supreme Court stage of the proceedings by Mary Robinson, later to become the first female President of the Irish Republic and, more recently, the United Nations Commissioner on Human Rights.

While Irish law did not make homosexuality *per se* a crime, a number of statutory provisions, passed in the nineteenth century by the Imperial Parliament at Westminster, did criminalise certain sexual activities. Section 61 of the Offences Against the Person Act 1861 criminalised what it called "buggery", while section 11 of the Criminal Law Amendment Act 1885 criminalised what it called "gross indecency between male persons" (*i.e.* sexual acts short of "buggery"). Notwithstanding the existence of these provisions, there had been no public prosecutions for some time except where minors had been involved or the acts were committed in public or without consent.

Norris first took his case to the Irish High Court. He argued that these provisions could no longer be regarded as law since Article 50 of the Irish Constitution stated that laws which were passed before the Constitution which were inconsistent with it, did not continue in force. He lost. On appeal to the Supreme Court, Norris argued that since Ireland had ratified the European Convention on Human Rights, its courts had to follow the European Court case of *Dudgeon v. U.K.* (1981) 3 E.H.R.R. 40, (1982) 3 E.H.R.R. 149, in which exactly the same statutory provisions (applied by the same Imperial Parliament to Northern Ireland) had been held to be contrary to the right to respect for private life as protected by Article 8 of the ECHR. His appeal was rejected on a 3-2 majority. The Chief Justice stated that the ECHR was an international agreement and could not form part of Irish law or affect the determination of questions under it until so determined by the *Oireachtas*. The Supreme Court considered the particular laws to be consistent with the Constitution and no right of privacy encompassing consensual homosexual activity could be derived from "the Christian and democratic nature of the Irish State". It is interesting to compare this finding with the US Supreme Court ruling in *Bowers v. Hardwick*, 478 U.S. 186 (1986) where, by a slim majority, that Court held that the right to privacy did not encompass a constitutionally protected "right to commit sodomy".

Norris then took his case to the European Court of Human Rights, which took a very different approach from that of both the Irish and the US Supreme Courts.

The first issue to be dealt with was title to bring the case. Under Article 25 of the ECHR a petition can only be made by a "victim", that is by a person who has suffered a violation of one of the rights set forth in the Convention. If Norris had not been prosecuted and there was little or no chance of him being prosecuted, could he really be considered to be a victim? The Irish Government argued that what Norris was seeking was an *actio popularis* or an *actio in abstracto*, neither of which was permitted under Article 25. The Court held, however, that while the risk of prosecution was minimal, there was no stated policy on the part of the authorities *not* to prosecute. The law *could* be applied if there was a change of policy. On that basis, Norris could claim to be a victim under Article 25 and so he had title to bring the case.

Article 8 is not absolute. The state is permitted to interfere with private and family life if it satisfies the conditions in Article 8(2), that is to say when the interference is in accordance with law, has one of the aims defined in the paragraph and is necessary in a democratic society (or, to put it another way, answers a pressing social need and is proportionate to the aim pursued—see *Handyside v. U.K.*, **Case 64**). The Government argued that whilst the criteria of pressing social need and proportionality were valid yardsticks for testing restrictions imposed in the interests of national security, public order or the protection of public health, they could not be applied to determine whether an interference was necessary in a democratic society for the protection of morals, since that issue was one uniquely appropriate for determination by the national authorities.

The Court held that in determining what is necessary in a democratic society, there should be an "assessment of the reality of the pressing social need implied by 'necessity'" and that every restriction imposed in this sphere must be proportionate to the legitimate aim pursued. The Court pointed out that while national authorities did have a wide margin of appreciation in moral matters, it was not unfettered. The

Irish Government was in effect seeking to draw a veil across its measures by pleading simply that they had been taken on the basis of morals. This was not acceptable to the Court.

The Irish Government did not put forward any arguments justifying the retention of the particular provisions additional to or of greater weight than those offered by the British Government in*Dudgeon v. U.K.* in attempting to justify the same statutes. In that case reference had been made to the Council of Europe's view of changing social *mores*. It was also stated that the authorities' refraining from prosecution did not display injury to moral standards in Northern Ireland or that there had been any public demand for stricter enforcement of the law. Applying this to *Norris* the Court could not accept that there was a "pressing social need" to make such acts criminal offences. While individuals who considered homosexuality immoral might be disturbed by private homosexual acts, this did not justify the application of penal sanctions.

Norris had sought damages under Article 50 in recognition of his suffering, but the court took the view that the finding of the breach of Article 8 was sufficient remedy. It had done this in*Dudgeon* but in that case a change had already occurred to Northern Ireland legislation. This was not the case with the Republic of Ireland. Homosexual acts in Ireland were not decriminalised until 1993.

The claim in *Norris* was not founded on Article 14 (prohibition of discrimination). The Court resisted for some time dealing with gay matters under Article 14, preferring to hold that, if a breach of Article 8 is found then it is unnecessary to go on to examine whether there is also unlawful discrimination. This was the Court's approach in *Dudgeon*, in *Lustig-Prean v. U.K.* [1999] I.R.L.R. 734 (the "Gays in the Military Case") and in *A.D.T. v. U.K.* [2000] 2 F.L.R. 697. Sexual orientation discrimination was finally recognised, and outlawed, by the European Court in *Da Silva Mouta v. Portugal* (2001) Fam. L.R. 2.

THE MARITAL RAPE CASE

Case 78: S. v. H.M. Advocate, 1989 S.L.T. 469
(High Court of Justiciary, Scotland)

Criminal law—Rape—Husband and wife—Art. 7, ECHR—Legal process

(See Jones, "Marital Rape", 1989 S.L.T. (Notes) 279).

Laws can change not only by statutory means, or by express judicial decision to overrule a previously settled rule of the common law, but also by the rule simply withering away as a result of fundamental changes in society. This is, however, very rare, and even rarer in the criminal than in the civil law. But an example of the phenomenon in the criminal law is the present case, dealing with the "Marital Rape Rule".

S was charged with raping E. His first line of defence was that, since he was married to E, he was immune from prosecution for her rape. No such charge had ever been brought before in relation to a husband and wife who were at the time cohabiting, though in *H.M. Advocate v. Duffy*, 1983 S.L.T. 7 and *H.M. Advocate v. Paxton*, 1985 S.L.T. 96 similar charges had been held relevant when the parties were married but separated. The lack of precedents was probably explained by the fact that prosecutors had long assumed that such a charge was irrelevant, either because a husband and wife were, in law, one person (which was never really the case in Scotland) or that a husband had dominion over his wife who had a duty, therefore, to obey. This understanding was translated into legal proposition by Baron Hume, writing in the early nineteenth century, in language typically opaque for the period. He had said that a husband "cannot himself commit a rape on his own wife, who has surrendered her person to him in that sort". What, exactly, is that supposed to mean?

Lord Mayfield, the trial judge, rejected the accused's objection to the relevancy of the charge, but granted him leave to appeal.

The High Court of Justiciary held that the validity of the view expressed by Hume depended entirely upon the reason that was said to justify it. They pointed out that if Hume meant that a woman, by marrying, consented to sexual intercourse, then this is no justification for the supposed rule since rape is an offence of violence, a type of aggravated assault, which cannot be said to have been consented to. If, on the other hand, Hume meant that a woman, by marrying, lost the right to refuse sexual intercourse because she had a duty to obey, then that justification no longer existed since the law no longer requires women to obey their husbands. Since the justification for the supposed rule has disappeared, so too has the supposed rule. The result in either case was that the rule of marital immunity to rape, if it ever had been a rule (which, in truth, was doubted by the Court) no longer existed today.

S was subsequently tried, and acquitted after a verdict of not proven.

The House of Lords followed this Scottish decision in an English case which resulted in a conviction: *R. v. R. (Rape: Marital Exemption)* [1991] 4 All E.R. 481. The so-called "marital exemption" had a firmer grounding in English law but that did not prevent the House of Lords rejecting it. The husband in this case, however, took the matter to the European Court of Human Rights, arguing that since Article 7 of the European Convention on Human Rights provides that no-one shall be found guilty on account of an act or omission which was not a criminal offence when done, the House of Lords had retrospectively and unlawfully created a new crime. In effect he was arguing that the House of Lords had deprived him of his right to rape his wife. Unsurprisingly, the European Court had little sympathy with this argument and it held (*C.R. v. U.K.; S.W. v. U.K.* [1996] 21 E.H.R.R. 363) that the progressive development of the criminal law through judicial interpretation, elucidation and adaptation to changing circumstances did not infringe Article 7.

A LOCAL STORY, FOR LOCAL PEOPLE

Case 79: Anderson v. The Beacon Fellowship, 1992 S.L.T. 111 (Outer House, Court of Session, Scotland)

Reduction of donation—Facility and circumvention—Fraud—Undue influence

What can you do if you want to get out of a contract, or if you want property back that you have given away? The short answer is nothing. A contract by definition is a legally binding agreement which, because it has been voluntarily entered into, creates an obligation which is enforceable even when a person subsequently changes his or her mind. A gift is the transference of ownership in property which, once it has taken effect, cannot be recovered. "The Moving Finger writes", the poet Fitzgerald reminds us, "and having writ moves on: nor all thy Piety nor wit shall have it back to cancel half a line, nor all thy tears wash out a word of it".

But all good rules have exceptions, otherwise the law would be both unjust and without humour. Contracts and donations can be washed out—in legal terms, reduced (*i.e.* the parties can be released from their obligations or the maker of the donation can get (what was) his or her property back) on a variety of grounds, such as fraud, nonage (the party was too young to enter into that particular legal transaction), mental incapacity or illegality (on this last, see *Morgan Guaranty*, **Case 89**). The ground that Ernest Anderson founded upon, in order to recover money that he had given away, was facility and circumvention.

Buckie, that grey little town in the north east of Scotland overlooking Spey Bay, attracts neither jet- or trend-setters, nor international travellers nor the rich and famous. It is a small isolated place, which subsists mostly through the fishing carried on by its sons. It is not easy living there; people by and large must make their own entertainment. Religious beliefs are rife. But it does have a hotel, and the hotel has a hall attached. In 1985 this hotel belonged to Mr Ernest Anderson. He, however, was not a well man. He had suffered from manic depressive illness since 1981 and, as a result of various prescribed drugs, was frequently in a state of confusion, upset and emotional vulnerability. The business suffered. He did, however, have a regular customer: the Beacon Fellowship, a religious association which maintained a pastor and elders and to which a number of local people adhered. The Fellowship hired the hall and, in due course, offered to purchase it from Mr Anderson. A price of £25,000 was agreed, entry to be on October 1, 1985. In the weeks before this date, members of the Fellowship took to visiting Mr Anderson in his times of need. It was averred that they offered to heal him of his ills. The pastor came and prayed over him, laying hands on him. The diagnosis was, it was averred, that Mr Anderson had too many worldly goods and far too much money. Money, preached the preacher, was valueless, but salvation was easy to achieve—by the renouncing of all his worldly goods Mr Anderson would be saved. And, it was averred, the Fellowship offered to make things easy for Mr Anderson—he could renounce his worldly goods by making them over to the Fellowship. Mr Anderson remained weak and vulnerable and confused. The week before October 1 he paid over to the defenders £9,000 in cash, and on October 1 (when, be it remembered, the defenders became due to pay him £25,000) he paid them a further £14,100.

Then he came to his senses, and wanted his money back.

He raised an action in the Court of Session seeking reduction of the donations he had made to the Fellowship, on the basis of facility and circumvention. His averments of facility (simplicity, suggestibility, vulnerability) were clearly relevant and could hardly be denied. The Fellowship, however, challenged the averments of circumvention. This word normally connotes fraud, that is to say deceit, and the Fellowship denied that there was anything in the pursuer's case which alleged that they had told him any lies. His case was that the Fellowship had told him that he would "achieve salvation" by giving them his property: the judge, Lord McCluskey, resisted the temptation to enter the philosophical mires of whether a statement of belief could be a lie just because it was false, or because it was irrational or ludicrous, and the practical mires of proving whether or not the members of the Fellowship actually did believe what they were (allegedly) saying to Mr Anderson. Lord McCluskey held that it did not really matter whether there was deceit or not. What was necessary was averments of pressure being put on the pursuer. For averments of undue influence are sufficient to set up a case of circumvention. He quoted Lord Blackburn in *Gibson v. Anderson*, 1925 S.L.T. 517 at 526: "It is not necessary that there should be deceit. It is enough that there should be solicitation, pressure, importunity, even in some cases, suggestion". The higher the degree of facility (and in the present case there was substantial facility) the less is required by way of circumvention.

The other point made by Lord McCluskey was that while facility and circumvention is usually pleaded against persons who are already in a confidential relationship with the pursuer, such as his or her solicitor or agent or doctor or minister, there is no strict categorisation adopted by the law and it is not a requirement that the relationship be professional or quasi-fiduciary. The factual circumstance that one party has influence over the other is enough.

In conclusion, Lord McCluskey found that the averments of facility and circumvention made by the pursuer were sufficient in law to warrant investigation, and so proof before answer was allowed. In other words, Mr Anderson was given the opportunity to prove the allegations that he made. It is not reported whether he was in the end of the day successful in getting his money back.

THE CASE OF THE SPANISH FISHERMEN

Case 80: R. v. Secretary of State for Transport,
ex parte **Factortame (No. 2)**
[1991] 1 A.C. 603; [1991] 1 All E.R. 70; [1990] E.C.R. I–2433
(European Court of Justice)

European law—Supremacy of European law—U.K. sovereignty

(See Oliver, "Fishing on the Incoming Tide" (1991) 54 Mod. L.R. 442; Wade, "Sovereignty—Revolution or Evolution?" (1996) 112 L.Q.R. 568; Allan, "Parliamentary Sovereignty: Law, Politics and Revolution" (1997) 113 L.Q.R. 443.)

It all began when experts perceived that there were less fish to fish in the Atlantic Ocean as a result of the growing number of fishing vessels on the water using modern fishing techniques. The European Community's "Blue Europe" common fisheries policy, agreed in 1983, was designed to conserve fish stock within Community waters allowing apportioned fishing quotas among the various member States. Each national quota was set according to the size, location, needs and traditional fishing grounds of each Member State's fishing fleet.

Following the accession of Spain and Portugal to the European Community in 1986, both the number of fishermen and the per capita fish consumption doubled in the Community. Quotas were accordingly fixed for the large fishing fleets of these new Member States. However, the system of separate quotas for national fishing fleets was quickly misappropriated by vessels which flew a certain Member State flag but which had no genuine link with that particular Member State. The problem arose when the Spanish fleet registered itself in Britain, and became thereby entitled to a share in the U.K. quota. To prevent this so-called "quota-hopping", the British Parliament passed the Merchant Shipping Act 1988. Under that Act, all fishing vessels were required to register anew which was a pre-condition to obtaining a license to fish under the quota permitted in the U.K. by the Community's common fisheries policy. However, in order to do so, all owners and operators of vessels had to satisfy conditions of British nationality, domicile and residence. That legislation would have the effect of disqualifying 95 Spanish boats from fishing from British ports. Factortame Ltd operated one of these boats and, together with other companies, they challenged the U.K. legislation.

The companies first requested judicial review of the refusal of the Secretary of State, in accordance with the Act, to re-register their Spanish controlled boats. They challenged the conditions for registration as being in breach of Article 52 EC (now 43) on freedom of establishment and Article 6 EC [now 12] on prohibition of discrimination on grounds of nationality. The Divisional Court ([1989] 2 C.M.L.R. 353) made a reference to the European Court of Justice under Article 177 EC [now 234] for a preliminary ruling on the proper interpretation of, among other things, Article 52 EC [now 43]. In the meantime, Factortame sought interim relief until such time as final judgment was given. The interim order made by the Divisional Court was appealed to the House of Lords, which held ([1990] 2 A.C. 85) that such an order could not be granted against the Crown. Indeed two rules of English law prevailed: (i) common law rules prohibit the grant of an interim injunction against the Crown and (ii) there is a presumption that an Act of Parliament is in conformity with community law until the European Court of Justice decides otherwise. The House of Lords, however, found it necessary to make a second reference to the ECJ under Article 177 to ascertain whether these procedural rules of English law should be set aside in the view of putative Community rights. In essence, the question referred concerned the extent of U.K. Parliamentary sovereignty.

The ECJ concentrated on the requirement of effectiveness of EC law and the obligation of national courts under Article 5 EC (now 10) to ensure its observance by setting aside procedural rules and principles of national law—even where the national jurisdictional limitations are of a constitutional nature. However, the Court gave the right for the House of Lords to specify the conditions under which a national remedy such as interim relief should be granted in a particular case in accordance with national principle. It made clear that a national rule, which prohibited absolutely the grant of interim relief, would contradict the principle of effectiveness.

By drawing on the idea of effectiveness, the ECJ articulated the fundamental principle of supremacy of Community law over national law. This decision has a particularly important impact in the constitutional order of the United Kingdom. With this sole decision, the

European judges limited parliamentary sovereignty, striking down the fundamental and historical principle on which British democracy is said to stand.

The substantive issues of *Factortame* could now be answered. The ECJ held that the nationality, residence and domicile provisions of section 14 of the Merchant Shipping Act 1988, even as amended following the Court's interim order, were contrary to Community law. As a consequence of this decision the fishermen affected by the discriminatory provisions of the 1988 Act raised an action for damages against the U.K. government for its failure to respect Community law. The High Court referred the matter (once more) to the European Court of Justice, which clarified its position on State liability ([1996] E.C.R. I-1029). Ultimately, it was held that compensatory damages were payable by the British Government to the Spanish fishermen.

THE ORKNEY "CHILD ABUSE" CASE

Case 81: Sloan v. B., 1991 S.C. 412; 1991 S.L.T. 530
(Inner House, Court of Session, Scotland)

Children's hearings—Exclusion of children—Flawed application to sheriff—Admission of press

(See Thomson, "*Sloan v. B.*: The Legal Issues", 1991 S.L.T. (News) 421; Sutherland, "The Orkney Case", 1992 J.R. 93; Norrie, "Excluding Children from Children's Hearings", 1993 S.L.T. (News) 67)

The Maid of Norway died in St Margaret's Hope, South Ronaldsay. So too, 701 years later, did the unquestioned approval that the Scottish Children's Hearing system had hitherto enjoyed. This system is the process whereby children who have committed criminal offences and children who have been the victims of abuse, neglect and other forms of bad upbringing are dealt with by a panel of lay persons trained in a welfarist philosophy which eschews punishment in favour of trying to effect change for the better in the child's life. Any system operated by people is subject to human error, but it was believed that the system itself was nearly foolproof in the procedural protections it afforded those who appeared before it. Until this case.

Early on a cold and (at that latitude) dark morning on February 27, 1991, representatives of the Orkney Social Work department visited four families who lived in and around St Margaret's Hope. They had warrants for the immediate removal of nine named children, aged between eight and 15 years, from these families. Policemen accompanied the social workers. The parents, and the children, attempted to resist, but to no avail. The children were taken to the mainland, where they were boarded at great distances both from their homes and from each other. The social workers were responding to concerns which they had developed as a result of on-going work with another family, members of which had implicated the St Margaret's Hope families. Allegations were made that the children were being subjected to serious abuse of a sexual and ritualistic nature, occurring in open fields and in a quarry, and overseen by the local Church of Scotland minister, dressed in a cloak and carrying a satanic staff. Had there been the least truth to these allegations then the children were most certainly at risk and the social workers were most certainly justified in acting to protect them. The problem was that there was no truth whatsoever to the allegations.

Children who are removed from home under the emergency provisions need to be brought shortly thereafter to a children's hearing, at which "grounds of referral" (that is to say the grounds for concern, laid down in what is now section 52 of the Children (Scotland) Act 1995) are put to both the child and his or her parents. The hearing has no jurisdiction to resolve disputes of fact relating to grounds of referral, and if they are disputed, or not understood by the child, the case will be referred to the sheriff for proof. If after proof the grounds are found established, or if the grounds were accepted by the parents and child, the hearing goes on to consider the case, and decide the outcome based on the best interests of the child. On March 5, 1991 the children's hearing was convened, the parents denied the grounds, and the matter was sent to the sheriff for proof. But where were the children? An earlier, informal, meeting of the members of the children's hearing had decided to dispense with the presence of the children on the grounds that meeting their parents in the circumstances of a hearing which was likely to be fraught would be against their interests, *and* that the children did not understand the grounds of referral. The statute (then the Social Work (Scotland) Act 1968) permitted the hearing to dispense with the presence of the child from the consideration of his or her case for the former reason; a referral to the sheriff was statutorily required if the latter reason existed.

On April 4, 1991 Sheriff Kelbie rejected the application for proof as incompetent. He pointed out that the statute required that the grounds of referral be explained to the children and that "thereafter" if the grounds are denied or not understood an application can be made to the sheriff. He interpreted this as imposing a requirement to explain the grounds to the children before deciding whether to send the matter to the sheriff. Since that had not been done in the present case, the application was incompetent. He also pointed out that the decision by the hearing that the children did not understand the grounds was meaningless and false since they had never seen the children to check their level of understanding, and at least one of the children was 15 years of age. In addition, in the presence of the press which he had invited into his chambers for the purposes of reading his judgment, he explained that he had seen the productions which would be led in evidence and severely criticised the manner in which the children had been interviewed in order to obtain the evidence: it was, he said, "repeated coaching" by interviewers that obtained responses from the children which would be used in evidence against their parents. He ordered the children's immediate release and, to great public rejoicing (for the parents had known how to get the press on their side, and had utilised this knowledge), reunions between parents and children took place later that day.

The reporter appealed to the Court of Session, though at the same time announced that he would be taking no further action in respect of the instant case. The Court of Session agreed to hear the appeal, though technically moot, because of its great importance to the Scottish system for child protection. The sheriff was overruled.

First, the Court held that it was not open to the sheriff to dismiss an application on the ground of incompetency unless it was based on an irregularity that could not be corrected. Secondly, the statutory requirement for the children's presence when the grounds of referral were being explained was dismissed as a mere technicality, not necessary when there would be no prejudice: there would be no prejudice in the present case since the matter was going to the sheriff in any case as the parents were denying the grounds of referral. Thirdly, the sheriff was not entitled to criticise the hearing's assessment of the children's competency to understand since that was a matter in the sole discretion of the hearing. Fourthly, he was wrong to express views on the productions before they had been led in evidence. The only thing he got right, according to the First Division, was in exercising his discretion to allow the press into his chambers. In addition, the Court held that the preliminary meeting of the hearing to dispense with the presence of the children was competent although it had no statutory basis.

In fact, the First Division was wrong on almost all counts. A child should attend a children's hearing because it is the *children's* hearing; it is impossible to know whether the case has to be sent to the sheriff until after the grounds have been explained, and therefore it is impossible to know whether the decision to exclude the child is competent until after the child has been excluded; to permit the children's hearing to assess a child's understanding without them ever seeing the child is, at least in the case of older children, simply ludicrous.

The vocal public concern over the whole affair led to a public enquiry, under the chairmanship of Lord Clyde (see Clyde, "Orkney Revisited: The Process of Inquiry", 1993 J.R. 229). His report was the basis of many of the changes in the law contained in the Children (Scotland) Act 1995. It is made plain there that children have an absolute right to attend their own children's hearing, and that the chairman of the hearing must explain the grounds of referral to the child and cannot avoid this by dispensing with the child's presence. "Business meetings", *i.e.* the sort of preliminary meeting to discuss procedural matters that had taken place in Orkney, were put on a statutory basis. And most importantly, the whole procedure for emergency removal of children was overhauled from top to bottom.

This is a disturbing case. Every agency involved, from the social workers on the ground, through the reporter, the hearing, the sheriff and up to the Court of Session itself, made mistakes. And children suffered, unsurprisingly, thereby. However, in many respects a worse case was the far less well-known one of *L., Petitioners*, 1993 S.L.T. 1310 and 1342 where children were kept away from their parents for some years (and the parents were not sufficiently articulate to mobilise the press on their behalves). There, no-one made mistakes in the application of the law. The system worked precisely as it was designed to do. But children were wrongly removed and the Court of Session had to invent a procedure for restoring the children to their parents (also now put on a statutory basis in the 1995 Act).

There is still strong support for and pride concerning the children's hearing system in Scotland. But as a result of the Orkney case that support can no longer be taken for granted. And that is as it should be.

THE HILLSBOROUGH DISASTER CASE

Case 82: Alcock and others v. Chief Constable, South Yorkshire Police
[1992] 1 A.C. 310; [1991] 4 All E.R. 907; [1991] 3 W.L.R. 1057
(House of Lords, England)

Delict—Negligence—Nervous shock

(See Lynch, "Nervous Shock Reconsidered" (1992) 108 L.Q.R. 367; Nasir, "Nervous Shock and *Alcock*: the Judicial Buck Stops Here" (1992) 55 Mod. L.R. 705.)

This litigation arose from the disaster at Hillsborough Stadium, Sheffield on the April 15, 1989. What was supposed to be a celebration of football in an FA Cup semi-final between Liverpool and Nottingham Forest developed into arguably British football's darkest day. The South Yorkshire Police were responsible for crowd control at the match, and in particular for supervising the admission of the Liverpool fans into the end reserved for them to watch the match—the Leppings Lane end. An excessive number of Liverpool fans were admitted and as a result the fans were crammed into the lower stand. In the resulting melee, 95 people were crushed to death and over 400 were physically injured. The game had already started as fans began to try to escape the carnage over the high mesh fencing enclosing them and separating them from the pitch. The match was being broadcast live on TV and scenes of the disaster were relayed to homes throughout Britain. A number of temporary morgues were set up at the ground and in the city to deal with the number of dead.

Now, this case was set in the context of the development of medical science and expertise in diagnosing a variety of forms of psychiatric illness, most notably post traumatic stress disorder (PTSD) and the law had also began to be less reticent in its willingness to accept "nervous shock" claims (the generic legal terminology for psychiatric illness claims), as evidenced in *McLoughlin v. O'Brien* [1983] 1 A.C. 410. However, in negligence law, the House of Lords was also taking steps to limit potential liability, conscious of the fear of the floodgates of litigation opening up.

In *Alcock*, 16 related actions by friends and relatives who suffered psychiatric illness as a result of "witnessing" the death of a loved one at the disaster made claims against the Chief Constable for nervous shock. At the outset it should be noted that the Chief Constable admitted the negligence of his force in supervising the crowd (*The Sun* newspaper has never been forgiven in Merseyside for originally blaming the incident on the loutish behaviour of the Liverpool supporters) but denied liability on the basis that he did not owe a duty of care to any of the particular plaintiffs to avoid causing them the particular injury (nervous shock) they were suing for. The House of Lords, expanding on the earlier case of *McLoughlin*, set out three criteria which need to be satisfied for a duty of care to be owed to a witness, or "secondary victim" to adopt legal terminology. First, the relationship between the person killed or injured and the secondary victim must be one of a "close tie of love and affection", and this would require to be proven in every case, although it would be presumed in parent/child and husband/wife relationships. The second and third criteria are related and require "proximity", *i.e.* the plaintiff has to be present at the accident or its immediate aftermath and have directly seen or heard of the accident or its immediate aftermath. These requirements are designed to limit the number of potential claimants and in this case none of the plaintiffs could succeed in overcoming all three obstacles. In one case a brother-in-law relationship did not satisfy the first test, whilst in others, "mere" attendance at the morgue to identify loved ones some nine hours after the disaster even where the plaintiff had witnessed or heard the disaster on TV or radio was insufficient as broadcasting ethics prevented the depiction of suffering of recognisable individuals.

The outcome in *Alcock* has been widely castigated although it was perhaps inevitable as the law in this area developed away from a straightforward reasonable foreseeability test. It certainly limited the possibility for secondary victims to sue in respect of their nervous shock, although it is widely accepted that the subsequent decision by the Inner House in *Robertson v. Forth Road Bridge Joint Board*, 1996 S.L.T. 263 is an over-strict application of *Alcock*. In that case, a fellow-employee was held unable to recover after witnessing his colleague falling out of a van and over the Forth Road Bridge as a twenty-year friendship was held not to amount to "a close tie of love and affection". In *Page v. Smith* [1995] 2 All E.R. 736 the House of Lords attempted to make a clear distinction between secondary victims, who would require to satisfy the criteria in *Alcock*, and primary victims who suffered nervous shock as a result of being in the "zone of physical danger" who would require only to satisfy the traditional test that some form of physical injury was reasonably foreseeable due to their proximity or active involvement in the incident (as in the older Scottish case of *Gilligan v. Robb*, 1910 S.C. 395, where the pursuer was confronted by a cow in her tenement close in Glasgow). As a result plaintiffs generally now attempt to portray themselves in the first instance as primary victims. This was the position in another important case in this area, also arising out of the Hillsborough disaster, *White v. Chief Constable, South Yorkshire* [1999] 1 All E.R. 1 in which a number of police officers involved in the disaster sued their Chief Constable in respect of nervous shock. The House of Lords, by a majority of 3–2 held that as the officers were not in the zone of physical danger they could not recover as primary victims (or rescuers even), and as none of them had a close tie of love and affection with the dead and injured they could not satisfy the *Alcock* criteria. Lord Steyn noted, with clear reference to *Alcock*, the sensitivities involved when he noted that the "claims of the police on our sympathy, and the justice of the case, were great, but not as great as that of others to whom the law denied redress". For policemen to receive damages for nervous shock caused by the police when relatives of the dead received nothing would be an impossible result to defend.

Cases arising from the disaster are still being decided, the most notable recently being the nurse who sued successfully on the basis that she was in the zone of physical danger as she feared for her life where she tended for the dying at the stadium. However, as Lord Reed noted in a recent Scottish "nervous shock" case (*Campbell v. North Lanarkshire Council*, 2000 S.C.L.R. 373), this area of law, as developed following the Hillsborough disaster, raises "difficult legal questions which turn on subtle, not to say tenuous, distinctions; between, for example, physical injury and psychiatric injury; primary victims and secondary victims; rescuers and bystanders; close ties of love and affection, and less close relationships." The House of Lords in *White* came close to accepting that the law in this area is beyond redemption.

TILTING AT TRIANGLES

Case 83: West v. Secretary of State for Scotland
1992 S.C. 385; 1992 S.L.T. 636
(Inner House, Court of Session, Scotland)

Administrative law—Judicial review—Scope of Court's supervisory jurisdiction

(See Himsworth, "Public Employment, The Supervisory Jurisdiction and Points *West*", 1992 S.L.T. (News) 257; Finnie, "Triangles as Touchstones of Review", 1993 S.L.T. (News) 51.)

Mr West was a prison officer. The terms of his conditions of employment meant that he could be transferred to any prison in Scotland. The reimbursement of the costs of moving house was at the discretion of the Scottish Prison Service. He was transferred from the Young Offenders Institution in Polmont to Saughton Prison in Edinburgh, but the prison service decided not to pay his removal expenses. He applied for judicial review contending that the decision was an unreasonable exercise of the discretion available to the department.

The importance of the case lies not in Mr West's plight but in the fact that Lord President Hope used the case as an opportunity to make a definitive statement on the availability of judicial review in Scots law and to clear up certain difficulties which had crept into judgments of the Scottish courts because of the influence of decisions of the English courts.

Lord Hope traced the development of the supervisory jurisdiction of the Court of Session from its institution in 1532, through its increased importance following the abolition of the Scots Privy Council in 1708 up to the introduction of the new procedure for judicial review in 1985 (Rule of Court 260B, now Rules of the Court of Session 1994, chap. 58). He concluded that the Court of Session has power, in the exercise of its supervisory jurisdiction, to regulate the process by which decisions are taken by any person or body to whom a jurisdiction, power or authority has been delegated or entrusted by statute or agreement; the purpose of the exercise of the supervisory jurisdiction is to ensure that the decision-maker does not exceed, abuse, or fail to exercise, his or her jurisdiction, power or authority; that cases where the exercise of the supervisory jurisdiction is appropriate involve a tripartite relationship which is constituted by the conferring, either by statute or private contract, of a decision-making power or duty on a third party to whom the taking of the decision is entrusted. So contractual rights and obligations, such as those between employer and employee, are not as such amenable to judicial review as the relationship involved is normally bipartite rather than tripartite.

He went on to say that to describe the supervisory jurisdiction as a public law remedy and to look for an element of public law as the test of whether it is available was to introduce concepts which had had no part in the development of the supervisory jurisdiction in Scotland over the last two centuries. The competency of an application for judicial review does not depend, as it does in England, upon a distinction between public law and private law. Nevertheless, there is no substantial difference between Scots law and English law as to the grounds on which the decision-making process may be open to judicial review. So reference may be made to English cases to decide whether there has been an excess or abuse of power.

Turning back to the facts of Mr West's case, Lord Hope said that he could find no element of a tripartite relationship. It was simply a case of a dispute between an employer and employee about the latter's conditions of employment, and as such Mr West's petition for judicial review was incompetent. So he did not get his removal expenses.

Although Lord Hope's judgment has made it clear that a public law element is not necessary in applications for judicial review in Scottish courts, the introduction of the tripartite test has caused some confusion and has led to some ingenious attempts to find a tripartite element in contractual relationships: see *Naik v. University of Stirling*, 1994 S.L.T. 449; *Blair v. Lochaber District Council*, 1995 S.L.T. 407; *Roonery v. Chief Constable, Strathclyde Police*, 1997 S.L.T. 1261.

ANOTHER DAY, ANOTHER DOLLAR

Case 84: CIN Properties Ltd v. Dollar Land (Cumbernauld) Ltd
1992 S.C. (H.L.) 102; 1992 S.L.T. 669
Cumbernauld & Kilsyth District Council v. Dollar Land (Cumbernauld) Ltd
1993 S.C. (H.L.) 44; 1993 S.L.T. 1318 (H.L.)
Dollar Land (Cumbernauld) Ltd v. CIN Properties Ltd
1998 S.C. (H.L.) 90; 1998 S.L.T. 992
(House of Lords, Scotland x. 3)

Landlord and tenant—Leasehold irritancy—Public right of way—Unjustified enrichment

After the Second World War, the housing shortage in the main Scottish cities was alleviated by the creation of five New Towns, of which Cumbernauld was one. In each case a Development Corporation was set up to oversee the development and growth of the New Towns, until the late 1980s when their functions were transferred to the local district councils, in Cumbernauld's case Cumbernauld and Kilsyth District Council.

The design of Cumbernauld Town Centre was very modern, mainly following the lines of development popularised by the French architect Le Corbusier. The fact that he designed for rather more benign climatic conditions than those pertaining in North Lanarkshire did not unduly bother the Development Corporation, which liked the idea that pedestrians and vehicles were kept strictly apart, the former moving through the town centre by means of overhead passageways. The town centre appeared in a rather good light in the film *Gregory's Girl*, and it attracted many architectural awards (the kiss of death to any development, as any cynic will tell you). After that, the story is one of deterioration of buildings, vandalism, and non-occupancy of property.

But in the 1970s, Cumbernauld was the place to be. As part of its strategy for the development of the town centre, the Development Corporation granted in 1979 a "Head Lease" to CIN Properties, under which CIN Properties would provide finance for the building of a shopping centre, in return for paying a nominal rent. CIN then subleased the development back to the Corporation, to rent out individual units to retailers (that rent being shared between the Corporation and CIN). In 1987 the Corporation sold their interest in the sublease to a company called Dollar Land (Cumbernauld) Ltd. Dollar Land probably congratulated themselves on a business coup, but the deal was to cost them dear, including the expenses of regular trips to the House of Lords accompanied by a coven of solicitors and advocates.

Their first mistake was, for some reason, to fail to pay the rent due under the sublease to CIN. In July 1988 Dollar Land sent a cheque to CIN for rent due in May, and then stopped the cheque. The next rent was due in November 1988 and that too was not paid. So on December 15, CIN wrote to Dollar Land demanding payment and informing them that "the lease ... may be terminated". Dollar Land may have read this as a threat to terminate the lease in the future, but in fact in Scots law a lease may be "irritated" (*i.e.* brought to an end by the innocent party) at any time if the conditions of the lease are not implemented to the letter. There is no significant body of Scottish commercial leasehold law, unlike in England where leases are governed by various Landlord and Tenant Acts. Put shortly, if you don't pay on time your leasehold right is irritated and the only defence is one of oppression. This was confirmed by the House of Lords in *Dorchester Studios (Glasgow) Ltd v. Stone*, 1975 S.C. (H.L.) 56.

(The doctrine of leasehold irritancy is not to be confused with the doctrine of feudal irritancy, which is very much less strict (and in any event was made unlawful by the Abolition of Feudal Tenure etc. (Scotland) Act 2000). No such legislation has abolished leasehold irritancies, although sections 4 and 5 of the Law Reform (Miscellaneous Provisions) (Scotland) Act 1985 made the law rather less severe in the case of a tenant who is merely slightly late in paying rent.)

Back to Cumbernauld town centre. CIN raised an action for declarator of irritancy and removing against Dollar Land. Dollar Land pleaded oppression, but this was rejected, and on appeal to the House of Lords (the 1992 case listed above) the irritancy of the lease was confirmed, in the light of *Dorchester Studios*. So Dollar Land had to vacate the shopping centre.

A year later, Dollar Land was back in the House of Lords, this time defending an action by Cumbernauld and Kilsyth District Council (the successor, be it remembered, of the Development Corporation). Dollar Land had acquired a right to a pedestrianised walkway through the town centre, but they closed it at nights and at other times in order to combat vandalism. The problem was, the public had used this walkway since its completion in 1966 and a public right of way was, after 20 years of continuous usage, thereby created. By closing the walkway, Dollar Land was interfering with the public right of way and this was challenged by the District Council. Dollar Land argued that there was no public right of way since they had been merely tolerating, rather than positively permitting, public usage. The First Division held that if a landowner allowed the public to cross his land he had to make them aware by some means that he was permitting this by licence rather than recognising a right. So Dollar Land took themselves back to the House of Lords (the 1993 case listed above), arguing that public use of a way had to be ascribed to tolerance by the landowner unless the usage was adverse to the interests of the landowner. Lord Jauncey described the appeal as "hopeless" and Dollar Land's arguments as "wholly unsustainable in law". So they lost again.

Hope triumphs over even very expensive experience. Dollar Land was still smarting over the loss of their original lease, and they noticed that CIN were making large profits from renting the shops in the shopping centre. So, having been unsuccessful defenders in two actions, they thought they would try their luck as pursuers. They raised an action against CIN on the ground that the latter had been unjustifiably enriched by the irritancy and that they, Dollar Land, were entitled to recompense for the loss of rents. The Lord Ordinary dismissed the action as irrelevant and Dollar Land reclaimed to the Inner House, arguing that, even though they themselves had been in breach of their original contract of lease, CIN had been disproportionately enriched by the irritating of the lease. They lost there too, though Lord Rodger, who knows about unjustified enrichment and was shortly to become Lord

President, dissented. Perhaps it was his dissent that encouraged Dollar Land to go, once again, to the House of Lords (the 1998 case listed above). But once again they lost. The contract of lease spelled out clearly the consequences of breach of its terms, and expressly allowed for CIN to take over the properties if the rent was not paid. CIN was indeed enriched, but since that was enrichment in terms of a contract it could not be said to be unjustified.

These cases represent a stern lesson in the power of leasehold irritancies, and a powerful lesson in the costs of tangling with the law.

THE HANSARD CASE

Case 85: Pepper v. Hart
[1993] A.C. 593; [1992] 3 W.L.R. 1032
(House of Lords, England)

Legal process—Statutory interpretation—Use of Parliamentary materials as aid to interpretation—House of Lords departing from established practice

(See Bates, "Parliamentary Material and Statutory Construction: Aspects of the Practical Application of *Pepper v. Hart*", 1993 Stat. L.R. 45; Walker, "Discovering the Intention of Parliament", 1993 S.L.T. (News) 121; Steyn, "*Pepper v. Hart*: A Re-Examination" (2001) 21 O.J.L.S. 59.)

It sometimes happens, indeed with some regularity in the House of Lords, that the actual facts of a case and even the substantive point of law are entirely irrelevant to the reason why the case is important. An example is the present case (another example is *London Street Tramways*, **Case 15**), where the point of law was whether a particular employment benefit was taxable while the importance of the case lies in how the courts are to use parliamentary materials in interpreting the law.

Teachers at a fee-paying school in England (called a "public" school there) were entitled under their conditions of employment to enrol their own sons at the school and pay one fifth of the normal school fees. This financial benefit was clearly an "emolument" for tax purposes and was therefore taxable under the Finance Act 1976. A dispute arose between the taxman and the teachers as to how to assess the value to be taxed. The taxman wanted to tax the benefit at the value of the saving to the taxpayer (*i.e.* the four fifths of the school fees they did not need to pay); the teachers argued that the amount taxable was the extra expense that the school was put to in educating their children (a very small amount indeed).

Now, the primary test for identifying the meaning of words and phrases in an Act of Parliament is the intention of Parliament. What, in other words, did Parliament mean to achieve when it used these words? Normally, this question is answered by applying the obvious, everyday meaning of the words because of the fairly strong presumption that Parliament means what it says. The teachers, however, wanted the court to apply a less obvious meaning, and they claimed that they would be able to show that Parliament intended the less obvious meaning, by looking at the parliamentary papers when the Act was being passed. But they had a problem: a rule of practice had grown up that in identifying the intention of Parliament the courts could look only at the words Parliament used in the statute, and they could not, in particular, look at the parliamentary debates which led to the passing of the statute. They could not, in other words, consult the official record of Parliamentary proceedings, known as Hansard. There were a number of reasons for this rule. Some were practical, such as that many court practitioners would not have access to Hansard. Some were theoretical, such as that statements in Parliament may be made for political reasons and not necessarily reflect the will of the whole of Parliament. Some were constitutional, such as that to allow the courts to go behind the words used by Parliament would be the courts questioning actions in Parliament, contrary to the 1688 Bill of Rights which provides for the separation of state functions between the legislature, the executive and the judiciary.

The House of Lords convened a larger court than normal to explore whether the practice of non-consultation with Hansard remained appropriate. Seven judges heard the argument and six of them (the Lord Chancellor dissenting) agreed that the rule against looking at parliamentary papers in order to determine the meaning of words in Acts of Parliament should no longer be followed. They held that Hansard and other parliamentary papers could be cited to the court for this purpose if (i) the legislation is ambiguous or obscure or led to absurdity, (ii) the material relied upon was ministerial statements or such material as was necessary to understand a ministerial statement, and (iii) the statement relied upon was clear. The House of Lords found no constitutional barrier to this approach: they were not questioning proceedings in Parliament, but merely finding out the correct intention of Parliament.

Having looked at the parliamentary background papers in the present case, the House of Lords unanimously found in favour of the teachers, who therefore made a substantial tax saving.

Parliamentary intent, it should be noted, is only one of the tools of statutory interpretation. At least as important today is the requirement in section 3 of the Human Rights Act 1998 to interpret Acts of Parliament (including Acts of the Scottish Parliament), if at all possible, to be consistent with the European Convention on Human Rights. There is also the Interpretation Act 1978, which provides presumed meanings to commonly used words and phrases (which meanings can be overturned if the evidence shows that Parliament intended different meanings). And there are other aids to construction than these statutes. For example, there is a presumption with criminal law statutes that prohibitions (being limitations to freedom) should be interpreted narrowly, and a strong presumption that Parliament does not intend to create crimes of strict liability (*i.e.* crimes which can be committed without *mens rea*, or a criminal mind: see *Sweet v. Parsley*, **Case 53**). In addition there is a presumption that Parliament intends not to infringe international conventions to which this country is party, with the result that if legislation is ambiguous the interpretation which satisfies rather than infringes international conventions is to be applied by the courts: see, in relation to the ECHR, *T., Petitioner* (**Case 91**) and, in relation to the UN Convention on the Rights of the Child, *White v. White*, 2001 S.L.T. 484.

TONY BLAND'S CASE

Case 86: Airedale NHS Trust v. Bland
[1993] A.C. 789; [1993] 2 W.L.R. 316; [1993] 1 All E.R. 821
(House of Lords, England)

Medical treatment—Termination of treatment—Best interests of patient—Patient in deep coma

(See Mason and Lawrie, "Management of PVS in the British Isles", 1996 J.R. 263; Keown, "Beyond *Bland*: A Critique of the BMA Guidance on Withholding or Withdrawing Medical Treatment" (2000) 20 Leg. Stud. 66)

Anthony Bland was the last victim of the Hillsborough Football Stadium Disaster (see **Case 82**), which occurred in 1989. Caught in the crushing crowd, his lungs were punctured and the interruption of the supply of oxygen to his brain left him severely and irreversibly brain damaged. From the date of the disaster he was in what has come to be known as a persistent vegetative state (PVS), from which he had no hope of emerging. The hospital authorities sought a declaration that it would be lawful for them to discontinue his life-sustaining treatment, including the termination of ventilation, nutrition and hydration by artificial means.

    The issue before the House of Lords was whether the principle of the sanctity of life would be infringed by removing life-support treatment in such circumstances. Their Lordships held that that principle was not absolute. The doctors were not under a duty to continue with medical care which conferred no benefit on the patient. The time had come when the patient had no remaining interest in being kept alive and so the justification for doing so had disappeared. As a result, the omission to perform that which had previously been a duty (*i.e.* to attempt to keep the patient alive) was no longer unlawful.

The case is hugely important in that it addresses the issue of decision-making on behalf of adults who cannot make decisions on their own and for whom one of the options is death. There are a number of possible approaches. The matter could be left to the patient's family, or to the medical personnel treating the patient. An alternative approach, exemplified in the well-known US case *Re Quinlan*, 355 A2d 647 (1976), is to require evidence to be led of what the patient him or herself would have wanted, so allowing the court to make what is called a "substituted judgment", deciding as the patient would have. None of these approaches was accepted and unanimously the House of Lords held that the approach to be adopted was to require life and death decisions of this nature to be made by a court of law, applying the principle of the best interests of the patient. That test had previously been applied to determine whether an adult incompetent should be sterilised (*Re F. (Mental Patient: Sterilisation)* [1990] 2 A.C. 1) but its application in the present circumstances was significantly more problematical. How can a "best interests" test be applied to a patient who, effectively, has no interests? Can it ever be better for a patient to die than not to die? Why is a court of law the body best able to determine "best interests" objectively in an area such as this when there is a variety of views as to what is best? The House of Lords resolved these dilemmas by holding that the lack of any benefit in continuing treatment took away the doctor's obligation to continue with that treatment. The question was not whether it was in the interests of the patient to die, but whether it was in the interests of the patient to be given further treatment. If that correct question can be answered in the negative then life-support treatment can be withdrawn. The fact that "best interests" is necessarily a subjective judgment was dealt with by their Lordships through the assistance of the case of ***Bolam v. Friern Hospital Management Committee* (Case 41)**: if a responsible body of medical opinion are of the view that it is not in a patient's interests to continue treatment then withdrawal of that treatment is not unlawful.

A few years after this case the Court of Session in Scotland was faced with the same question in *Law Hospital NHS Trust v. Lord Advocate*, 1996 S.L.T. 848 and though procedurally the reasoning was rather different the end result was the same. Unlike the English courts, the Court of Session retains *parens patriae* jurisdiction over children and the insane, whereby it represents the Crown as natural and legal guardian of the incompetent. In making a decision about an incompetent's medical treatment the test to be applied was whether the proposed course of action was in the best interests of the patient. In the present case of a PVS patient if continuing life-support treatment could not be of any benefit to her, then there were no longer any best interests to be served by continuing it. There have been a number of subsequent English cases in which patients have been in varying degrees of PVS: declarations that it would be in the best interests of these patients to terminate treatment have been granted whenever the evidence has shown that the patient is experiencing no meaningful life: see *Frenchay Health Care NHS Trust v. S.* [1994] 2 All E.R. 403, *Re B.* [1998] 1 F.L.R. 411, and *Re H. (Adult: Incompetent)* [1998] 2 F.L.R. 36. A similar case from New Zealand, though one in which the patient retained some brain function, is *Auckland AHB v. Attorney General* [1993] 1 N.Z.L.R. 235.

SPANNER

Case 87: R. v. Brown
[1994] 1 A.C. 212; [1993] 3 All E.R. 75; [1993] 2 W.L.R. 556
Laskey, Jaggard and Brown v. U.K. (1997) 24 E.H.R.R. 39
(House of Lords, England; European Court of Human Rights)

Criminal law—Causing actual bodily harm—Consent—Human Rights—Right to private life—Art. 8, ECHR

(See Giles, "*R. v. Brown*: Consensual Harm and the Public Interest" (1994) 57 Mod. L.R. 101; Bamforth, "Sado-Masochism and Consent" [1994] Crim. L.R. 661; "*Laskey v. U.K.*: Learning the Limits of Privacy" (1998) 61 Mod. L.R. 77.)

There really is no accounting for taste. Many people find it astounding that others take pleasure in watching boxing, or foxhunting, or that people are willing to take part in these activities. Human kind would, of course, be irredeemably dull if we all liked the same things, but while some differences in taste are readily understandable and acceptable, others are far less so. This is especially the case when the taste involves matters sexual.

Most people, given the choice, would rather have a nice cup of tea than have their genitals rubbed with stinging nettles, or their nipples branded with hot irons, or their penises nailed to benches. But, surprising though it may seem, not everyone would take the tea. In the town of Bolton there had been in existence for some years a group of men, some fifty strong, who enjoyed doing and having done to them the activities described above, and far more besides. They were sadomasochists who willingly and indeed enthusiastically participated in the commission of such acts against each other, all for sexual gratification. There are many descriptions one could come up with in judging the morality, decency or even the common sense of these acts, but the question that the present case concerned itself with was: were the acts criminal?

None of the men complained to the police. None was forced to take part. All were of an age when they could consent to sexual acts. No act was done in public. However, as part of the complete sexual experience offered by these men to each other, videos were taken of the activities which, quite accidentally, fell into the hands of the police. They passed the videos to the Director of Public Prosecutions, who prosecuted seven of the men on a charge of causing actual bodily harm. Now, the difficulty was that the prosecution could not establish lack of consent. Quite the reverse, for the men were willing and enthusiastic participants in the activities. Nevertheless, they were convicted and sentenced to lengthy terms of imprisonment. On appeal to the Court of Appeal and then to the House of Lords, the convictions were upheld.

This case is not the first time that such an issue has arisen. Courts have long held that there are certain crimes which are not defensible merely by pleading consent. Euthanasia remains murder, notwithstanding the consent of the "victim". There is established authority that assault for sexual pleasure is not innocuous because of consent (*R. v. Donovan* [1934] 2 K.B. 498, where a man paid a woman to allow herself to be "spanked", and the court held that her consent would not prevent a charge of assault). A slight variant is the Scottish decision in *Smart v. H.M. Advocate*, 1975 S.L.T. 65, the "square-go" case, where two men agreed to fight each other and that agreement was held to provide no defence to a charge of assault by one against the other. In neither case was the consent so readily given as here. Both involved some public disturbance (street prostitution and street fighting) which was entirely absent here: in the present case a much stronger argument could be made that what went on was a matter of private choice in which the state had no interest. And yet the decision went the same way as in the earlier cases.

The House of Lords held, though by a slim majority, that while lack of consent was an essential element to the common law crime of assault, it was not essential to the crime that the men had been charged with. They had been prosecuted under the Offences Against the Persons Act 1861, where the crime was merely causing actual bodily harm, which had been shown: consent was not relevant to the existence or otherwise of "bodily harm". There might be a defence, the Court held, if there was good reason to cause the injury, such as for example in contact sport or in surgery, but the satisfaction of sado-masochistic sexual desires did not constitute good reason. Lord Mustil dissented on the ground that the activities in question were to be judged by the standards of private morality rather than by the criminal law, and he suggested that there was no public interest to be furthered in prosecuting these men. He could not see where to draw the line between "rough play" and criminal injury. Lord Slynn agreed with him, but the other three judges, though declaiming any role in judging morality, held that the activities were clearly criminal.

The men complained to the European Court of Human Rights, arguing that their convictions amounted to a breach of their right to respect for their private lives, as protected by Article 8 of the European Convention on Human Rights. The Court held that not every sexual activity carried out in private falls within Article 8, though they accepted that sexual orientation and activity concern an intimate aspect of private life. They doubted whether there really was "private life" in a case involving a group of 50 men who advertised what they did and invited new participants, but since the matter had not been disputed they accepted for the sake of argument that the convictions amounted to an infringement of private life. The question was whether that infringement was justified under Article 8(2) which allows interference with family life if this is necessary in a democratic society for the protection of public health and/or public morals.

Following well-established case law (see especially *Handyside v. U.K.*, **Case 64**), the Court held that "necessity" implies a pressing social need and that it must be proportionate to the legitimate aim pursued. They accepted that the state may legitimately control harmful activities, even when these activities are sexual, and they held that it was for the state to balance the extent to which interference was justified by the legitimate aim of the protection of health. So the men's convictions could not be said to be a breach of Article 8. The Court refused to decide, as being unnecessary, whether protection of morals was a further legitimate aim. It is interesting to note that all the domestic judges explicitly denied that they were judging the morals of the men involved, and the European Court explicitly refused to do so, notwithstanding that "protection of morals" is expressly mentioned in Article 8(2). Courts, domestic and international, have lost their appetite for giving "moral" leadership. Yet a moral judgment was undoubtedly made here by the judges. There is nothing inherently unlawful in putting oneself in danger. Indeed, the stunt man, the astronaut, the man—or woman—who climbs Everest is hailed as Hero. Why is it that exposing oneself to danger, or exploring the limits of one's own endurance, renders one a hero in one context and a criminal in another? The answer is that heroes, by definition, are asexual. In the present case the activities of the accused outraged the judges' sense of sexual decency and propriety and that is what turned the acts without victims, in any realistic sense of the word, into crimes.

DISREPUTABLE HABITS

Case 88: Kamperman v. MacIver
1994 S.C. 230; 1994 S.L.T. 763; 1994 S.C.L.R. 380
(Inner House, Court of Session, Scotland)

Marriage—Irregular marriage—Cohabitation with habit and repute—Succession

(See Norrie, "A Habit that Brings Scots Law into Disrepute" (2000) 5 S.L.P.Q. 301).

Scotland, bizarrely, continues to recognise not only those marriages that are conducted in accordance with the civil procedures laid down by the Marriage (Scotland) Act 1977, but also those which come into existence by the application of the old common law doctrine known as "marriage by cohabitation with habit and repute". Originally Scots law recognised three forms of "irregular marriage" (the irregularity lying only in the constitution and not in the consequences of the marriage, which is entirely valid for all purposes): (i) marriage by consent *de praesenti*, under which a couple would be married merely by their exchange of present consent to be married; (ii) marriage by promise *subsequente copula*, under which a man became married to a woman the moment he achieved sexual penetration, if that was permitted by the woman solely on the basis of his promise to marry her; and (iii) marriage by cohabitation with habit and repute. The Marriage (Scotland) Act 1939 abolished the first two methods of getting married, but retained the third. The Scottish Executive, at the beginning of the Third Millennium and for no good reason, has determined again to retain this method.

The basic requirements for this method of getting married is for a couple who have capacity to marry each other to live together as if they were married and for a general repute to exist that they are indeed married. The theory is that marriage requires both the mental element of consenting to be married and an outward or factual element; that the latter is usually constituted by a marriage ceremony but that it may be constituted by living together in circumstances in which a general repute holds the parties to be married; and that this repute creates a (rebuttable) presumption that the necessary consents have been exchanged. It is not required that the repute be universal—merely that it be general. It is required that the cohabitation be for a "considerable period", a phrase deliberately kept vague, though in *Shaw v. Henderson*, 1982 S.L.T. 211 a period of 10 months and 23 days was held in the Outer House to be sufficient. The present case was a typical irregular marriage case, though with one speciality.

Mrs Lillian Kamperman and Mr James Jackson fell in love. They wanted to have sex. Unfortunately, they were both married to other people. Nevertheless, they started to live together in May 1984. Mrs Kamperman was divorced in February 1986 and Mr Jackson was divorced in February 1989, from which moment they were free to marry each other. But the point is that they didn't. Seven months later, Mr Jackson died. Mrs Kamperman, wishing to succeed to the man's property, sought declarator that they were married by cohabitation with habit and repute. For under the law of succession, widows receive a generous portion of a deceased's estate, while paramours receive nothing. The issue for decision in the part of the case that is reported was whether there had been sufficient cohabitation. While the parties had lived together in fact for five years, they had only lived together while free to marry for seven months: the question to be decided was whether the whole period or only the latter period counted. In the Outer House, it was held that the "considerable period" of cohabitation was required at a time the parties were free to marry, and that seven months was not "considerable". However, this was reversed on appeal. The Inner House held that cohabitation for the purposes of the doctrine was a matter of fact and that the important issue was the nature of the cohabitation. Mrs Kamperman and Mr Jackson had in fact lived together as husband and wife for five years, even although for most of that period they could not lawfully marry. So the first instance judge was overruled, and Mrs Kamperman given the opportunity to prove her case.

The doctrine is typically regarded as part of the law of marriage, yet in reality it is an aspect of the law of succession. What is happening in the vast majority of cases is that a cohabitant, on the death of their partner, is informed that she or he has no claim to any portion of the estate; but that the law will grant a claim if she or he can prove that they had tacitly agreed to be married (even although they never went through the ceremony of marriage) and that they were generally reputed to be married. In other words, the law is attempting to ameliorate the harsh and unfair position that cohabitants would otherwise find themselves in. Of the cases in the 1990s, the defenders were executors or heirs on intestacy in *Mullen v. Mullen*, 1991 S.L.T. 205, *Donnelly v. Donnelly's Exr*, 1992 S.L.T. 13, *Gow v. Lord Advocate*, 1993 S.L.T. 275, and in the present case of *Kamperman*. In only two, *Dewar v. Dewar*, 1995 S.L.T. 467 and *Walker v. Roberts*, 1998 S.L.T. 1133, was the dispute between the cohabitants themselves at the end of their relationship (in *Dewar* the claim was for aliment and in *Walker* the claim was for financial provision on divorce). This is the reality of these claims. They are, however, successful or unsuccessful on the basis of facts irrelevant to the real issue, which is whether it is fair, just and reasonable that one person should have a claim out of the estate of another, or whether it is reasonable to assume that the deceased would have wanted a portion of the estate to go to the surviving partner. Whether the parties' acquaintances believed them married or not may be one small element in the reasonableness of the claim, but it can hardly be determining. The doctrine is a clumsy and unfair method of ameliorating the effects of tying in financial benefits to the status of marriage rather than to the realities of the relationship between parties. It gives benefits to those who hide the truth, and denies the benefit to those who are open and honest. The existence of this doctrine bring the law into disrepute and ought to have no place in a modern legal system.

A COMEDY OF ERRORS

Case 89: Morgan Guaranty Trust Co of New York v. Lothian Regional Council
1995 S.C. 151; 1995 S.L.T. 299; 1995 S.C.L.R. 225
(Inner House, Court of Session, Scotland)

Unjustified enrichment—Condictio indebiti—Error of law—Illegal contract—Precedent—Court of Five Judges

(See Evans-Jones and Hellwege, "Swaps, Errors of Law and Unjustified Enrichment" (1995) 1 S.L.P.Q. 1; Evans-Jones, "Receptions of Law, Mixed Legal Systems and the Myth of the Genius of Scots Law" (1998) 114 L.Q.R. 228.)

This is one of those cases in which the basic facts are fairly straightforward but in which the law appears to be unnecessarily complicated. Luckily, the judges recognised the complications and consciously set out to simplify the law. It is also one of those cases in which a layperson, hearing the facts, would think the solution to be obvious (rather like one of the cases cited in the Opinions here— *Woolwich Equitable Building Society v. Inland Revenue* [1993] A.C. 70, in which the Building Society tried to recover monies it had paid to the Inland Revenue as a result of demands from the taxman but which were not, in fact, due. Why did we need the House of Lords to say that yes, of course, the money should be repaid?) But the problem is that rules of law developed to reflect equity and justice in one factual situation may not be so reflective of what is right in even a slightly different scenario (see also *Lord Advocate v. Royal Bank of Scotland*, **Case 65**). If a rule of law is binding on a court which, for equitable reasons wants to avoid it, then judges are all too often tempted to bend and contort the law to suit the individual circumstances. Over the years, decades and sometimes, as this case shows, centuries, the contortions of the contortions multiply the complications so that the justice of the layman's answer may well be obvious even to the court but the way to that answer is hidden behind a thick forest of doctrine. Welcome to the law of unjustified enrichment.

First, the facts. Lothian Regional Council entered into a complicated financial contract, known as a "swap agreement", with Morgan Guaranty, a New York bank. The contract proved lucrative for the local authority, and in just over two years it had brought them a total of over £350,000. But in 1989 swap agreements were held to be *ultra vires* of local authorities and therefore unlawful. Morgan Guaranty sought the return of the money they had already paid out.

The judge at first instance held that the loss must lie where it fell, because in an action for recovery of money paid in error, equity permits recovery only if the error is one of fact and not one of law. Here the error was one of law (the interpretation of the local authority's statutory powers). *Glasgow Corporation v. Lord Advocate*, 1959 S.C. 209, a First Division decision, had so decided and he was bound by the rules of precedent to follow this case. On appeal to the Inner House, council for Morgan Guaranty could question the equity of the rule but he could not challenge the rules of precedent. However, the Court of Session is a collegiate court (not for nothing are judges designated Senators of the College of Justice) and the whole court can be convened to overrule inconvenient precedents. A practice has grown up (as the size of the Whole Court has increased) that a Court of Five Judges can overturn a Division; a Court of Seven Judges can overturn a Court of Five, and so on. In the present case, in order to get around *Glasgow Corporation*, a Court of Five Judges was convened. The leading Opinion was delivered by the Lord President.

Lord President Hope pointed out that if a party, who has paid money in terms of a contract or a purported contract, wants his money back, he must argue under the general principle of unjustified enrichment which, in Scots law, takes three basic forms: restitution (if the pursuer is seeking the return of an item of corporeal property), repetition (if the pursuer is seeking the return of money which he or she has already paid over) and recompense (which is a sort of compensation if in some other way the defender has been enriched at the pursuer's expense). These three forms overlap to some extent with each other but all three are trying to do essentially the same thing, which is to balance the equities of a situation. Lord President Hope said that the law would be needlessly complicated if there were a limitation to one which did not apply to the others. It would lead to pursuers trying unrealistically to force their claim into one head rather than the other (as the pleading showed here). He held that the present case was clearly one of repetition, or *condictio indebiti*, as the Romans had it. The problem for the pursuer was that *Glasgow Corporation* had held that in an action for repetition (though not for recompense) payments made under an error of law could not be recovered even when the correct law said that no payments were due.

But the Court held that this limitation was illogical and, indeed, based upon a misunderstanding of the true law. The illogicality comes from the fact that the rule is based on the maxim *ignorantia juris neminem excusat*, or ignorance of the law excuses no-one. This maxim, sound in itself, had been translated into the artificial presumption that everyone knows the law. Applying this interpretation of the maxim meant that Morgan Guaranty was presumed to *know* that the contract under which they paid the money was void, with the result that they could not now complain. That might well be so if *in fact* they knew the law, but *in fact* they didn't. Lord Cullen pointed out that the purpose of the maxim was to enforce the true law against a person seeking to avoid its consequences, not to compel a person to live with the consequences of the application of bad law. But in addition, it always had been a mistake to assume that the error of law rule was a part of Scots law. An old case, *Stirling v. Earl of Lauderdale* (1733) Mor. 2930, had allowed recovery of money paid in error of law, but it was so poorly reported in *Morison's Dictionary* that when Lord Brougham was referred to it in *Dixon v. Monkland Canal Co* (1831) 5 W. & S. 445 he was able (with the help of English authority) to dismiss it as absurd. It is Lord Brougham's views that founded the decision in *Glasgow Corporation*. But in the present case, counsel located the original papers from the *Stirling* case in the Advocates' Library and proved that the statement in *Morison's Dictionary* was both accurate and well-considered by the judges. So the error of law rule had, itself, been an error all along. *Glasgow Corporation* was overruled. Morgan Guaranty recovered their money.

SECRETS AND LIES

Case 90: Re B. (Adoption Order: Jurisdiction to Set Aside) [1995] 3 All E.R. 333 (Court of Appeal, England)

Parent and Child—Adoption—Revocation of adoption order

B was born in March 1959, to an unmarried Roman Catholic woman. The birth took place in a nursing home in Manchester, to which the mother had been sent by her priest, so that she could give birth without anyone knowing. The Matron of the nursing home dealt with many cases like this. She knew people who wanted to adopt children whose mothers could not keep them.

The Matron knew of a childless couple, Mr and Mrs R, rather old to adopt perhaps, but full of love and desperate for a child. She liked them. They were good people. The baby was handed over. The court made the adoption order with the consent of the child's birth mother. He was given a stable and secure and loving upbringing. Everything worked out for the best in this best of all possible worlds.

Did that justify the secrets and lies? For the Matron had lied. Mr and Mrs R were devout and Orthodox Jews, and they wanted a Jewish child. So the Matron had had B circumcised and had told Mr and Mrs R that his father had been of Syrian Jewish stock. She knew they would not take the child otherwise. Mr and Mrs R brought B up within their community. But secrets will out. The Beth Din knew or discovered the truth when B was 9, and informed his parents. They were shocked and upset but, good people, their love for B was unaffected. They had him formally instructed into their faith and when he was 11 he was formally received into the Jewish Faith and Community. Some years later he started University, graduating in 1983 with a degree in Semitic languages and literature. His mother died in 1988, and his father in 1991.

B developed a deep interest in Israel and travelled there with a view to emigration. But he was not made welcome. He was viewed with suspicion, and accused of being an Arab and a Palestinian spy and terrorist. He was eventually asked to leave Israel. At this point, knowing that he had been adopted, he began to make enquires about his background, and he discovered more than his parents had ever known. He contacted his ex-mother, and learnt that his genetic father was an Arab from Kuwait, and a Muslim. He wanted to visit Kuwait to trace his father, but was not allowed to due to his previous travels in Israel. The political, religious and racial enmities in the Middle East had the unfortunate consequence for this young man that to the Israelis he was an Arab, and to the Arabs he was a Jew.

In these circumstances, now 35 years of age and the parents who had nurtured him and brought him up to man's estate now dead, B applied to the court for the setting aside of the adoption order. He argued that the mistake made by the applicants (Mr and Mrs R) went to the root of the adoption order. He contacted his ex-mother and persuaded her to say in the witness box that she would never have given him up if she had known that he would go to working class Jewish people, instead of nice middle-class English people. The whole adoption process, B argued, was flawed.

He failed.

The Court of Appeal held that there was no flaw. Procedurally the adoption could not be challenged. The fact that the adopters did not know the truth about the child's genetic background was irrelevant. To allow such a claim would be to undermine the whole basis of the concept of adoption, where orders are designed to be final and absolute.

But the Court did not close the door completely to the setting aside of adoption orders. It might have been different had fraud been involved, that is to say a deliberate attempt to harm the parents by deceit, rather than a well-intentioned, if rather foolish, Matron trying to do the best in the circumstances. It would be different if there were some procedural flaw, such as a failure to seek the birth mother's consent. The Scottish court had some years previously faced a similar claim in different circumstances. In *J. and J. v. C's Tutor*, 1948 S.C. 637 adoptive parents attempted to have the adoption order set aside when they discovered that, contrary to what they had been told, the child was not healthy but was, in fact, severely mentally disabled. The action was dismissed, with some contempt. Being a parent is a risk and there is no difference between becoming a parent by adoption and becoming a parent by natural means. On the other hand, an adoption order was set aside in *Re K. (Adoption and Wardship)* [1997] 2 F.L.R. 221 in which a young orphan child was rescued from the Bosnian war and brought to England. The foster carers then adopted the child but some time later, when Bosnia emerged from the chaos of tormenting war, relatives came forward to reclaim the child. This is an unusual (though not unique) case and in general it will be next to impossible to have an adoption order reduced once it has been properly made.

The Gay Adoption Case

Case 91: T., Petitioner, 1997 S.L.T. 724; 1996 S.C.L.R. 897 (Inner House, Court of Session, Scotland)

Adoption—Qualifications of adopter—Dispensing with consent—Homosexuality

(See Ross, "Attitudes to Sexual Orientation in Adoption Law" (1997) 1 Edin. L.R. 370; Norrie, "Parental Pride: Adoption and the Gay Man", 1996 S.L.T. (News) 321).

A little boy, known to the Court as "S", was born in Manchester in November 1990, sadly disabled due to his mother's taking drugs during pregnancy as treatment for her own epilepsy. His elder sister had previously been removed from the mother due to her inability to care for children, and when S himself was born he too was placed with foster carers and the search for a permanent home commenced. The mother, recognising her own utter inability to look after her children, did not object but nor did she co-operate in any way, preferring to withdraw into herself.

Due to S's fairly severe disabilities, Manchester Social Services had some difficulty in finding a suitable permanent carer for him, but towards the end of 1994 the boy was placed, in Scotland, with T, a qualified nurse who had looked after both children and adults with physical and mental disabilities. The intention of this placement was to allow T to apply to adopt S. Two years later T presented his petition to the Court of Session. No-one objected; everyone involved considered that this was best for the little boy. Everyone, that is, except the judge, Lord Gill.

The minor worry that Lord Gill had was that the mother had not expressly agreed to the adoption. Now, when a parent does not agree, the court can dispense with her or his consent if it is being withheld unreasonably. But Lord Gill pointed out that while the mother had not agreed, nor had she withheld agreement—rather she had simply refused to express any view. The Inner House had little difficult in overruling Lord Gill on this point and held that the refusal of the mother to take any part in the process could be regarded as a refusal to agree to the adoption. This issue was, however, a mere appetiser to the real point of the case.

Lord Gill drew attention to the undenied fact that T was a gay man, living with another gay man in an admittedly sexual relationship.In his view, there was a fundamental question of principle as to whether the statutory process of adoption should be sanctioned by the court in circumstances where it is expressly proposed by a single male prospective adopter that the child should be brought up jointly by himself and by a third party with whom he cohabits in a homosexual relationship. The Adoption (Scotland) Act 1978 does not allow two men (or two women, or a man and a woman who are not married to each other) to apply to adopt a child, though it does permit unmarried persons to apply singly, which is what T was doing. Lord Gill was concerned that the welfare of a child could never be secured in a case in which a gay man or a gay couple were, with the sanction of the court (which can only be given in the interests of the child), bringing up a child. He did not, of course, explicitly indicate what he feared for the child, but other judges in custody disputes had previously expressed fears of the paedophile gay man and the proselytising lesbian—in other words, gay parenting is bad for children because the men will attempt to sexually interfere with the boy children, and the women will attempt to turn the girl children into little lesbians. In *Early v. Early*, 1989 S.L.T. 114 (affm. 1990 S.L.T. 221) a Scottish judge had removed a child from the mother with whom he had always lived and delivered him to a father who had never looked after him and who had two convictions for child neglect. These convictions were perceived to be less of a risk to the child than the fact that the mother had now entered into a lesbian relationship.

Thankfully, the decision of Lord Gill in the present case was overturned on appeal. Had it not been so, the boy would have been removed from his home and returned to the care system in Manchester, for adoption law requires the removal of children from unsuccessful adoption petitioners. This would have been so even if all the professionals were convinced that the best care for this needy child would be provided by the petitioner, which would indicate quite clearly that the law is more concerned to express its disapproval of gay men and lesbians than with the welfare of individual children. But in an important judgment, which has proved to be a watershed, the Inner House dismissed Lord Gill's concerns as worthless.

Lord President Hope pointed out that the Adoption (Scotland) Act 1978 has nothing to say about homosexuality. This means that, since there was nothing to make the present petition incompetent, the decision was to be made on the basis of the welfare of the child. But that test requires an assessment of the actual facts before the court rather than an application of preconceived notions which might or might not be relevant in the individual case. Appeal judges very seldom feel it appropriate in their reported judgments to castigate the judge from whose decision the appeal is being made (though what is said in private may well, for all one knows, be quite different). But Lord President Hope did so in this case: "what [a judge] must not do", he said, "is to permit his own personal views, or his own private beliefs, to affect his judgment. These views or beliefs are irrelevant to the issue which he has to decide". He went on: "This clearly is a difficult area of jurisprudence, so it is particularly important that the judge should base his decision strictly on the information which is before him in the case". Of course, if there is a fear that the particular petitioner will constitute a risk to the particular child, then it is open to any party to raise it and prove it. But the court cannot simply assume that a person is bad, or is likely to harm a child, based on nothing more than the person's sexual orientation.

Since this decision, courts in both England and Scotland in both adoption and residence cases have been far more relaxed at the prospect of gay parenting, and have not been able to presume that it is something to be avoided unless the contrary be proved. The European Court of Human Rights in *Da Silva Mouta v. Portugal* (2001) Fam. L.R. 2 subsequently held that it was unlawful discrimination, contrary to Articles 8 and 14 of the European Convention on Human Rights, for a court to use sexual orientation to decide a child custody dispute. *Early v. Early* is dead; long live *T., Petitioner*.

THE STORY OF RAYMONDO

Case 92: Jones v. Tower Boot Co Ltd
[1997] 2 All E.R. 406; [1997] I.C.R. 254
(Court of Appeal, England)

Employment law—Racial Discrimination—Vicarious liability

A 16-year-old of mixed race, Raymondo Jones, started work in his first job as a last operative in the shoe factory of Tower Boot. He resigned a month later, having been subjected to an horrific catalogue of physical and verbal abuse by two fellow workers, Messrs Clements and Cotter. The verbal abuse was in crude racist terms. The physical abuse included some serious incidents, one involving burning an arm with a hot screwdriver for which Mr Clements was eventually convicted of causing actual bodily harm. Mr Jones had complained to his supervisor, Mr Ablett, about this particular incident. Mr Ablett's response was to remove him to another part of the factory and to instruct the other two men to "stop the horseplay". As well as reporting the incident to the police, Mr Jones raised an action against Tower Boot for race discrimination under the Race Relations Act 1976. While racial harassment, racial abuse or racially motivated violence are not expressly covered by the Act it is accepted (i) that such treatment can be direct discrimination under s.1 of the Act, which prohibits less favourable treatment on racial grounds, and (ii) that it can amount to a breach of the employer's duty under s.4 of the Act not to discriminate against an employee by subjecting him or her to a detriment. The Act, by s.32(1), also provides that "anything done by a person in the course of his employment shall be treated for the purposes of this Act…as done by the employer as well as by him, whether or not it was done with the employer's knowledge or approval". Mr Jones claimed compensation for race discrimination on the basis that the company was responsible for the actions of Messrs Clements and Cotter.

The industrial tribunal found in favour of Mr Jones, apparently equiparating s.32(1) with the common law concept of vicarious liability (on which, see **Case 49**). They found that Clements and Cotter were authorised to use the screwdriver with which they had inflicted the injury so that its use to injure Mr Jones was an improper mode of carrying out an authorised function. However, this was overturned by the Employment Appeal Tribunal, who similarly founded on the common law of vicarious liability but held that the acts of abuse could not be considered to be a mode of carrying out authorised work, but were themselves unauthorised. They remitted the case back to the tribunal to consider whether the supervisor's "wholly inadequate" response was taken on racial grounds. The EAT had followed an earlier decision of the Court of Appeal, *Irving v. The Post Office* [1987] I.R.L.R. 289, in which it had been held, applying the common law of vicarious liability, that the Post Office was not responsible for the action of a postman who had scrawled a racist drawing and message on an envelope he was sorting which was addressed to his neighbours, Mr and Mrs Irving, since this action could not be considered an improper mode of carrying out his duties and were not part of the performance of his duties. When Mr Jones appealed the decision of the EAT, the Court of Appeal found that the earlier case was based entirely on the common law and that the statutory term "in the course of employment" at issue in the present case should be interpreted as the lay person would interpret it and should not have the "gloss" of the common law imposed upon it. A wider interpretation was justified for a number of reasons. The scheme and policy of the Act (and also of the Sex Discrimination Act 1975 and the Disability Discrimination Act 1995 in relation to sex and disability discrimination respectively) is to make employers responsible for the prevention of discrimination including harassment at work. In addition, unlike the common law concept of vicarious liability, the conscientious employer has a statutory defence under s.32(3) if the employer proves that "he took such steps as were reasonably practicable to prevent the employee from doing that act, or from doing in the course of his employment acts of that description". Needless to say, Mr Ablett's "wholly inadequate" response to the abuse of Mr Jones would not allow Tower Boot to make use of this defence. Accordingly the Court of Appeal decided that the EAT had been wrong to overturn the tribunal's decision, and both the finding in Mr Jones' favour and the award of £5,000 compensation were re-instated.

The employer's responsibility to ensure that there is no racial or sexual abuse or harassment at work was also re-enforced in *Burton and Rhule v. De Vere Hotels* [1996] I.R.L.R. 596, but in that case the employer was held to be personally liable directly under ss.1 and 4 of the Act. Two black waitresses, Freda Burton and Sonia Rhule, were working at one of the company's hotels at a dinner organised by the City of Derby Round Table at which the guest speaker was Bernard Manning, a performer who had built a reputation on sexist and racist material and who made sexist and racist remarks in the course of his speech, including one directed at the two women. After the performance one guest made an offensive sexual and racial remark to Ms Rhule, while another guest attempted to put his arms round Ms Burton. The assistant manager intervened, and the following day the hotel manager apologised to the two women. They raised an action against the company on the basis that it had subjected them to the harassment they suffered. The tribunal found against the two women on the basis that it was guests of the hotel who had committed the actions and there was no vicarious liability for the actions of guests. The EAT, however, held that an employer who causes or allows harassment to occur in circumstances in which he or she can control the situation is guilty of subjecting their employees to the harassment. The foreseeability of the situation (as here since the performer Manning's reputation was well known) was relevant to whether or not the employer had the necessary control. The employers should have adopted employment practices which would have protected the waitresses from Mr Manning and the guests. The EAT had in mind "keeping a look-out" and withdrawing the waitresses "if things became unpleasant". It may be thought that not permitting offensive material in the first place would be more effective.

THE MOTHER OF DISPUTES

Case 93: Rafique v. Amin, 1997 S.L.T. 1385 (Inner House, Court of Session, Scotland)

Heritable property— Common property—Law of the tenement

When you read case reports or legal textbooks you will see that some lawyers like to use Latin. The version lawyers use often bears no relation to classical Latin, and if you were to hear the terms spoken, you would discover the pronunciation owes little to classical Rome. This book does not use much Latin. However, for this case we make an exception.

There is an old Latin maxim that all home owners (and their lawyers) should learn. *Communio est mater rixarum*. It is surprisingly absent from the case reports. But it is important, for it translates (fairly literally) as "co-ownership is the mother of disputes".

This is no idle boast. When two people share ownership of a thing they *have to* work together. The "property owning democracy" may be a political aspiration but there is no democracy within property ownership itself. The law requires decisions to alter, repair, use, or carry out any act in relation to the property must be made not by a majority of the co-owners, but by the unanimous agreement of them all. Whilst people are normally willing to co-operate with each other, it appears that most of us can only work together for so long. And when arguments start, legal disputes arise.

We offer only one illustration of this maxim. It involves two flats in Rose Street, Aberdeen. When people own separate flats under the one roof a special legal regime known as the law of the tenement applies. Under the law of the tenement while neighbours owe obligations to each other to provide shelter and support (meaning a lower flat owner could not remove supporting walls, or an upper flat owner could not refuse to repair the roof), flat owners are broadly left to their own devices. Aside from the common stairway providing access to the flats the flat owners do not share ownership of any part of the block. Each flat owner owns their internal walls, and the walls, floor and ceiling surrounding the flat. They can, in effect, do what they like with their flat. However, the law of the tenement only provides background rules. If people make different provision in the title deeds affecting the property, this will supersede the background law of the tenement. In conveyancing practice many flats are owned subject to these express provisions in the titles. Ignoring the warning contained in the Latin maxim, titles will often provide that much of the property is to be co-owned by all of the flat owners (when so owned this is known as "common property").

The flats in Rose Street, Aberdeen were owned in this way. Their title provided that "the solum on which the building is erected, the foundations, outside walls, gables, roof and chimney heads of the building and rhones, gutters, spouts, main drains, solid and water supply pipes and electric mains, cables and wires which are or which may be used in common ... the internal division walls, ceilings and floors separating the subjects" were all to be co-owned by the flat proprietors Rafique and Amin.

The case illustrates the dangers of creating co-ownership. Amin wished to build a new stair inside his flat. To construct the stair, Amin required to insert steel beams into a gable wall. Rafique raised an action to prevent Amin's proposed alterations. He relied on the general principle of common property that all co-owners must agree for an alteration to be carried out. Rafique did not wish the steel beams in the gable wall.

Amin had little hope. He therefore relied on one limited exception to the general rule of unanimity. If a repair were very trivial, the court would not require the consent of all co-owners. In the case law this allowed a person to screw a brass nameplate to property owned by co-owners. Amin argued that the insertion of steel beams into the gable wall and into the foundations was like the insertion of a screw into a wall, in being so trivial as to be not worth bothering about. This received short shrift from the court. The right of veto was absolute and unanimity was held to be necessary for alterations or repairs to co-owned property.

However, Lord Justice-Clerk Ross noted that if the flat owners had left the common law of the tenement untouched Amin would have been able to proceed with his repairs without difficulty. He said, "It is somewhat ironical that if, instead of making these elaborate provisions regarding common property, the granter had allowed the more usual law of the tenement to prevail, many of these difficulties would not have arisen."

The moral of the case is clear. Think carefully before co-owning property, because in co-owning property you are required to work in co-operation with your fellow owners. And if that co-operation should fail, then remember the warning that co-ownership is the mother of disputes.

NOT SO SHARP PRACTICE?

Case 94: Sharp v. Thomson
1995 S.L.T. 837, 1995 S.C. 455, 1995 S.C.L.R. 683 (IH)
reversed by 1997 S.C. (H.L.) 66; 1997 S.L.T. 636;
1997 S.C.L.R. 328
(House of Lords, Scotland)

Heritable property—Sale—Delivery of disposition—Floating charge—Transfer of Ownership

(See Reid, "Jam Today: *Sharp* in the House of Lords", 1997 S.L.T. (News) 79, "Equity Triumphant: *Sharp v. Thomson*" (1997) 1 Edin. L.R. 464; Rennie, "*Sharp v. Thomson*: The Final Act" (1997) 42 J.L.S.S. 130)

A normal house purchase proceeds as follows: A contract of sale (known as the missives) is agreed by the seller and purchaser some time before the day the purchaser hopes to move in ('the date of settlement'). A disposition is prepared for signature by the seller, which will narrate that the seller is transferring ownership of the house to the purchaser. Come the date of settlement and the purchaser (or rather his or her solicitor) will hand over the purchase price to the seller (or rather the seller's solicitor). In return the signed disposition of the house will be handed over from seller to purchaser. The purchaser will then register the disposition in the property register. The registration of the disposition will usually take place within a few days of the date of settlement. The purchaser thereby acquires ownership of the house. The seller will get the purchase price. Everyone is happy (at least until the central hearing breaks down a week after the purchaser moves in, but that's a different story).

When brother and sister, Steven and Carol Thomson, purchased 10 Whinhill Road, Aberdeen, it was not a normal house purchase.

At first, things appeared to proceed smoothly. The Thomsons obtained a loan from the Woolwich Building Society. They found a flat in a leafy, but central, part of the Granite City. Albyn Construction Ltd (a property developer) had built five flats on the plot. Albyn and the Thomsons concluded missives. The sale was due to settle on April 14, 1989. On that date the Thomsons duly paid over £40,000. However, no disposition was delivered. Time passed. There was still no disposition. A new year dawned, and still no disposition. Time continued to pass. In fact, the disposition was not delivered until August 9, 1990. This was the day before Albyn, who had granted a floating charge (on floating charges, see *Lord Advocate v. Royal Bank of Scotland,* **Case 65**) six years before, went into receivership. On August 21 the disposition in favour of the Thomsons was finally registered. The Thomsons had granted a standard security (mortgage deed) over the flat in favour of the Woolwich, to secure the Woolwich's loan. This was registered on the same day.

The receivers argued that because the floating charge had attached to Albyn's property on the appointment of a receiver, it attached before registration of the disposition by Albyn in favour of the Thomsons. This meant that it attached while Albyn still owned the house. Accordingly, they argued that they should be able to sell the house, and remove the Thomsons. The Thomsons would then be unsecured creditors of Albyn for the return of their money (which Albyn did not have).

The Thomsons and the Woolwich defended the action. They argued that the floating charge should not attach the flat because the price had been paid in full, and the disposition had been delivered before the charge attached. On delivery of the disposition they acquired a special right that prevailed against attached floating charges and would protect purchasers in insolvency processes. Accordingly, the receivers had no right to sell the flat.

At issue before the courts was the most fundamental question of property law. When does ownership transfer? If ownership transferred on registration of the disposition (as had been assumed at least since the case of *Young v. Leith* (1847) 9 D. 932, approved by the House of Lords in (1848) 2 Ross L.C. 81) then the receivers would be successful since registration occurred after the floating charge attached. However, if ownership transferred on delivery of the disposition then the Thomsons would be successful, because a floating charge can only attach property owned by the debtor.

The receivers were successful in the Outer House before Lord Penrose.

The decision provoked considerable consternation in the profession. There was a flurry of articles. Some criticised the approach of the decision, and believed that if the receiver won and was able to sell the Thomson's home this would be unfair. The Thomsons had paid the money, received the disposition and should be protected. Others believed that property law required to be based on clear and certain principles. The focus should not be on fairness between the parties to the transaction, but on creating certainty for third parties. They believed that creating a special rule for the Thomsons would cause problems for independent third parties (such as creditors) looking to rely on the property register.

On appeal to the Inner House Lord Penrose's decision was upheld. Lord President Hope stressed that in Scots law there were only two types of rights—personal rights, rights enforceable against persons; and real rights, rights in things, enforceable against any challenger. The Thomsons could not have a right midway between the two. Lord President Hope stressed that Scots law was unititular. There could only be one real right of ownership in any one thing at any one time. Following *Young v. Leith* that real right of ownership did not transfer until registration of the disposition.

The Woolwich Building Society appealed to the House of Lords and varied their argument. They now argued that the crucial issue was interpretation of the Companies Act 1985, s.462—the section that gave statutory authority to companies to grant a floating charge.

The House of Lords accepted Woolwich's new argument and overturned the decision of the Inner House on the basis of statutory interpretation. A company can only grant a floating charge over the assets in its "property and undertaking". It was held that "property and undertaking" did not include heritable property where the company has the real right of ownership, but has delivered a disposition to a purchaser, and has accepted payment of the price. So in the end the Thomsons got to keep their flat.

On the fundamental question of property law—when does the real right of ownership transfer?—the House of Lords appeared to leave the decision of the Inner House untouched, though differing views were expressed by Lords Jauncey and Clyde on the question of competition between a purchaser holding a delivered disposition and the unsecured creditors of an insolvent seller. Following a long line of authority, Lord Clyde said that a trustee in sequestration (or liquidator) and the purchaser required to race to the register. Whoever registered first acquired the real right of ownership and could deal with the heritable property. Lord Jauncey, on the other hand, argued that if a purchaser had a disposition delivered prior to sequestration or liquidation they were protected and had no need to start racing with anyone. The trustee or liquidator was not entitled to acquire the real right of ownership in preference to them. The purchaser had a "beneficial interest" that prevailed in insolvency. Despite this difference, the other Law Lords agreed with both speeches. So *Sharp* left more questions than it answered.

It is now not clear exactly what assets are attached by a floating charge, nor whether the approach in *Sharp* can be applied to other types of property (such as incorporeal property rights), nor is it clear what would happen in a competition involving insolvency and a purchaser holding a delivered disposition.

This last point was at issue in *Burnett's Trustee v. Grainger*, 2000 S.L.T. (Sh. Ct) 116 where there was a competition between the holder of a delivered disposition and a trustee in sequestration who reached the register first. The judgment of the sheriff principal appeared to do the impossible and reconcile the speeches of Lords Jauncey and Clyde. His conclusion was—controversially—that there was no race to the register. The holder of the delivered disposition prevailed. The decision has been appealed, but any result may not last. The Scottish Law Commission has now been invited to carry out a review of *Sharp v. Thomson* and its aftermath by the Scottish Executive. A discussion paper (Scot. Law Com. DP No. 114) has been published. It seems likely that legislation will follow.

FOETAL RIGHTS AND WRONGS

Case 95: Kelly v. Kelly
1997 S.C. 285; 1997 S.L.T. 896; 1997 S.C.L.R. 749
(Inner House, Court of Session, Scotland)

Abortion—Interdict—Father's right—Unborn child's right—Arts. 2 and 8, ECHR

(See Russell, "Abortion Law in Scotland and the Kelly Foetus", 1997 S.L.T. (News) 187)

It is a basic principle of the Scots law of persons that an unborn child has no legal personality: this means that it cannot be party to any legal transaction, including litigation, nor can it be the victim of a crime. But the foetus in the womb does exist and its existence does have legal consequences. Its life is protected by the crime of abortion; if someone injures it and it is subsequently born alive, the living child has an action for damages (see *Hamilton v. Fife Health Board*, 1992 S.L.T. 1026) and if it subsequently dies it has been the victim of the crime of culpable homicide or (perhaps) even murder: *McCluskey v. H.M. Advocate*, 1989 S.L.T. 175; *Attorney General's Reference (No. 3 of 1994)* [1997] 3 W.L.R. 425. The "*nasciturus*" principle allows the child to succeed to property even although the succession opens before he or she is born: see *Cox's Trs v. Cox*, 1950 S.C. 117; *Elliot v. Joicey*, 1935 S.C. (H.L.) 57. The question in the present case, however, was whether an unborn child, or someone acting on its behalf, has title to seek interdict to prevent harm being done to it while still in the womb—particularly, to prevent its abortion?

James Kelly and his wife Lynn Kelly separated, and were planning a divorce. However, Mr Kelly found out that Mrs Kelly was pregnant and there was no suggestion that it was not his child. Mrs Kelly was seeking an abortion and when he discovered this Mr Kelly raised an action against both her and the Edinburgh Royal Infirmary NHS Trust, seeking interdict against the carrying out of the termination. At first instance, Lord Easie, after an *ex parte* hearing (*i.e.* a hearing in the absence of one of the parties), granted interim interdict (which is granted not on the basis of an assessment of the legal rights at issue but in the present case for the necessity of keeping the situation stable until a full hearing could be arranged). However, six days later, after hearing all parties, Lord Easie withdrew the interim interdict. Mr Kelly immediately appealed to the Inner House, which heard the case two days later, and the next day they rejected his appeal.

Mr Kelly's argument was set out in stages, most of which the judges readily accepted. He argued as follows: a child, suing through his or her legal representative (which includes the father if he has parental responsibilities), can seek damages for injuries caused *in utero*; if the causing of such injury is a wrong, it can be interdicted before it occurs; interdict can seek to prevent death as well as injury short of death. He argued that the abortion being sought by his wife would cause the death of the child and that he, as the child's legal representative, had title to seek to prevent that occurrence. The Court accepted that interdict is available to the representative of a person to prevent injury or death to the person in circumstances in which that injury or death would sound in damages. They also accepted that the father of an unborn child would be entitled to take proceedings on behalf of the foetus *if* abortion was an actionable wrong. But the problem for Mr Kelly was that the Court did not accept that abortion was an actionable wrong. The Court said that Mr Kelly's question—if it is legally wrong to damage a foetus, shouldn't it be capable of being interdicted as a wrong?—simply begged another question: accepting that the child, once born, can sue for the wrong, does it necessarily follow that injury to the foetus before birth is actionable? The answer to this question, said the Court, depended on whether the law conferred a right on a foetus to remain in the womb. And Scots law recognises no such right. As a result, no person can invoke the power of the court to vindicate such a right.

That was sufficient to reject Mr Kelly's claim, and the Court was careful to do so by strict legal analysis. But they were conscious throughout of the social, moral and even political context in which the case was argued. Abortion is lawful in Scotland within the terms of the Abortion Act 1967 and any judicial recognition of rights not contained in and controlled by that Act would have implications (of which the Court were fully aware) far beyond the boundaries of that Act and involving the whole regulation of pregnancy and pregnant women. The courts in both Scotland and England have shied away from arguments which would have the effect of limiting the freedom of women to conduct their pregnancies as they think fit.

The decision in *Kelly* is in line with similar decisions in many other countries: see for example *Paton v. British Pregnancy Advisory Service*

[1979] 1 Q.B. 276 and *C. v. S.* [1988] Q.B. 135 (England); *Tremblay v. Daigle* (1990) 62 D.L.R. (4th) 634 (Canada); *Attorney General of Queensland ex rel. Kerr v. T.* (1983) 46 A.L.R. 275 (Australia); *Wall v. Livingstone* [1982] 1 N.Z.L.R. 734 (New Zealand). The losing father in the *Paton* case complained to the European Commission of Human Rights, arguing that the unborn child in that case was being deprived of its right to life (as protected by Article 2 ECHR) and that he was being deprived of his right to family life (Article 8). The Commission rejected the complaint (*Paton v. United Kingdom* (1980) 3 E.H.R.R. 408) on the basis that the interference with the father's family life was justified by the need to protect the rights of the mother, and that the right to life was subject to limitations which, though not necessary to specify in the present case, clearly covered lawful abortion. There is little doubt that the present position of the foetus in Scots law is in conformity with the ECHR.

SEXUALLY TRANSMITTED DEBT

Case 96: Smith v. Bank of Scotland
1997 S.C. (H.L.) 10; 1997 S.L.T. 1061; 1997 S.C.L.R. 765
(House of Lords, Scotland)

Contract—Good faith—Reduction of contract—Intimate personal relationships—Judicial legislation

(See Gretton, "Sexually Transmitted Debt", 1997 S.L.T. (News) 195 (with acknowledgements for the above title, which he acknowledges he pinched); Dunlop, "*Smith v. Bank of Scotland*: Spouses, Caution and the Banks" (1997) 42 J.L.S.S. 446; Dickson, "Good Faith in Contract, Spousal Guarantees and *Smith v. Bank of Scotland*", 1998 S.L.T. (News) 39).

Though it is no longer the case that a husband is liable for his wife's debts, it is true that many spouses end up paying their partner's creditors. This often appears to be a matter of choice—you might not want to see your partner become bankrupt, preferring to spend your own money to avoid it, or you might choose in a commercial transaction to guarantee the debts of your partner, to give him greater financial flexibility. The question is, how free is this choice given the social environment in which family relations operate? To what extent should commercial considerations be compromised by the realities of domestic life?

Mr Mumford and Mr Smith were partners in a business, known as Kestrel, which they operated in Glasgow. The firm needed an injection of capital and so they approached their local bank, the Knightswood branch of the Bank of Scotland. "What security can you offer, if we lend you money?" asked the bank manager, as bank managers have asked since time immemorial. Mumford and Smith looked at each other, then replied, "all we have is the houses we live in". "That will do nicely", said the bank manager.

The problem for Messrs Mumford and Smith was that they were both married, and their respective wives had interests in the houses they were offering the bank as security. Mrs Mumford had no title since her husband was the sole owner, but she did have possession rights under the Matrimonial Homes (Family Protection) (Scotland) Act 1981; Mrs Smith was joint owner, with her husband, of their home. So in both cases the husbands required the consents of the wives, which they obtained, effectively making the wives cautioners (or guarantors) of the firm's debts, in the sense that their financial interests could now be accessed by the bank if the firm defaulted on the loan. On this basis, the bank made the loan. Came the dawn. The wives realised what they had done—they had put their homes at risk for the sake of their husbands' business. They reassessed their priorities and decided that they would rather preserve the former even at the expense of the latter. So they sought reduction of the securities, insofar as these related to their own interests. The ground for reduction was that the husbands had induced them to sign the guarantees by materially misrepresenting to them the purpose for which the guarantees were required: the wives alleged that the husbands had merely said they needed their signatures to get a loan, and that they were given no opportunity to peruse the documents, nor advised to seek separate financial and legal advice. Now, the difficulty the wives faced was that they were seeking reduction against the bank, on the basis that their husbands had not been entirely honest with them —but of what concern was that to the bank?

A very few years previously, the House of Lords in an English case had been faced with a very similar claim: *Barclay's Bank v. O'Brien* [1994] 1 A.C. 180. There it was held that when a creditor knows that a guarantor is in an intimate relationship with the primary debtor then the creditor is put on notice that the guarantee might have been extracted through undue influence: it followed from that that any right to have the guarantee set aside is pleadable against the creditor as well as against the debtor. Interestingly, the concept of "intimate relationship" was recognised to be wider than husband and wife and might include cohabitants, opposite-sex or same-sex.

In the present case, the wives asked the Scottish court to follow this English decision. The Lord Ordinary (1994 S.L.T. 1288) and the First Division (1996 S.L.T. 392) refused to do so, on the ground that undue influence could only be pleaded against a creditor if there were averments to show that the creditor knew that the primary debtor was exercising undue influence over the cautioner. Since there was no such suggestion in the present case, the action must fail. At this point, exhausted, Mrs Mumford dropped out of the case; but battling Mrs Smith (who had, be it remembered, more to lose) fought on. And she won in the House of Lords.

The Inner House's decision was overruled, on the basis that there was no ground for refusing to extend to Scotland the protections of guarantors introduced into English law by *O'Brien*. That protection was found, at least in Scots law, in the concept of good faith in contract: a creditor who accepts a cautionary obligation (*i.e.* a guarantee by A of B's debts) is required by law to show good faith to the cautioner. So, if the circumstances of the case are such as to lead a reasonable person to believe that owing to the personal relationship between the debtor and the proposed cautioner the latter's consent may not be fully informed or freely given, then the creditor should take steps to remain in good faith, such as by advising the potential cautioner of the consequences of the transaction and advising her or him to take independent advice.

The leading speech in this case was given by Lord Clyde who, interestingly, accepted that the Inner House had applied "existing Scottish law" (and he should know, having applied it for years himself). But that did not stop him extending the English law, created only three years previously, to Scotland so reversing, without legislative authority, existing law. The surprise is either (i) that people have found this surprising or (ii) that Lord Clyde was so honest about what he was doing. It may be noted that the High Court of Australia refused to follow *O'Brien* in *Garcia v. National Australia Bank Ltd* (1998) 72 A.L.J.R. 1243.

INFLUENCING ETERNITY

Case 97: Osman v. United Kingdom
[1999] 29 E.H.R.R. 245; [1999] 1 F.L.R. 193
(European Court of Human Rights)

Delict—Negligence—Public policy—Police immunity—Right to a fair trial—Art. 6, ECHR

(See Monti, "*Osman v. U.K.*: Transforming English Negligence Law into French Administrative Law" (1999) 48 I.C.L.Q. 757; Giliker, "*Osman* and Police Immunity in the English Law of Torts" 2000 Leg. Stud. 372; Gearty, "Unravelling *Osman*" (2001) 64 Mod. L.R. 159.)

This case arose out of a tragedy which the domestic law of England was unable to respond to appropriately. Ahmet Osman was a school boy who had the misfortune to attract unwanted attentions from a disturbed teacher, Paget-Lewis. The teacher took photographs of the boy in the street and followed him home. He daubed sexually explicit graffiti in the boy's neighbourhood. On being warned by the education authority about his behaviour, Paget-Lewis threatened to "do a Hungerford" (referring to a shooting massacre some years previously). Ahmet's parents complained to the police, who interviewed Paget-Lewis but did not arrest him. In 1988 Paget-Lewis stole a gun, went to the Osmans' home and fired at both the boy and his father. The father was killed, and Ahmet was seriously injured. Paget-Lewis was subsequently sent to a secure mental hospital.

Ahmet and his family then raised an action against the police for failing to protect them from the known danger of Paget-Lewis. Though accepting that the plaintiffs had an arguable case in that the proximity between the police and the Osman family was such as to impose a duty of care on the former, the English court struck the action out, following an earlier House of Lords decision, *Hill v. Chief Constable of West Yorkshire* [1989] A.C. 53. In that case, the plaintiff was the mother of the last victim of Peter Sutcliffe, the Yorkshire Ripper, who had sued the police for not tracking down Sutcliffe soon enough to prevent her daughter being murdered. The Court held that the police owed no duty of care to the plaintiff's daughter since there was insufficient proximity between the police and members of the public who may be victims of crime; more importantly, however, the Court held that public policy prevented the imposition of a duty of care by the police in the investigation and suppression of crime. The Court was worried that the imposition of a duty of care would lead to defensive policing and distract officers from their core functions. A similar argument was used in relation to social workers (*X. v. Bedfordshire County Council* [1995] 2 A.C. 633) and the army (*Mulcahy v. Ministry of Defence* [1996] 2 All E.R. 758), though more recently the courts have been more sceptical of this argument, for example in relation to other emergency services like the fire brigade (*Capital and Counties plc v. Hampshire County Council* [1997] Q.B. 1004).

However, *Hill* was successfully used by the police in the present case to defend themselves against the action by the Osman family (*Osman v. Ferguson* [1993] 4 All E.R. 344). The Court of Appeal, having struck the action out while accepting that proximity might be established, appeared to be applying a blanket immunity for any negligence by the police in the investigation and suppression of crime. The Osmans took their case to the European Court of Human Rights, arguing that the application of such an immunity in these circumstances was a disproportionate restriction on their right of access to the courts and was therefore an infringement of their right under Article 6 of the

European Convention on Human Rights to a fair trial. The European Court agreed. They did not, however, hold that immunity from suit was in all cases contrary to the European Convention. Rather, they required that any immunity justified by public policy had to be applied in any particular case in a proportionate manner, taking account of competing policy considerations. It was the fact that the English court struck the action out without considering any arguments against doing so that rendered the decision a breach of Article 6. Other courts, even before the decision of the European Court in the present case, were not dismissing actions quite so readily. In *Swinney v. Chief Constable of Northumbria Police* [1997] Q.B. 464 the Court of Appeal took account of the need to protect police informants as a consideration of even more import than that accepted in *Osman v. Ferguson* and *Hill*. In *Costello v. Chief Constable of Northumbria Police* [1999] 1 All E.R. 550 the Court of Appeal, while denying that they were undermining *Hill* in any way, held that the notion of common sense should be placed in the balance against the imposition of the *Hill*-type immunity. And in the Scottish case of *Gibson v. Orr*, 1999 S.C. 420 it was pointed out that the immunity in *Hill* was there limited to the investigation and suppression of crime and did not, therefore, apply in the present case which involved negligence in respect of the police force's civil operational tasks (failing to close a road leading to a collapsed bridge). In addition, *Osman* has been used to justify a departure from the immunity granted to other professions than the police, such as barristers and advocates: see *Hall v. Simons* [2000] 3 W.L.R. 54.

So even before the European Court gave their judgment, the immunity for which *Hill* had been authority and which was automatically applied in the domestic *Osman* case was being chipped away by the domestic courts. Nevertheless, the European Court's judgment remains hugely significant for a number of reasons. First, the European Court took jurisdiction over domestic notions of public policy, a matter which previously they had been inclined to leave to national authorities as part of the "margin of appreciation" (see **Handyside v. U.K., Case 64**). Secondly, the case illustrates that European Human Rights law has the potential to influence the development of purely domestic aspects of law like delict or tort: not just in procedural aspects but also in the substantive law—both are elements relevant to the question of whether a domestic legal system affords individuals a "fair trial". And thirdly, the case shows that the jurisprudence of the European Court can render previous domestic precedents, even those, like *Hill*, from the House of Lords, of little continuing value.

The emerging test for the imposition of liability in both Scots and English law, the fair, just and reasonable test, is entirely consistent with the European Court's decision, for that requires the weighing up of competing considerations in order to determine where the demands of justice lie in any individual case and so it was held, by the European

Court, in the subsequent case of *Z. v. U.K.*, May 10, 2001. Indeed, in that case the Court held that its previous judgment in *Osman* has to be reviewed in the light of the clarifications provided by the fair, just and reasonable test, which eschews the concept of a blanket immunity such as was imposed in *Osman*. At the end of the day, perhaps the case illustrates the danger in relying too heavily on one aspect of the claim for negligence (the duty of care) at the expense of the other aspects, such as standard of care, causation and remoteness. Had the English court accepted that Ahmet Osman was owed a duty of care, but that the police's failure to arrest Paget-Lewis was not in the circumstances a breach of that duty, then the case would never have reached the European Court. But then that court would not then have had the chance to expand its jurisdiction into domestic issues of public policy and substantive law.

THE GENERAL, THE JUDGE AND THE PENALTY SHOOT-OUT

Case 98: R. v. Bow Street Magistrates, *ex parte* Pinochet (No. 1) [2000] 1 A.C. 61; [1998] 3 W.L.R. 1456 (No. 2) [2000] 1 A.C. 119; [1999] 2 W.L.R. 272; (No. 3) [2000] 1 A.C. 147; [1999] 2 W.L.R. 827

Extradition—Crimes against humanity—Torture—Legal process—Judicial bias

(See Turns, "Pinochet's Fallout: Jurisdiction and Immunity from Criminal Violations of International Law" (2000) 20 Leg. Stud. 566; Malleson, "Jurisdictional Bias and Disqualification After *Pinochet (No. 2)*" (2000) 63 Mod. L.R. 119; Middleton, "*Pinochet* and the House of Lords: A Turning Point in International Human Rights Law?" (1999) 3 Edin. L.R. 380.)

General Augusto Pinochet, the Chilean dictator, was Head of State of that country from 1973 until March 1990. He took power through a *coup d'etat* and maintained power by an oppressive regime of kidnap, torture and murder of opponents. He finally gave up power in 1990, but retained significant political influence in Chile, becoming a Senator for Life.

In October 1998, he came to the U.K. in order to undergo medical treatment. The judicial authorities in Spain immediately issued international warrants for his arrest. It was alleged that during his time in power various crimes against humanity including torture, hostage-taking and murder had taken place, for which he was knowingly responsible and of which various Spanish citizens were victims. It was alleged, not that Pinochet personally committed any of these acts himself, but that agents of the *Direction de Inteligencia Nacional* (the Chilean secret police) undertook and arranged the killings, disappearances and torturing of victims on Pinochet's orders. Pinochet was duly arrested and sought to have the warrants quashed. One of the warrants was quashed. In relation to the second one, it was quashed also but a stay was allowed pending an appeal to the House of Lords.

The major difficulty was the notion of state immunity from prosecution. In public international law theory, all States are legal equals (*par in parem non habet imperium*). This means that it is legally unacceptable for one sovereign power to exercise authority over another sovereign power, and because the State and sovereign are synonymous this immunity extends to the sovereign him- or herself. In addition, section 20 of the British State Immunity Act 1978 conferred personal immunity upon a head of state, and on his or her family and servants. Such immunities include under Article 31 of the Vienna Convention on diplomatic privileges "immunity from the criminal jurisdiction of the receiving state".

The Spanish Government accepted that a foreign Head of State, during his or her tenure of office, enjoyed immunity for certain acts from arrest or trial. However, it argued that once this tenure ceased, immunity also ceased and arrest and prosecution for crimes committed during the period of leadership was possible. Pinochet maintained that the immunity he had for his actions while in office continued even after he had left office. The House of Lords held that immunity for a former head of State from the criminal jurisdiction of the U.K. continued after he left office with respect to acts performed by him in the exercise of his functions as a Head of State. After an analysis of the State Immunity Act 1978 and other relevant instruments the question became: were the actions complained of "functions of a Head of State"? Lord Nicholls thought not: "it hardly needs saying that torture of his own subjects, or of aliens, would not be regarded by international law as a function of a head of state ... [I]nternational law has made plain that certain types of conduct, including torture and hostage-taking, are not acceptable conduct on the part of anyone. This applies as much to heads of state, or even more so, as it does to everyone else; the contrary conclusion would make a mockery of international law". Lord Steyn agreed, pointing out that the development of international law since World War II indicated that by the time of the 1973 *coup d'etat* which brought Pinochet to power, international law condemned genocide, torture, hostage taking and crimes against humanity as international crimes deserving of punishment. Two other judges (Lords Slynn and Lloyd) disagreed and held that Pinochet enjoyed immunity. So the case climaxed in a dramatic fashion with the casting vote being left to Lord Hoffmann. He decided against immunity for Pinochet. Lord Hoffmann's pronouncement brought audible cheers and gasps from the public benches. It was characterised as having all the excitement of a football penalty shoot-out. Critics of Pinochet and his regime, as well as human rights lawyers in general, heralded the decision as a major boost to the fight against torture.

However, more controversy was to follow. Shortly after the case, it emerged that Lord Hoffmann had links with Amnesty International. This organisation had, unusually, been given the right to intervene in the proceedings against Pinochet. General Pinochet argued that such links might well have given the appearance of bias against him. Though there is, technically speaking, no appeal from the House of Lords, the House decided to allow Pinochet's points to be heard on the ground that as ultimate court of appeal the House had the power to correct any injustice caused by one of its earlier orders. The House held that the absolute impartiality of the judiciary had been compromised by Lord Hoffmann's links with Amnesty International and that the case, therefore, had to be heard all over again, this time with seven judges sitting. *Pinochet (No. 2)* is a strict interpretation of the requirement on judges to be neutral and to be seen to be so.

Consequently, in *Pinochet (No. 3)*, the House of Lords once again considered the substantive matter. This stage could never hope to emulate the excitement of the first case and the somewhat dampened feeling which surrounded it is reflected in the legally technical nature of the decision. Lord Browne-Wilkinson took the view that there were two issues: (i) were the crimes allegedly committed by General Pinochet "extraditable crimes" which would trigger a U.K. court's jurisdiction over him; and (ii) if they were, was Pinochet immune from trial for committing those crimes?

Section 2 of the Extradition Act 1989 defined an "extradition crime" and Lord Hope took the view that of the offences alleged, and in the particular circumstances libelled, the charges relating to hostage-taking did not constitute extradition crimes. Although murder was adjudged an extraditable crime, Pinochet was not alleged to have killed anyone personally, and so the question was whether conspiracy to do so was such a crime. Lord Hope indicated that in certain circumstances it might be. In relation to torture and conspiracy to torture these could be extraditable crimes provided that certain conditions had been met. The U.K. was a party to the Torture Convention but it had only been enacted into U.K. law by the Criminal Justice Act 1988, which gives U.K. courts extra-territorial jurisdiction over acts such as those Pinochet was accused of. (This is an exception to the general rule that criminal jurisdiction is territorially confined—for other exceptions, see ***Attorney General of Israel v. Eichmann*, Case 43**). Because most of the crimes alleged against Pinochet had occurred before the coming into force of the 1988 Act, there remained jurisdiction over only a very few alleged acts of torture.

The first question having been answered (to a limited but sufficient extent) in the positive, the next question was whether Pinochet had immunity in respect of the torture and conspiracy to murder charges. In relation to the murder and conspiracy to murder allegations the Court held that no reason had been advanced as to why the ordinary rules of immunity should not apply and consequently Pinochet was entitled to such immunity. But in relation to torture, the Court held as it had held before: a former Head of State enjoyed immunity but only in respect of acts done by him as Head of State as part of his official functions as Head of State. So the question, again, was could torture form part of Pinochet's official duties? Lord Browne-Wilkinson asked rhetorically: "how can it be for international law purposes an official function to do something which international law itself prohibits and criminalises?' If torture were an official function then the immunity would extend far beyond the Head of State and would cover those who had actually carried out such "official business". This would have frustrated the aims of the Torture Convention which defines "torture" as acts carried out by state officials. Consequently Pinochet was not entitled to immunity for such acts, and although the judges did not agree on the exact date when immunity ended, they were broadly agreed that it was late 1988.

So, Pinochet was liable to extradition, though in relation only to a small number of the original charges. The last step was consent of the Home Secretary. This was ultimately withheld, on the grounds of the General's deteriorating physical condition. So he was allowed to fly home. The Chilean Government undertook to prosecute the former dictator for criminal acts carried out on his orders during his time in power.

Since the *Pinochet* case a number of developments have taken place endeavouring to ensure that there is no impunity for human rights infringements. An arrest warrant was issued in Belgium against an individual named Abdulaye Yerodia Ndombasi who was the Foreign Minister of the Democratic Republic of Congo and who was charged with serious violations of international humanitarian law. These included the making of speeches inciting racial hatred which contributed to the massacre of hundreds of individuals of Tutsi origin. Given the many obstacles and legal wrangling experienced in *Pinochet* and the slow progress of the proceedings against Ndombasi, perhaps the best solution is seen in the establishment of the International Criminal Court which within Article 27 of its statute excludes official capacity such as Head of State from excusing criminal responsibility under the Statute. This sends a message that crimes which are abhorrent to mankind will not be allowed to go unpunished.

DISTRIBUTING JUDICIAL FAVOURS

Case 99: McFarlane v. Tayside Health Board
2000 S.C. (H.L.) 1; [2000] 2 A.C. 59; 2000 S.L.T. 154
(House of Lords, Scotland)

Delict—Wrongful birth—Economic loss—Consequential losses

(See Thomson, "Abandoning the Law of Delict?' 2000 S.L.T. (News) 43; Norrie "Failed Sterilisation and Economic Loss: Justice, Law and Policy in *McFarlane v. Tayside Health Board*" (2000) 16 Professional Negligence 76).

In 1989, Mr George McFarlane underwent a vasectomy operation, having decided with his wife that after four children their family was now complete. After the operation he submitted a sample of his semen for a sperm count. Unfortunately, as a result of an alleged administrative error at the hospital, he was wrongly informed that his operation had been a success and that he was now sterile. Consequently, he and his wife, Mrs Laura McFarlane, stopped taking contraceptive precautions and predictably (though—and this is the point—not to them) in 1991 Mrs McFarlane became pregnant. In May 1992 she gave birth to a fifth child, whom they called Catherine. Both Mr and Mrs McFarlane sued the Health Board responsible for the hospital at which the sperm count was carried out for their losses; the defenders said, "what losses?"

Actions for what have come to be called "wrongful birth" had become fairly common in England in the 1980s, arising from a variety of acts of negligence, such as the negligent carrying out of an abortion (*Sciuriaga v. Powell* (1979) 123 S.J. 406), the negligent carrying out of a sterilisation operation (*Emeh v. Kensington and Chelsea and Westminster Area Health Authority* [1985] Q.B. 1012) or the negligent failure to advise of the risk that fertility might spontaneously reassert itself even after an initially successful sterilisation operation (*Thake v. Maurice* [1986] Q.B. 644). In some early cases defendants had attempted to argue either that the birth of a healthy child could not, in law, constitute a "loss" or that even if it did there were policy reasons why the law should not provide monetary compensation for people who acquired the inestimable blessing of parenthood. After initially being attracted by these arguments, the English courts by the mid-1980s were accepting that while the child itself could not be regarded as a compensable "loss" nevertheless the unwelcome consequences of its birth could be so regarded, including both the physical consequences (such as the discomfort of pregnancy and the pain and suffering of childbirth) and the economic consequences (such as the extra costs involved in bringing up an unplanned child). No case before the present had, however, reached the House of Lords, and indeed the House of Lords had refused leave to appeal to it in *Thake v. Maurice* (which suggests that they were, then, quite happy at the way the lower English courts had been developing the law). However, discomfort remained, to be heightened after *Salih v. Enfield Health Authority* [1991] 3 All E.R. 400 where part of the recovered costs of bringing up the child included the school fees the parents intended to pay in educating their unplanned child.

When the present case reached the Court of Session, the Outer House judge, Lord Gill, dismissed the action on the basis that the normal consequences of pregnancy and childbirth could not, in law, be characterised as "loss" and that any economic disadvantages suffered as a result of having to bring up an unplanned child were more than cancelled out by the benefits of parenthood. That decision was reversed by the Inner House, which chose to follow the existing English approach, if expressed in rather more Scottish terms. They held that the physical effects of pregnancy and childbirth were clearly manifestations of *damnum* for which Mrs McFarlane could claim, and that the economic costs were also recoverable by both parents, without any deduction for the intangible benefits of parenthood. The Health Board appealed. The House of Lords had the choice of confirming previous practice in the lower courts or putting the law on a whole new track. They chose to do the latter.

This is one of those cases in which the Court is clearly seeking a compromise in a dispute in which both sides have almost unanswerable points. From the defenders' perspective it could hardly be said to be fair that the costs of bringing up a child were switched wholly from the parents to the Health Board—that is not what people pay tax and national insurance for in times of long waiting-lists, nursing shortages, and crumbling hospitals. From the pursuers' perspective, to leave the loss where it fell would mean that they were facing precisely those costs which they had relied on the defenders to relieve them of, and which they now faced as a direct result of the defenders' negligence (if established). The compromise that the House of Lords came up with was to allow the claim to proceed as far as the physical injuries suffered by Mrs McFarlane were concerned (plus directly consequential economic losses such as her loss of earnings, extra medical expenses, costs of clothing for her and the new baby), but to reject it as far as the other economic costs were concerned. The dynamic of the case comes from their Lordships' attempts to draw a rational distinction between the two types of claim. Lord Millett dissented on the basis that there was no rational distinction and that, therefore, both claims must either stand or fall together (and he was for letting them fall).

The distinction that the majority founded upon was the fact that the economic costs were so economic as to fall into the category of irrecoverable economic losses (see *Hedley Byrne v. Heller & Partners*, **Case 46**). As such, they would be permitted only if it were fair, just and reasonable to permit them, and in the circumstances the Court held that it would not be. Lord Hope, oddly, held that it would not be fair, just and reasonable to allow the claim for the costs of upbringing because the level of damages would be out of proportion to the minor act of negligence (which does not usually amount to a defence or to a mitigation in civil cases); Lord Steyn, even more oddly, held that in terms of what he called "distributive justice" (basically, a theory that says the law of delict is not about applying set rules but about allocating the costs of accidents fairly across society) it was fairer to let the parents pay for the upkeep of their own child. The case was followed in *McLelland v. Greater Glasgow Health Board*, 2001 S.L.T. 446 where the child had been born handicapped: illogically, the defenders had conceded that they were liable to pay the difference between the costs of bringing up a handicapped child and those for bringing up a "normal" child.

Once again, a Scottish case which reached the House of Lords has fundamentally affected the development of the law of England for there is no doubt that, though their Lordships were purporting to state the law of Scotland, they were also laying down (and changing) the law of England. In the process, the "fair, just and reasonable" test for allowing new claims to succeed, developed in England, was firmly embedded into Scots law. The "distributive justice" approach to claims for damages will, one assumes, wither on its gnarled and unattractive vine.

THE FOXHUNTING CASE

Case 100: Whaley v. Lord Watson of Invergowrie
2000 S.C. 340; 2000 S.L.T. 475
(Inner House, Court of Session, Scotland)

Constitutional law—Scotland Act 1998—Power of court to regulate Scottish Parliament

In July 1999, within days of the Scottish Parliament reconvening after an absence of almost 300 years, the Scottish Campaign Against Hunting with Dogs approached a Member of the Scottish Parliament, Lord Watson, and invited him to sponsor a Bill to make hunting with dogs an offence. He was happy to do so. The Campaign offered him legal and administrative assistance in drafting the Bill and dealing with his correspondence concerning the Bill. In September 1999 he submitted a draft proposal for a bill entitled the "Protection of Wild Mammals Bill", the main purpose of which was to make it an offence to hunt wild animals, like foxes, with dogs.

Three individuals, whose livelihoods were to some extent dependent on hunting, sought interim interdict against Lord Watson from introducing the Bill to the Parliament. They argued that, by introducing the Bill, Lord Watson would be in breach of the rules governing members' interests. Article 6 of the Scotland Act (Transitory and Transitional Provisions) (Members' Interests) Order 1999 (S.I. 1999 No. 1305) prohibits MSPs from doing anything in their capacity as members of the Parliament to further the interests of those from whom they receive remuneration. The petitioners argued that the support and assistance given to Lord Watson by the Scottish Campaign Against Hunting with Dogs amounted to "remuneration". They had to bring the matter to court by way of petition seeking interim interdict since section 28(5) of the Scotland Act 1998 would prevent them challenging the bill after it was passed, for that section provides that the validity of any Act of the Scottish Parliament is not affected by any invalidity in the proceedings of the Parliament leading to its enactment.

In response, Lord Watson argued that it was incompetent for the Court to investigate or consider the internal workings of the Scottish Parliament because it had been allowed by the Scotland Act to regulate its own proceedings. In addition, it would also be incompetent to grant interdict because of the provisions of s.40 of the 1998 Act, which prevents courts from making various orders, including interdicts, against the Parliament or, in certain circumstances, against a member of the Parliament.

Lord Johnstone in the Outer House dismissed the petition. He accepted that the Court of Session had jurisdiction to oversee the Parliament but held that s.40 was designed to prevent interference with its activities by the back door, which was exactly what the petitioners were trying to do. The petitioners appealed to the Inner House.

In the Inner House there were two main arguments: jurisdiction and title. In relation to jurisdiction the Court held that Lord Johnstone, though coming to the correct decision, had given insufficient weight to the fundamental character of the Scottish Parliament. The Lord President pointed out that it is a body created by statute and derives its powers from statute. Like any other statutory body it must work within the scope of its powers and if it does not do so the courts may intervene. The Scottish Parliament has simply joined the wider family of parliaments created by the Westminster Parliament. Counsel for Lord Watson had urged the court to exercise a self-denying ordinance in relation to interfering with the proceedings of the Scottish Parliament but the Lord President held that to do so would be to fail to uphold the rights of other parties under the law. Lord Prosser agreed with the Lord

President, confessing that he found it hard to grasp the contention that the court had no jurisdiction to deal with the issues raised. The contention seemed to him to be based on the view that the Scottish Parliament, being a Parliament rather than a local authority, was in some way immune from judicial regulation. But he could not accept that contention. In so far as Parliament and its powers had been defined and limited by law, it was self-evident that the courts had jurisdiction in relation to these definitions and limits; all the more so when the body had very wide powers like the Scottish Parliament. He found baffling the suggestion that the courts should exercise a self-denying ordinance, for that might allow the Parliament to exercise powers beyond its legal limits. A defined Parliament is there to do not whatever it wants but only what the law has empowered it to do.

The second, and crucial, issue was whether the petitioners had title and interest to seek the interdict at all. Lord Watson argued that the members' interest order was designed for the benefit of the Parliament and not the public. But the Lord President disagreed. The Parliament, he said, had been created for the benefit of the people living in Scotland; and the public interest could be pointed out by the fact that breach of the order was a criminal offence. So *prima facie* the petitioners had the necessary interest to pursue the proceedings. However, in the end they were not entitled to do so. While the public did have an interest in the order, there was nothing to suggest that this interest conferred a *civil right* on members of the public to secure compliance with the order. Breach of the order was a matter for the criminal courts, and the Parliament itself had additional disciplinary powers. This suggested that members of the public were not entitled to have the right to institute civil proceedings for breach of the order, nor the right to prevent members from breaching the order: therefore Parliament could not have intended to confer a right to bring proceedings for interdict to prevent a threatened breach.

Lord Prosser agreed. Any interest of the petitioners would be infringed only after many other acts had taken place beyond Lord Watson's act of presenting the Bill (including the Parliament actually passing the Bill). So the necessary causal connection between the apprehended breach and the eventual detriment they claimed they would suffer did not exist.

The limited nature of the Scottish Parliament, confirmed in this decision, is perfectly obvious to anyone with a knowledge of constitutional law. The pre-1707 Parliament of Scotland never claimed the absolute sovereignty that the British Parliament at Westminster claims, and it had no apparent difficulty in passing legislation purporting to bind itself for the future: APS II, 335 provided that any future Act inconsistent with the doctrines of the church of Rome would be of no effect. (Political reality, in the shape of the Reformation, did of course supersede any constitutional doctrine—which might be a lesson to bear in mind when considering the conflict between the sovereignty of the U.K. Parliament and the requirements of E.C. and European Human Rights Law). The post-1999 Scottish Parliament follows this tradition. The Scottish Parliament is not sovereign (but then few Parliaments are sovereign in the democratic world, in the sense of being entirely free to do as they please without judicial scrutiny) and it has not been established for its own benefit, but rather for the benefit of the public. The clear statements from the judges in the present case should dispel any contrary notions in the minds of both MSPs and the popular press.

INDEX